TOWARDS A FULLER VISION

VISION

*My Life & The Ethiopian
Orthodox Church
(A Short History: Part One)*

Brahana Selassie
Ordained Ethiopian Orthodox Priest

UPFRONT PUBLISHING
LEICESTERSHIRE

TOWARDS A FULLER VISION: *My Life & The Ethiopian Orthodox Church (A Short History: Part One)*
Copyright © Brahana Selassie 2000

ISBN 1 84426 096 8

First Published 2000 by
MINERVA PRESS

Second Edition 2003 by
UPFRONT PUBLISHING
Leicestershire

TOWARDS A FULLER VISION

VISION

*My Life & The Ethiopian
Orthodox Church
(A Short History: Part One)*

Preface to the second edition

In the June of this year I received correspondence that Minerva Press who published the first edition of my book had ceased trading and went into liquidation. The files that I had with them were passed onto Upfront Publishing, and by mutual agreement we have agreed to publish a second edition.

As a first time author this gives me the opportunity to make some small amendments to the original manuscript. I have added a tables of contents, made some changes to the beginning (Acknowledgements), and at the end (Epilogue) of the book. I have also corrected some grammatical mistakes and incorrect dates I found once the book was published on 25 January 2000.

Table of Contents

Acknowledgements

The initial creative waves of inspiration for this book began thirty years ago. It was early March 1972 and I was a seventeen year old African-Caribbean teenager attending South Shore High School in the Carnasie neighbourhood of Brooklyn, New York City. Born in the middle of the decade of 1950's in Grenada in the South-Eastern Caribbean, I left at the age of nine and travelled to London where I lived for six years. I had been brought up in the Roman Catholic Church, and by the time I became a teenager in 1968, for my peer group, and myself, the expression of Roman Catholic Christianity became bankrupt against the de-colonisation decade of the 1960's when the British Empire lost almost all its colonies in Africa and the Caribbean. Because we were caught up in this process as we grew into adults on the religious plane, one quest dominated our consciousness: Africa had two nations, Egypt and Ethiopia, with multiple biblical references, especially in the Old Testament. Did these communities with their biblical roots still exist in the 20th century, and if they did, could we make living contact with them?

In 1970 my family moved to Brooklyn, New York City, and it was two years later that this question was answered for me when I had my first exposure to the Ethiopian Orthodox Church (E.O.C.).

The book's construction and production grew out of the massive collections of notebooks I made when I joined the Church in March 1976 in London, and more formally when I was being educated and prepared for entry into the priesthood of the E.O.C. between January 1977 to June 1980.

During these years I lived in the Holy Trinity E.O.C. located at 140-142 West 176th Street in the Morris heights neighbourhood of the Bronx. Of course the twin towers of the World Trade Centre were still in existence then. The cataclysmic events of the morning of 11 September 2001 were a long, long way in the future.

My original plan was to produce one enormous book of about 800 pages, but with the passage of years I came to see that it would be more effective as a trilogy: part one, links to part two, and part two.

Before I proceed any further I must acknowledge the role that the clergy and the faithful parish members of the Holy Trinity E.O.C. contributed to helping me. I must confess that I have not had any contact with some of them since August 1982, and many of the older generation that I knew may have passed away in death. I must mention my teachers and mentors. First of all there was Abba Petros (Peter) Gebre Selassie. Then, Abba Laike Mariam Mandefro. In January 1979 he became Archbishop Yesehaq (Issac) the head of the newly created E.O.C. Archdiocese of the Western Hemisphere (Europe, North America, and the Caribbean).

He was the one chosen by the Holy God in Trinity to bestow upon me through the sacrament of ordination both the ministry of the deacon and the priesthood.

Once I became a priest my name changed from that I was given at birth, Danford Elmo Anthony Briggs-Romain, (Tony is the one my family chose to use of my three first names) to Brahana Selassie, the name I am now legally known by. However, in my family I am still known as Tony.

★

It makes me sad now to admit that the relationship between us since he became an Archbishop suffered a series of conflicts over the events of the 1974 Ethiopian revolution and its effects on the life of the Church. Since 1985, the relationship between us has broken down beyond repair. This is a matter that I will discuss in greater detail in the next two instalments. However, I should point out here that since 1992 when Abuna Paulos (Paul) was elected and enthroned as the 5th Patriarch of the E.O.C. he had been very hostile towards this administration until his rank of Archbishop was suspended in 1995. It was the publication of his highly controversial book 'The Ethiopian Tewahedo Church: an Integally African Church' by Vantage Press in 1989, a copy of which I obtained and studied the following year, that finally made me decide on the title for my book.

The next teacher and mentor that I must mention is Liqe Siltanat, Abba Elias Abebe, who became my confessor father when I was ordained as a deacon on 16 September 1979, and as a priest on 13 July 1980. Today, Abba Elias is now Archbishop Nicodemus, the secretary of the Holy Synod of the E.O.C.

I cannot forget my confessor mother either, the Ethiopian Orthodox Nun, Imahoy Christos Semra, (Mother Wisdom as we all called her). She passed away in death in December 1980. May the Holy God in Trinity grant her a peaceful rest in her grave until the time for the final judgement on the last day that will separate the sinners from the righteous forever. In that awesome moment when all the dead will rise up from their graves, may my confessor mother, together with all those countless millions of faithful men, women, young people, children and infants, be invited to inherit an eternal life in the presence of the Holy God in Trinity, which the New Testament authors call the Kingdom of Heaven.

Gashey Asefa Yemane Brahan, the distinguished Ethiopian Orthodox icon painter; Mother Palmer (Wolleta Tinsae); Kes Gebre Eyesus; Kes Gerzehai Gebre Selassie; the Evangelist, Bro Aria Selassie; Deacon Wolde Ab Wode Selassie; and last, but certainly not least, in this list must come Abba Gebre Kedan.

The memory of the martyred Patriarch, His Holiness Abuna Theophilos, must also be acknowledged. My discovery of the Ethiopian Orthodox Church as a seventeen year old in March 1972 while attending South Shore High School in Brooklyn, New York, is directly linked with this great twentieth-century African Church father. One can say that, although I never met him at all, my entire orientation as a convert from Roman Catholic Christianity towards ordination into the Ethiopian Orthodox Church has been to make known the theological and spiritual world of Abuna Theophilos: his efforts to continue to build enduring structures for the newly formed independent Ethiopian Orthodox Patriarchate which started with the administration of the previous Patriarch, Abuna Basilos (1959–70); his efforts to strengthen the relationships with the other Orthodox Churches of the Oriental Orthodox family (in Syria, India, Armenia and Egypt); his efforts in the formation of the Theological Commission for Union between the Oriental Orthodox and Eastern Orthodox Churches; and finally, his efforts towards developing a more effective presence and impact for the Orthodox Churches upon the work of the World Council of Churches, and the wider ecumenical movement.

I must also mention some of the staff of Minerva Press who worked on my manuscript before this publishing firm ceased trading in June and went into liquidation in July 2002. First of all there is Julia Coekerham and Angelina Anton who were the first Minerva Press staff I had contact with in April 1997 when their offices were in Knightsbridge south-west London. When the Press moved to Canberra House, Regent Street in the heart of London, Angelina Anton became one of two managing directors and introduced me to Rebecca Ward, Rachel Barlow, Alix Percy and Sally Wench. It was these staff members who helped to get my manuscript ready for publication and did the initial publicity and advertising drive when it was published on 25 January 2000.

I now wish to thank all the staff of Upfront Publishing for helping to produce this second edition.

There are three other people I must acknowledge. The first one is His Eminence Archbishop Matthias, the Ethiopian Orthodox Archbishop of Jerusalem from 1979 to 1982 and of the USA from 1993 onwards. The Holy Spirit brought him into my priesthood at a very special time. We have not seen each other for many years now, but I want to thank him and the faithful of the Ethiopian Orthodox community of Washington DC, the capital of the USA, for all the help and support they gave me between November 1985 and August 1990. He is one of the few Christlike persons I have met in my life.

I now come to mention my mother, Jean Briggs. More than any other human being, she has had the most influence on the formation of my Christian identity. Throughout my life she has always been there when I was in need. She has been there again with a loan when I needed the finance to produce this book. The most important thing I have learnt from my mother is this: Christianity is the life of the sacraments, prayer and worship. When my mother is praying she does not just recite words to the Living God. I have always felt that she was having a holy dialogue with the Lord himself. Sometimes when I hear her sing holy songs, her voice has the sweetest melody I have ever heard. There is a belief among Syrian Orthodox Christians in Damascus that the prayer of 'Our Lady Mary', following the annunciation to her by the Archangel Gabriel that she will become the mother of our Lord Jesus Christ, which is preserved in St Luke's gospel (1:46–55), was a hymn of praise and rejoicing whose melody has been kept alive by communities of nuns in Damascus. I have heard a recording of these nuns singing this holy song and their voices made me think that the melodic sweetness of St Mary's, our Lord's Holy Mother, voice must have been similar. Sometimes when I hear my mother sing, I think of these Syrian Orthodox nuns and I think of St Mary as well.

I want to say a deep word of thanks to Father Ken Leech, the well-known Church of England Priest, theologian and author of many best-selling books like: *Soul Friend, True Prayer, True God, Youthquake, Pastoral Care & The Drug Scene, Keep The Faith Baby, The Social God, Spirituality & Pastoral Care*, just to name a few of his publications.

When I first met him in January 1985 he was attached to the Board of Social Responsibility of the Holy Synod of the Church of England. His office was in Church House, Great Peter Street, Westminster. He was one of its Race Relations Field Officers. At this time Father Ken gave me a lot of help with the deportation case that I was facing. This case was mounted by the Archbishop who ordained me, two officials in the church headquarters in Addis Ababa, and the administrator of the Church here in England over my efforts to publicize the murder of Abuna Theophilos and some of our other Church leaders in the campaign of persecution of the E.O.C. inside Ethiopia, undertaken by the government of Mengistu Haile Mariam. While I was raising my voice and writing articles, these other Ethiopian

Orthodox Church officials chose to remain silent and pretended that no such killing or persecution was taking place at all.

Father Ken would remain in his post on the board of Social Responsibility for another two years. Prior to my meeting with him he held several positions with parish-based ministries at Holy Trinity Church Hoxton, St Matthew Bethnal Green, both in East London and St Ann's in Soho. He had helped to establish the Jubilee Group. He served St Augustine's College in Canterbury Kent as its Chaplain.

When he left the Board of Social Responsibility in 1987 he became the Director of the Runnymede Trust and in 1991 he was appointed M.B. Reckitt Urban Fellow and Community Theologian based at St Botolph Church in Aldgate, East London. This is a position he still holds. Since the time we met we have kept in touch with each other. In the second instalment: 'Links to Part Two' I will say more about the deportation case and help that Father Ken gave me which caused a friendship to develop between us.

Finally, I dedicate Part One of this two-part work to my wife, my son and my daughter.

Foreword by Father Ken Leech

I am delighted to commend this book by Father Brahana Selassie, whom I have known for about fifteen years. I first encountered him when he was under threat of deportation because of political divisions within the Ethiopian Orthodox community, and I was glad to be involved in preventing an act of injustice which would have had damaging effects on his developing pastoral ministry. Father Selassie belongs to a generation of Christians who have been led to the Orthodox faith in the form represented by Ethiopian Orthodoxy, and he has been a key figure in helping to draw a community of Caribbean origin into this ancient tradition of Christian practice.

In this book Abba Brahana begins to introduce this tradition and looks at its early historical and theological formation. This will, I trust, lead on to a critical evaluation of the present situation to which we all look forward. For we are witnessing in our day the resurgence of many ancient traditions of spiritual life, and the revived interest in 'Oriental orthodoxy' is one facet of a wider shift in the centre of gravity in the Christian world. In a recent study of religion in an inner-city area of East London, only the Orthodox, among the 'mainstream' churches, showed increases in membership.

The appeal of the Ethiopian Orthodox tradition to young black people is linked with many cultural changes: the Garvey movement, the rise of Ras Tafari, the quest for a form of Christology which does not present a white Christ and a white symbolic framework, and so on. In this shift, Father Selassie has played an important role, and I commend both his writing and his continuing ministry for serious attention by Christians and all people of good will.

Kenneth Leech
Community Theologian
St Botolph's Church, Aldgate, London
July 1999

Chapter 1
Early Experiences Before Discovering and Joining the Ethiopian Orthodox Church (EOC)

Belonging as I do to a group of over one hundred and twenty priests and deacons who are not Ethiopian by birth, but are of African descent born in the Caribbean, North America or England, I shall begin with a short account of my early life before I discovered the Ethiopian Orthodox Church and became a priest in it. From the date of my ordination I adopted a new name, 'Brahana Selassie', which was totally different from Danford Elmo Anthony Briggs-Romain, the name I was given by my parents at birth, and which appears on my birth certificate. Of all the names given to me, the one which all my family used was Tony, the shortened form of Anthony.

The route that led me to discover the EOC was a historical route. In fact I would say that history, alongside English Literature and Composition, was my favourite subject in my school days. One of the charges made against me by many of my school friends was that I had a tendency to linger in the past. My preoccupation with history was because of two decisive events: the death of my father, Dennis Romain, on 29 January, just about one month before my third birthday on 26 February 1958. The second preoccupation I had with the study of history was due to the fact that I shared the same birthday as an aunt, Catherine Joyce Briggs, who was my mum's second oldest sister. So this created in me a longing to learn more about both sides of my family.

The house where my older sister, Sharon Briggs-Mcdougall,

and I were born, with the small plot of land on which it stands, was located on Sendall Street, Grenville, the capital of the parish of St Andrews, Grenada. It belonged to my mother's family from at least 1907, when my maternal great-grandmother, Maria Belmar, who belonged to the Belmar family of Noel's Hill, Grenville, got married, and my great-grandfather, Robert Ellis, who came originally from St Vincent, purchased it. My maternal great-grandmother's father was from Carriacou, while her mother was Grenadian.

Great-grandma Maria had six sisters: Lousia, Emily, Etta, Sophia, Lylia and Linda. Her only brother, Philip, had served in the British West Indies Regiment during World War One, but never returned and was officially declared 'missing in action'.

My maternal great-grandfather, Robert Ellis, was quite a re-markable man. He came to Grenada from St Vincent as a highly skilled joiner, and he eventually owned a business that supplied furniture to most of the wealthy families not only in Grenville and St Andrews, but in the other five parishes of the Island as well. When he met great-grandma, Maria Ellis, he taught her his art, and after a while she worked along with him. She had become so proficient that when he died she carried on the business.

★

In economical and technological terms Grenada was, and still is, a very small and undeveloped island. However it was always known as the spice centre of the Caribbean. It produced one third of the world's nutmeg (a hard tiny seed with a fragrant smell, covered by an outer shell) and Grenville had the island's largest nutmeg station. Cinnamon, cloves and vanilla are the other well-known spices exported internationally.

When I was born Grenada was the residence of the British Governor of the Windward Islands. Grenville ('La Baye' is the old name; 'Rainbow City' is the more modern one) is situated in the eastern tip of the parish of St Andrews. It had the status of the second town after St George's, the capital. Our family house was located on Sendall Street, not far from the town centre which began on Jubilee Street. It overlooked the sports ground. The old disused Roman Catholic Church, established by Fr Angelo Leoni in 1841 and around which Grenville was built, was located at the junction of Sendall Street and Cook Hill Road. This building could be seen when standing on our veranda. It is now under repair.

From the window of our living room, overlooking the sports ground, we could watch all the football, cricket and athletic teams who came from other parts of the island to compete against each other.

Grenville's town centre itself was approximately two square miles in size and consisted of around seven main roads (Gladstone Road, Jubilee Street, Victoria Street, Albert Street and Seton James Street) with food and clothes shops, restaurants, a market and a cinema. The Methodist and Anglican Churches had schools in the town centre too.

Several government offices such as the revenue and tax office, the sanitation department, a post office, a crown court and a police station were located here as well. Grenville had its own harbour behind the police station which operated a daily steam ship service to Carriacou and Trinidad during the 1950s. Since I have become an adult these ships have been upgraded.

The parish of St Andrews was the largest and wealthiest of the island. It has the longest coastline and the most estates which produced Grenada's main export crops (cocoa, nutmegs, bananas, vegetables, coconuts and fruits).

The island's only airport – Pearl's Airport – was located in St Andrews as well. Opened in 1943, it stayed in use until 1984 when Point Salines replaced it. Built originally on an old Arawak settlement, since its closure quite a few archaeological excavations have been carried out on and around Pearl's Airport by the Grenada National Trust & Historical Society, and it has attracted international attention. The parish is also famous for the Marquis (or Mount Carmel) waterfalls, the highest on the island, Grand Etang Forest Reserve, and two horse race courses at Telescope and Sea Moon.

★

For the first twelve years of my life, trying to reconstruct a full-length biography of my father's life, his character and his work consumed me. I was fortunate in that I lived for four years with my paternal grandmother, Elvie Slinger-Romain, after my mother, Jean Briggs-Romain, (who was a schoolteacher) came to England in 1960.

My paternal grandfather, Alfred Romain, was a native of Victoria, the main town of the parish of St Mark's, the smallest of all the six parishes of the island. He had died before I was born, so I knew very little about him.

My paternal grandmother, Mama Elvie, was like the centre of the little community. Her house was on St David's Road in Victoria, and it is in this house that my father and his brothers and sisters grew up. Unlike Grenville, Victoria was mainly a small seaside fishing town that was an extinct Carib settlement. We knew this because as children, I and several of my cousins would see many stones with faces carved on them, all along the coastlines where we played. It was our relatives who taught us that these stones were Carib stones. This is now an established fact and is published in all presentations that deal with the history of the parish of St Mark's.

Those natives of Victoria who were not involved with the fishing industry worked on the large Tufton Hall, or Belmont estates, just outside Victoria, or smaller ones which grew cocoa, bananas, nutmegs, other spices, fruits and yams.

Located in a valley, Victoria is surrounded by mountains, and Grenada's highest mountain, Mount St Catherine, (2,756 feet above sea level) could be reached in about three hours' walk, heading south-west from my grandmother's house.

I remember very well how Mama Elvie had very extensive knowledge of herbal medicines, as many of the local people would come to our house to consult her. On some occasions I was asked along with some of my cousins to deliver some of these remedies. She also did a lot of voluntary work for the local parish church. Living with her we had access to a paternal aunt, Nora Romain, and four uncles, Neville, Arnold, Gordon and Septie, who still lived in Grenada. We had several other paternal aunts and uncles who were living in Trinidad, the US and in England.

This meant our father's side of the family was without question much bigger.

★

On my mother's side of the family (the Briggs), we had two aunts, Catherine Joyce and Daphney; and one uncle, Karl, who still resided in Grenville. My maternal grandmother, Ethiel Ellis-Briggs, (or Mizzie as she was called by everyone) was born in 1907. She was a very prominent woman as well. She had extended our family house on Sendall Street into one of the largest bakeries and butchering establishments in Grenville. However, when I was born she was living in the Dutch West Indies Island of Aruba, together with my youngest maternal aunt, whose name was Pearl, and an uncle, whose name was Hayden. All three had left Grenada in 1951. My maternal grandmother remarried while living in Aruba, and in 1960 she and uncle Hayden and aunt Pearl went to live in Brooklyn, New York, following the death my grandfather Cyril Briggs, who came originally from St George's. Of our maternal relatives still in Grenville, aunt Daphney, who was married, taught in the Methodist school. Later she became the headmistress of the Paraclete School.

Her husband, uncle Pat Gilbert, came originally from St Paul's, in the parish of St George's, and held a government post as the Head of the Sanitation Department for St Andrews. One vivid memory that I had from this time was his supervision of the massive job of disposing of a whale that was washed up on the shore near our home in January 1960.

Aunt Joyce was also a school teacher, while my uncle Karl taught at the Grenada Boys' Secondary School in the capital, St George's. My oldest maternal aunt, whose name was Cicely, was already married and living in Trinidad before I was born.

Of our paternal uncles, three were in the Grenada Police Force. Uncle Arnold was the inspector for St Andrews. Another one, Uncle Gordon, was the head of the fingerprint section for the CID in the capital. And the third one, Uncle Neville, had just joined this same department.

My other paternal uncle, Septie Romain, owned a blacksmith establishment on Albert Street, Grenville. The only paternal aunt I had in Victoria, aunt Nora, owned a dressmaking shop, and helped our grandmother, Mama Elvie, look after us, because when my sister and I went to live with her, she had six other grandchildren living in the household.

Therefore the link into the history of the island came to me from these aunts and uncles. They are the ones who gave me the knowledge that my father was a civil servant who worked as the Assistant to the Chief Immigration/Customs & Excise Officer stationed at Pearl's Airport.

In his spare time my father was a cricket coach, and he helped to finance the Victoria, and then the Grenville, cricket teams. He was also apparently an avid reader of classic English authors like Geoffrey Chaucer, John Milton, Sir Edmund Spenser, John Dryden and Sir Walter Scott. His favourite writer was apparently P.G. Woodhouse.

My maternal grandfather, Cyril Briggs, was born and grew up in St George's, the capital, as I mentioned earlier. As a young man he joined the Grenada Telephone Company as a technician, and later became the Chief Engineer responsible for telephone operations in the entire western part of Grenada. This is when he moved to Grenville and met my maternal grandmother.

These details of my family's history taught me a vital lesson as I grew older about the nature of historical research; almost all studies of the past (political/military/economic, etc.) begins with family biographies, usually of three generations (grandparents' generation/parents' generation/children's generation) living in a specific geographical cradle. The historian's aim is to trace the journey of those family members who distinguished themselves, as their lives spread outwards from their family base in wider overlapping concentric circles that compose the society around them, carried along by the arrows of time and motion, birth and death.

★

The history and geography of the island that my relatives, as well as the teachers we had at Roman Catholic school, shared with us was very interesting.

Grenada is situated in the south-eastern part of the Caribbean Sea, one hundred miles north of Venezuela on the South American mainland. On navigational charts it is 12 degrees north of the equator, and 61 degrees 40" west longitude. From the earliest recorded times it was always grouped with Carriacou, Petit Martinique, St Vincent and the other tiny islands that make up the Grenadines in the Windward Island chain. It is very near Trinidad & Tobago. In fact it is the southernmost island in the Windward Island chain. The three islands of Grenada/Carriacou/Petit Martinique now form a three-island state that covers an area of 133 square miles. The other islands of the Grenadines are governed by St Vincent.

Grenada itself is a mountainous island, twelve miles wide and twenty-one miles long, with thickly wooded forests, wild streams, rivers and a number of waterfalls. The central mountain range is composed of a number of ridges, some of which contain crater basins. It has a population of around 95,000, and English is the main language spoken. Some of the older citizens speak a dialect of French patois or Creole.

Grenada was first inhabited in the first century AD by the Amerindian Arawaks who originally came from central Asia. They constructed their first settlement near Point Salines International Airport. Coming to the island from the Amazon basin in South America, and being good seafaring and farming people, they migrated along a north-east route to the northern coastline of Venezuela and Guyana before landing on Trinidad, Tobago, and the Windward Islands (Grenada, St Vincent & the Grenadines, Dominica and St Lucia). Caribbean and native Grenadian historians state that many more of these Arawaks settled in the Windward Islands than in the other islands of the Caribbean Sea further north.

The next group to migrate to Grenada were the more warlike Caribs who came around 700 AD from central Brazil and Guyana. They went on a conquest of the island and destroyed all the Arawak men. Having succeeded, they made all the Arawak women and children their wives and servants. It was a mixture of these two Amerindian tribes that made up the population by the time Columbus arrived towards the end of the fifteenth century, with the Caribs firmly in control.

During the sixteenth century Grenada's history is a history of bitter conflicts between the French and the Caribs. By 1650 the French settlers had destroyed almost all the Carib communities and were in full control of the island. They ruled it until 1763 when it was handed over to the British monarchy at the Treaty of Paris that ended the Seven Years' War between England and France.

From this time onwards English and French language and cultural zones were created, and both governments competed with each other in bringing African slaves to Grenada as well as to other locations in the Caribbean. In 1779 the French recaptured it, but five years later (1783) it was returned to the English. Census figures taken at the end of the eighteenth century estimated that there were around 9,752 African slaves distributed over 337 plantation estates to produce spices, sugar, coffee, cocoa and rum.

As in other parts of the Caribbean region which the British monarchy controlled, by the time slavery was abolished in Grenada between 1834–38, the slave population numbered approximately 23,536. The British ruling class on the island was very small: probably not over one thousand. They controlled a population that was a mixture of French, Africans and Indian migrant workers brought in from the Indian subcontinent.

★

According to letters by the Governor, Robert Melville, to his masters back in London around this time, the African slave population included around five hundred maroons who had broken away from several plantations before slavery was abolished.

Melville seems to blame them, as well as some Frenchmen rebelling against the French control of Martinique, for inspiring the larger slave population to take part in a slave uprising between 1795 and 1796 against the British rule of Grenada. This uprising was led by Julian Fedon, a free black Grenadian of African and

24

French descent. Fedon owned a coffee and cocoa estate in Belvedere, in St John's parish. The forces under his command took possession of almost all of Grenada, except St George's. They were in control for about fourteen months. It took a naval force under the command of Sir Ralph Abercromby to end this movement. But Julien Fedon himself was never captured.

★

The complete abolition of slavery in 1838 did not improve the quality of life for the former slaves, nor did it mean the end of the two linguistic and cultural zones.

In fact, I was shocked when one of my uncles told me that when he was a small boy in the 1930s, for the majority of Grenadians, employment was still tied to the land, and workers were paid slave wages daily: 25p for women, and 40p for men.

In my life time, which has seen the government of the Prime Ministers Eric Gairy, Maurice Bishop, Herbert Blaise, Ben Jones, Nicholas Braithwaite, George Brizan, and now Keith Mitchell, the majority of the population still work off the land, and still earn very low wages.

★

During the last two decades Grenada has been most known in international circles as the little island in the southern part of the Caribbean Sea which was invaded by the US in October 1983, at the request of several Eastern Caribbean governments, following the murder of the Prime Minister Maurice Bishop and members of his New Jewel Movement government. After these tragic events a savage power struggle broke out which led to civil war and thousands lost their lives. This was the background which led to the invasion of the US troops. A film with Clint Eastwood in the leading role called *Heartbreak Ridge* was made in 1986 about this 1983 US invasion.

Prior to this, the two most internationally known Grenadians were probably Lord Pitt of Hampstead, London, England. He was the chairman of the former Greater London Council (GLC), as well as serving as president of the British Medical Association (BMA) before he died in 1995. The other prominent and internationally known Grenadian was Jennifer Hosten who won the Miss World Beauty Competition in 1970 and was crowned by the American celebrity host, Bob Hope.

The first twenty years of my life (1955–75), before I discovered the Ethiopian Orthodox Church, can be called the years that finally saw the death and burial of the British Empire. In these years I moved from the house I was born in on Sendall Street, Grenville St Andrews, to my paternal grandmother's house on St David's Road, Victoria St Marks, to live in Fulham, Plumstead and Tottenham in London from 1964 to 1970; and then to Brooklyn, New York City, in the USA from 1970 to 1975 when I first participated in a worship service of the Ethiopian Orthodox Church. The countdown to the end of this Empire began during the 1920s and 1930s, but did not become a formal process until the decision was taken by the Labour government of Clement Atlee just after they won the election in July 1945 to grant India its independence. This, however, did not happen until 15 August 1947 when Nehru led India to independence.

After the independence of India, decolonisation in other parts of the British Empire, in Asia, Africa and the Caribbean, was bound to speed up. This occurred during the twenty-year period when my generation grew up into young adulthood.

Studying the process of how these Africans and Asians both in their home continents, and in the Diaspora, threw off the British colonial yoke in the first twenty years of my life, was like observing two groups of scientists in a history laboratory mixing specially chosen chemicals to regenerate the lives of two ailing ancient races of peoples.

Knowing of the decision of the Atlee government to grant India its freedom before the 4th Pan-African Conference opened in Manchester, England, in November 1945, the African and African-Caribbean delegates who attended the conference were also determined to reject the colonial yoke and issued a militant six-point declaration to the colonial powers in control of Africa and its Diaspora to relinquish its role. Key figures at this conference who would also play a leading role over the next decade were

Kwame Nkrumah of Ghana, George Padmore and R.T. Makonnen from the Caribbean, the distinguished W.E. DuBois from the US, Jomo Kenyatta from Kenya, and Peter Millard.

From the year of my birth in 1955, until I was ordained to the priesthood on 13 July 1980, television and radio networks, newspapers, current affairs magazines, even the film industry, in the three places where I lived, could not ignore this decolonisation process. And the type of information that was made accessible had many layers of history to uncover.

The study of this kind of contemporary history was more meaningful to me than the history of the English monarchy, the Roman Catholic Church, the French and Industrial Revolutions, that we were being taught in RC Church and other schools that I attended.

Let me just make a short list of some of the key events in the African international world that the different forms of communication media mentioned above would initially transmit, and in some cases repeat, in the first twenty years of my life. Some of these events occurred when I was very young, and seeing them repeated several times as I grew made a huge impact on me and my entire generation.

- The short-lived Federation of the West Indies was formed in 1958. Also in that year was the 1st Conference of Independent African States in Ghana.
- In 1960 seventeen African colonies gained independence.
- The crisis in Congo that led to the murder of the Prime Minister Patrice Lumumba, and UN General Secretary Dag Hammarskjold in 1961.
- The islands of Jamaica and Trinidad gained independence in 1962. Also in this year, we saw the squabble between the leader of the now extinct USSR, Nikita Kruschev, and President John Kennedy of the USA, over Cuba that led to the threat of the releasing of missiles by Kennedy. The Federation of the West Indies was disbanded.
- The Inaugural Meeting of the Organisation of African Unity (OAU) in Addis Ababa, Ethiopia, in 1963.
- The trial and imprisonment of Nelson Mandela by the

apartheid government of South Africa in 1964. Also in this year was the merging of Zanzibar and Tanganyika to form Tanzania.

- Ian Smith's decision to take what was then Southern Rhodesia outside the sphere of British control in 1965. The brutal murder of Malcolm X in the same year in New York City.
- Barbados and British Guyana became independent in 1966.
- The US officials stripped one of our childhood heroes, Muhammad Ali, of his World Heavyweight title for refusing to go to Vietnam to fight with the US forces there in 1967.
- Newspaper photographs of Kenneth Kauanda, the President of Zambia, and James Baldwin, the African-American writer, addressing the 4th General Assembly of the World Council of Churches in Uppsala, Sweden, in 1968. Also that year I remember very well the 'Black Power' salute of the American sprinters Tommy Smith, John Carlos and Lee Evans at the Olympics in Mexico on the winners' rostrum after winning gold medals.
- The assassination of Martin Luther King Jr in the same year of 1968 in Memphis, Tennessee.
- The British MP Enoch Powell proposed the repatriation of all non-white immigrants out of the British Isles in 1969.
- The death of Kwame Nkrumah of Ghana in 1972.
- The independence of the Bahamas, as well as the Ethiopian famine, in 1973.
- My island of Grenada became independent in 1974; also the Ethiopian Revolution in September of that same year.

These are just a few of the events that I recall from these years that the media transmitted once or several times as we were growing up. The impact that they made upon my generation was massive and long lasting. We grew up seeing black African and Caribbean men and women in leadership roles, a thing that my mother's generation did not observe at a similar stage of their growth into adulthood.

It was the meaning of these epoch-changing events, along with our consciousness of the biblical history we were taught at school, where we saw the names of the African countries – 'Ethiopia' and 'Egypt' were mentioned in several places – that led me and many others to discover the living world of Ethiopian Orthodoxy. It was a gradual process really. My first vague conscious memory of Ethiopia was a news programme on the CBS television network in the USA, not too long after we arrived at my grandmother's house at 342 Hawthorne Street, Brooklyn, from our previous home at 80 Kitchener Road, Tottenham, in North London, on 9 May 1970. This news programme must have been at the end of May or the beginning of June, as I distinctly remember the newsreader, Walter Cronkite, announcing the results of an African sub-committee hearing of the US government in Washington.

He said something to the effect that within the context of the changes in the power politics in the Horn of Africa, the sub-committee decided that the Nixon administration was no longer committed to the territorial independence of Ethiopia or Somalia, against moves by the now defunct government of the USSR to bring either African nation into its orbit of influence.

★

Contact with the Ethiopian Orthodox Church for me occurred two years later in 1972. I was seventeen and now living at 534 East 96th Street, on the section that went from Church Avenue to Linden Boulevard, Brooklyn, New York, while attending South Shore High School on Ralph Avenue, at the junction with Flatlands Avenue in the Carnarsie section of Brooklyn. One day in March 1972 when school was over, I went home with one of my closest friends, Frank Johnson, who lived five minutes from us on East 95th Street, on the section from Church Ave to Wilmot Street.

When I arrived at his house, his mother was preparing dinner and we were in the living room which had a few book cases. We were listening to some of Marvin Gaye's music. On a small table were some Church magazines. I started to flick through them and I eventually saw a copy of the World Council of Churches magazine, *The Ecumenical Review*, of 1971. It was the first time I had ever seen any publication of the WCC. I recalled that the only previous time that I had heard of the WCC was while attending Roman Catholic schools in London, especially in 1968, when our teachers told us of the fourth assembly that was held in Uppsala, Sweden. Some of the daily newspapers carried clippings of President Kaunda of Zambia, and the African-American writer James Baldwin, addressing the delegates.

Frank's father and one of his maternal uncles had been very active in the Baptist Church in Macon, Georgia, as preachers before moving to Brooklyn, so I assumed the magazine belonged to one of them.

This issue was entirely dedicated to the meeting of the Central Committee of the WCC which was held in Addis Ababa in January 1971 by the host church, the Ethiopian Orthodox Church. As I flicked through it, I did not read much of it, as the language was not what I was used to.

I only remember reading the short speech of the head of the Ethiopian Orthodox Church, Abuna Theophilos. The parts of his speech that stuck with me is where he mentioned that the EOC had accepted the Christian faith over sixteen centuries ago; that it was one of the original establishing member Churches of the WCC, a fact which was confirmed by the former General Secretary, W.A. Visser't Hooft, in his response. Abuna Theophilos also mentioned some of the burning problems then facing the African continent that he hoped the WCC could offer help in overcoming.

He was holding the office of Patriarch in an acting capacity; it was only when I joined the Church, that I learned that the previous Patriarch, Abuna Basilos, had died in October 1970, and the Synod of the EOC had not yet held elections for the new Patriarch.

What also caught my attention in this issue of *The Ecumenical Review* was an article of a new WCC project called 'The Programme to Combat Racism' (PCR), that had been authorised by the Central Committee at its August 1969 meeting in Canterbury, England.

I remember the article outlining that the main aim of the PCR was to identify with, and offer support to, those peoples who were being racially oppressed. It called for a study of biblical teachings regarding race, and for research into the race problems in India, Latin America, and the Aboriginal community in Australia. There were also some descriptions of the then current problems in Mozambique, Guinea Bissau and South Africa.

I also read how the work of the PCR was to be carried out by an international committee which the Central Committee had appointed, and I remember there were several African and African-Americans on this committee.

I remember saying to my friend Frank, that if the EOC had embraced the Christian faith over sixteen centuries ago, then this brought it back to the fourth century.

We wondered if maybe, just maybe, it was possible that it was linked with the Baptism of the Ethiopian Treasurer mentioned in Acts of the Apostles chapter 8:26–end, although from Abuna Theophilos's speech, we could not be certain a Christian community was in existence in Ethiopia since then.

If the confession of faith this Ethiopian Treasurer made, in declaring his belief that Lord Jesus Christ is the Son of God, before St Philip baptised him, could be proved to be the historical base upon which the Church in Ethiopia came into existence, then it meant that this Treasurer's faith had grown organically out of an ancient Ethiopian Old Testament background, as he was met by St Philip reading the scroll of the Prophet Isaiah. But Abuna Theophilos's speech did not throw any light on this aspect as he said nothing about this Ethiopian Treasurer.

Furthermore the narrative clearly stated that the Treasurer belonged to the highest level of Ethiopian royal ruling class; he was in charge of the Queen of Ethiopia's Treasury. We had the notion that maybe the present Ethiopian Orthodox Church that Abuna Theophilos now led could be connected in an unbroken historical chain with this early New Testament episode, even if no Church community was in existence in Ethiopia then.

As teenagers in this time, we were exposed to the thoughts of African thinkers like Kwame Nkrumah, and African-Americans like Angela Davis, Maya Angelou, the Soledad Brothers, Bobby Seale and Hewey Newton of the Black Panther Party, Stokely Carmichael, and historians like John Hendrick Clarke, and Yosef

Ben-Jocannan. The music of James Brown, Sly and the Family Stone, The Temptations, Marvin Gaye, Aretha Franklin, Dionne Warwick, the Supremes, Kool and the Gang, Earth Wind and Fire, Curtis Mayfield, Otis Redding, and Edwin Starr were also powerful media that carried uplifting messages for us.

This made us view Abuna Theophilos' speech, and the context in which it was made (the meeting of the Central Committee of the WCC being held in Addis Ababa), along a historical line of thought that forced us to re-assess the origins of Christianity as starting in a Northwest Asian–Northeast African geographical cradle.

We therefore decided to adopt Abuna Theophilos as our African spiritual father, although at seventeen neither of us had any great desire to find or join the Ethiopian Orthodox Church.

Upon leaving Frank's house, we could not help wondering if there was any connection as well between the origins of the Christian faith in Ethiopia and Egypt. Abuna Theophilos did not mention this aspect either in his short speech.

But we clearly now remembered the story of the flight of the Infant Lord Jesus Christ to Egypt with St Mary, His Virgin Mother, and St Joseph, His guardian, to escape Herod's genocide policy that is recorded in the second chapter of St Matthew's gospel.

If there was any living connection between these two early New Testament references to African exposures to the life of the Lord, then it meant that the Christian communities in Ethiopia and Egypt, however large or small, existed from the first century.

Through the power of this realisation, both Frank and I experienced a total transformation in our entire historical outlook about how the origins of Christianity had occurred, as we walked from his house to mine. From the bare kernels of these historical facts, it meant that Christianity was not a European religion at all, in spite of the fact that the land of Canaan/Palestine/Israel, and Egypt, at the time that the Lord Jesus Christ lived on earth, was dominated by a fusion of Hebrew and Greek culture (Hellenistic Judaism) and were colonies of the Roman Empire whose civilisation was the base upon which the future nations of Europe would be erected. It also meant that, unlike other parts of the

African continent, Ethiopia and Egypt were not introduced to Christianity by European missionaries during the eighteenth and nineteenth centuries' missionary movements.

In the world of teenage African-American Brooklyn of the early 1970s, these were revolutionary facts with which to be armed.

The following year (1973) the Emperor of Ethiopia, His Majesty, Haile Selassie I, came to the US for a meeting with President Nixon concerning the way in which his administration had allowed the Soviet Union to supply arms to Somalia. On this trip the news media gave a short history of the Solomonic dynasty to which he belonged. Reference was made to the fact that in the Orthodox Christian communities of Egypt, Armenia, Syria and India, besides his native Ethiopia, the title of 'Defender of Faith' had been conferred upon him because of this commitment to the Orthodox Christian faith, and also the fact that he was the only living Orthodox Christian leader of a government.

*

So as you see I discovered the living world of Ethiopian Orthodoxy from reports of the meeting of the Central Committee of the WCC, published in the *Ecumenical Review* of 1971. I mention this here because from the time I started to study for the priesthood, in January 1977, I had a burning passion to learn more about Abuna Theophilos. The discovery also made me interested in the work and structure of the Church HQ in Addis Ababa as well as the WCC.

That 1971 copy of the *Ecumenical Review* where I saw Abuna Theophilos's speech further taught me that maybe it was possible to have an authentic African Christian experience of God, grounded in biblical history that was Orthodox, and neither Roman Catholic, or Anglican, or Methodist, or United Reformed, or Presbyterian, etc. But I did not pursue investigating the history of the Ethiopian Orthodox Church. I was seventeen years old and other things occupied my mind.

*

I did not make any physical contact with an Ethiopian Orthodox Church community until May 1975. I was twenty years old. The site was in London where a congregation worshipped at a Methodist Chapel on Denbigh Road, off Westbourne Grove, in West London.

The congregation was composed of Ethiopians, African-Caribbeans, young black men and women born here in England, and some people from the Rastafarian community. It was one of my cousins, Burge Francis, and some childhood friends, who introduced me to it, after I was back in London following my discharge from the US Marine Corps and was thinking of going to Angola as a freedom fighter. They told me about the St Mary of Zion Ethiopian Orthodox Church which met at the Methodist Chapel on Denbigh Road, and invited me to attend a worship service. I agreed to go.

Looking back now, the thing that I recall the most about this first exposure to an Ethiopian Orthodox worship service is how sacramental it was.

It reminded me of the Roman Catholic worship that I knew from childhood, where the entire focus of the worshippers was concentrated in a mood of sacred reverence on to an altar where the body and blood of our Lord Jesus Christ was being prepared. This was a welcome change from the pulpit-centred sanctuaries I experienced in many of the African-American Churches in the USA, where the preacher's sermon and the collection bowls were the centre of attention.

Here in this plain and bare Methodist chapel, a mystical transformation would occur and a traditional Ethiopian Orthodox sanctuary with colourful portable icons would come into existence. Icons were hung everywhere, along the walls, the ceiling and in the window ledges.

I recall also the colourful, royal-looking robes of four deacons around a portable altar who chanted prayers either in unison or solo throughout the service. One held a huge processional cross. I remember especially the two Ethiopian priests who were leading the service. They would make periodic processions around the portable altar, distributing a thick smoke-filled aroma of frankincense from their censers, over the sacrifice of the Lord's body and blood, wrapped in white cloths in the form of bread and wine mixed with water, on the altar, before it was ready to be distributed to the faithful.

Once these two priests came outside the altar sanctuary, accompanied by the deacon with the processional cross, and distributed the smoke-filled aroma of the incense over all in the congregation. The whole service looked very dignified.

Experiencing this incense ceremony for the first time locked my mind on the narrative of St Luke chapter 1, which described the episode of Zacharias the Priest, standing in front of the altar in the Temple of Jerusalem, worshipping and distributing frankincense till a thick cloud was formed. It was in this cloud of the frankincense that the birth of his son, John the Baptist, was announced by an angel to him and his wife, Elizabeth.

From this time onwards in 1975, I decided that I wanted to learn more about this ancient African Orthodox Christian Church, so I started attending regularly. I was confirmed a full member the following March 1976 and given the Ethiopian Christian name Brahana Selassie (a name which means 'Light of the Holy Trinity') after attending worship services, bible and sacrament classes at the home of the priest from the time that I was introduced to it.

The meaning of the name 'Brahana Selassie' overpowered me at first and I felt very uncomfortable about using it for about two years after receiving it.

As I gained more knowledge about the Church, I began to understand that the particular historical entry point into the world of Ethiopian Orthodoxy that now confronted me was very turbulent. Three years had elapsed (in 1973) since the devastating famine in the northern provinces that led to what Ethiopians called the 'creeping revolution' between February and September 1974.

From the time of this famine in 1973, constant pressure was exerted on the two oldest institutions of Ethiopian civilisation, (the Church and the Solomonic/Orthodox Christian Monarchy) by frustrated sectors of the Ethiopian population (students and teachers, the armed forces, labour union members, and the taxi drivers of the large towns).

The unrelenting pressure from these groups was mainly over the slow pace of the reforms promised by the Emperor's government and the Church. The pressure eventually forced cracks to appear, then shattered the union of Church and State on 12 September 1974.

This was a union that had been in existence over 3,000 years of recorded history, when its Old Testament origins was taken into account. But on 13 September 1974 this union no longer existed. A group of middle ranking army officers destroyed it by taking control of the power to govern and by beginning a programme to eliminate its opponents one by one. They started to declare in slogans over all the fourteen provincial capitals 'Revolutionary Ethiopia or Death. There is no other choice for Ethiopians now besides these two. Revolutionary Ethiopia or Death.'

In 1975–76 the Ethiopian, African-Caribbean and English born young men and women of African-Caribbean parents, together with the Rastafarian sections that made up the membership of the St Mary of Zion EOC in London, were still debating the consequences of the 12 September 1974 revolution in the life of the Church, while the two Ethiopian-born priests and deacons refused to be drawn into any discussion about it.

I returned to Brooklyn, New York, in November 1976 and headed for the Holy Trinity EOC at 140–142 West 176th Street in the Bronx. I was received by Abba Laike Mariam Mandefro. The following January, in 1977, I would start my education to become a priest in the Ethiopian Orthodox Church. I was joined by four others. We were all around the same age, give or take a year or two, and were very aware of what we wanted to do once ordained as priests.

We wanted:

1. To gain and share the knowledge of the Church's rich biblical heritage.
2. To visit Ethiopia to study there and learn properly Ge'ez and Amharic, the languages in which its theological manuals were composed, so that we could do some translations to build up a body of the Church's literature in English.

3. To write essays presenting its theology and philosophy as one of the original African Christian theological and philosophical traditions.
4. To chart the spiritual journey we had travelled that led us to the EOC, and share it with as many centres of learning and libraries as possible.

The next five and a half years of my life would be spent at this Holy Trinity parish on West 176th Street in the Bronx. In Part Two of this book, I will give more details of this period of my life.

Chapter 2
A Description of my studies for the Priesthood

My mind wanders back to 1978 now, when I was in my second year of studying the history, theology, liturgy, monastic and sacramental spirituality of the Ethiopian Orthodox Church at the North American headquarters of the five year old Ethiopian Orthodox Diocese of North America and the Caribbean, under the leadership of His Grace, Abuna Athanasius, whose residence was in Trinidad.

The church where I received my training was the Holy Trinity Parish Church located at 140–142 West 176th Street between the intersections of Popham and Montgomery Avenues, in the Morris Heights section of the Bronx, the northernmost borough of the New York metropolitan area. It had been located there since 25 December 1969 when the premises and an adjacent plot were purchased by the faithful. The first Holy Trinity parish was actually located at 43 West 126th Street and Lennox Avenue, in Upper Manhattan, when His Holiness Abuna Theophilos (then Archbishop of Harar, Deputy Patriarch, and also then one of the Presidents of the WCC) acting under instructions from the Patriarch, His Holiness Abuna Basilos, officially registered its establishment with the New York State and City governments at City Hall in Lower Manhattan on 25 October 1959. There was also another parish dedicated to the Archangel Mikael, located on 726 Gates Avenue in Brooklyn which was established around the same time. But when I started my studies it was no longer there.

The course of studies that I was fortunate to undergo was the second time it was taught. The graduate candidates from the first course had been ordained for the parishes in the Caribbean where

I come from. The growth of Ethiopian Orthodoxy was more prolific in this region in the 1960s than in other areas of the diocese.

When I started my studies the teaching staff consisted of the Archbishop of the Ethiopian Archdiocese of the Western Hemisphere from 1979 to 1993, His Eminence Abuna Yesehaq, who was then Abba L.M. Mandefro; three other priests of our Church; another Orthodox priest from our sister Church of India; two deacons; a nun; and a distinguished Ethiopian icon painter. From June 1979 we also had the former head of the Holy Trinity Cathedral in Addis Ababa, Ethiopia, and another priest who had come from our Church in Jerusalem.

We also attended lectures by Orthodox clergymen and professors at New York Theological Seminary in Manhattan, St Vladimir's Orthodox Theological Seminary in Crestwood, Iona College, and the College of New Rochelle, in New Rochelle.

Besides these formal programmes we also had access to the older members of the congregation who helped shape our ideas as well, because we lived in the Church building, as well as the large Orthodox Christian community of the New York City Metropolitan area which was made up of the Coptic, Armenian, Syrian, Greek and Russian Orthodox parishes.

My fellow brother students and I knew that, like the first group who had graduated and had been recently ordained, we were to be trained and prepared to serve as future ordained clergy and teachers of the Diocese of North America and the Caribbean.

★

This course of studies was designed and fully approved with the blessing and the grace of His Holiness, Abuna Theophilos, the Patriarch of Ethiopia; the Holy Synod of the Ethiopian Orthodox Church; the Bishop of the Diocese, His Grace Abuna Athanasius; and the other senior priests working in the diocese, after the three-week visit of the Patriarch and some of the senior officials of the Holy Synod to nine states of the USA in May 1973. The highlights of the New York stage of this trip were:

a. The visit to St Vartan Armenian Orthodox Cathedral on East 34th Street and 2nd Avenue in Manhattan where he and his entourage were received by Archbishop Torkom Manoogian, the head of the Armenian Orthodox Archdiocese in the USA; the HQ of the National Council of Churches in the USA, on Riverside Drive, near the Union Theological Seminary and Columbia University of the Upper West Side of Manhattan.

b. His visit to the UN Headquarters at E42–E43rd Street and 1st Avenue in Manhattan where he was received by the Secretary-General, Kurt Waldheim.

c. His visit to the headquarters of the Greek Orthodox Archdiocese of North and South America on E79th Street, near the Metropolitan Museum of Art on 5th Avenue overlooking Central Park on the Upper East Side of Manhattan, where he was received by Archbishop Iakavos, the head of the Greek Orthodox community.

I was not associated with the Church when this visit was made. When I started to study for the priesthood, we were told that during this 1973 visit, the Patriarch, Abuna Theophilos, and the Synod officials who came with him from Ethiopia were able to see for themselves the urgent need to train and educate those non-Ethiopian-born members of the parishes of the diocese like myself, who, through their parish priests, expressed a strong desire to dedicate their lives to the mission of establishing and building up the Ethiopian Orthodox Church in this young diocese.

During his visit to the Holy Trinity parish in the Bronx on 19 May 1973, the Patriarch, Abuna Theophilos, had told the faithful that the life of the Ethiopian Orthodox Church is a living tradition inseparable from the original African Apostolic Christian experience of God. During His earthly ministry, he further told them, the Lord Jesus Christ entrusted His message and plan for the salvation of the world to a group of disciples, who also became witnesses of His Crucifixion, Resurrection and Ascension; and who also received the gift of the Holy Spirit on the great day of Pentecost. St Philip was one of the members of this original Apostolic community who also baptised the Ethiopian Treasurer, as is recorded in the New Testament book, *The Acts of the Apostles*, Chapter 8:26–39. Without the transmission of this experience, the Christian faith in Ethiopia would have died. Furthermore if devout Ethiopian Christian men and women did not first try to learn from the Incarnate Saviour Himself, if they had no concern throughout the ages of the Church first to preserve, and then to transmit the teachings of Christ, the Ethiopian Orthodox Church would not have reached this part of the world, nor would the faithful here have any connection with the living historical reality of the earthly life of the Lord Jesus Christ, through the grace of the Holy Spirit, in the life of the Church.

★

This is only a summary of the Patriarch's main message to the faithful on that occasion. The notes that I made and kept in a notebook of the Abuna Theophilos's actual speech, as dictated to us by Abuna Yesehaq, while in the course of our studies, were lost when my room in the Holy Trinity Church was broken into in December 1981 and this notebook was taken, together with my main library which contained over 350 books, plus copies of the chronicles of various Ethiopian Emperors including Yekuno Amlak, Amde Zion, Dawit I, Zera Yacob, and Fasilades. Besides these, many Orthodox theological journals, articles and pamphlets from Ethiopia, and essays dealing with the International Conferences of Ethiopian studies were lost too. Some of these items were given to us as presents by our teachers, and others by Coptic and Armenian Orthodox priests and scholars who frequently visited our parish. This entire collection was stolen.

In fact even this book that I am now writing, I have had to reconstruct from the two huge boxes of other notebooks that I kept in the basement of my aunt Cicely's house at 4009 Amundson Avenue at the intersection of Strang and Edenwald Avenues in the Eastchester neighbourhood of the Bronx, near the border with Mount Vernon. The other huge boxes that were full of notebooks were kept in the basement of my sister's house on Snyder Avenue at the intersection of East 35th and East 36th Streets in the Flatbush neighbourhood of Brooklyn. What a blessing this turned out to be, especially when I think that the only reason why I stored them in these places was because there was no more space to put them in my room at the Holy Trinity Church.

As a result the reader will find that in almost all of this book I am not able to give precise footnotes as I would have liked to. This makes the book read like a historical narrative done in the manner of a 'scissors and paste job', to use the jarring phrase of the English historian, philosopher and archaeologist, R.G. Collingwood (1889–1943), to describe those disjointed works of history that he had read, in his book *The Idea Of History*. Collingwood used this phrase to describe the method that previous generations of historians adopted in merely cutting out sections from the sources they were using and pasting them together in their new narratives. This is the major setback that I have had to overcome, and I apologise to my reader, especially as I know only too well that the primary sources of the Ethiopian Orthodox Church's literature and history which were given to us by our teachers, and by Coptic and Armenian Orthodox priests, were made from the few English translations of Ge'ez or Amharic that they brought with them from Ethiopia. Most of this information dealing specifically with the history of the EOC using the work of the Church's scholars is almost impossible to come by in public libraries and book shops in America and England where I have lived since ordination. One can obtain this information in specialised research libraries like the British Museum library in London, the Bodleian library in Oxford, the library of Cambridge University, here in England, and similar specialised libraries like the Frobentius Institute in Frankfurt, Germany; the Africa Institute of the Academy of Sciences of Moscow; the University of Paris; the Pontifical College in Rome; Howard University in Washington DC, and Hill Monastic Microfilm Library, at St John's University in Collegeville, Minnesota, in the US.

However to gain access to these libraries the reader would have to be attached to some institution of learning as a research scholar, and would have to be a fluent reader in a combination of Ge'ez, Amharic, German, Italian, Slavonic, French and English.

Two of the more notable areas where this lack of knowledge of Ethiopian orthodoxy in the English language is strongly felt are in the introduction of the Christian faith into the Axumite Kingdom of Ethiopia in the first century with the visit of the three Magi, and also with the Baptism of Queen Candace's Treasurer by St Philip recorded in the New Testament book, *The Acts of the Apostles*.

Most public libraries and bookshops that I know in the USA and England do not possess books that deal with this aspect of the Church's historical origins from the Ge'ez and Amharic texts; as a result the introduction of Christianity into Ethiopia is pushed back until the second decade of the fourth century during the reigns of the twin brothers Abraha and Atsbeha (who as monarchs took the names Ezana and Shaiazana), with the arrival into Ethiopia of St Frumentius during the reign of King Ella-Amida I from AD 294 to 325. His training for the ordained ministry in Alexandria from 326 to 330, and his eventual ordination as the first Archbishop of Ethiopia by St Athanasius, the twentieth Patriarch of Alexandria, took place on the feast of Pentecost in AD 330. This view that Christianity was first introduced into Ethiopia during the fourth century after the birth of Christ by St Frumentius is still upheld on pages 117–118 of the last book *Imperial Unity*, published in 1989 by Fr John Meyendoff, the distinguished and prolific Orthodox scholar/priest who was on the teaching staff for over three decades and Dean of St Vladimir's Orthodox Seminary from 1984 until he died in 1992.

The affairs of Church in the Non-Solomonic Zagwe era, which lasted from the ninth to the thirteenth centuries, is the other historical period where this lack of knowledge is felt. Starting with the English historian Edward Gibbon (1737–94), this period is referred to as the 'Dark Ages' by quite a few European scholars like Dillman, Cheesman and Jager. The only Zagwe monarch discussed in any detail is Emperor Lali-bela because of the remarkable rock-hewn churches built in his time. With a title like the 'Dark Ages' the assumption is made by these writers that 'Ethiopia's real Christian history' after the sacking of Axum in the ninth century does not resume until Emperor

Yulkunno Amlak restores the Solomonic-Orthodox Christian dynasty when he ascends the throne in 1270.

★

Another central problem with the construction of a history that focuses on the religious life of the Ethiopian Orthodox Church is this. Because the royal courts of Ethiopia's Emperors always arranged for the Coptic Orthodox Synod of Alexandria in Egypt to assign Metropolitans or Archbishops to govern the Ethiopian Orthodox Church from the time of St Athanasius in the fourth century until this century, the temptation has been to build up a narrative that focuses only on this relationship. So over the centuries the EOC has been called the Ethiopian Coptic Church.

Mengistu Haile Mariam's 'Red Terror Surgeon', Abebaw Yigzaw, who ran the Church HQ from the summer of 1982 until 1988 and performed his brand of 'Ethiopian Marxist surgery' upon members of the synod of Patriarch Tekla Haimanot, made much of this fact in an interview with Peter France, the narrator of a programme called *Priests and Propagandists*, which was broadcast on BBC television on 2 March 1986 in an 'Everyman' series of programmes named *The Hammer and the Cross*.

(A) Into the Cradle of Human Civilisation

When we began our formal studies in January 1977, I remember quite well one of our teachers, Abba Petros, telling us that the scope of our studies was enormous.

First we would have to study the entire history of Ethiopian Orthodox Christianity, including its Old and New Testament biblical references.

When Liqe Siltanat Abba Elias Abebe came in 1979, he also told us the same thing. He was the priest who took over the administration of the Holy Trinity Cathedral in Addis Ababa after Abba Habte Mariam Workernesh was deposed and imprisoned by Mengistu's Haile Mariam government in 1976.

★

Our initial studies would make us look at the human fossil discoveries which established the Great Rift Valley (stretching from Transvaal in Southern Africa to Ethiopia in the North Eastern part of the continent) as the undeniable location of the origin of human civilisation from the 1920s to the 1970s, when European palaeontologists such as Hans Reck, Raymond Dart, Robert Broom, Louis and Mary Leaky, and the American, Donald Johanson, made their discoveries of the remains of the first human ancestors dating from about four million to one and a half million years before our age. These discoveries were made all along this massive 3,500 mile long Great Rift Valley.

Let me summarise the content of these studies, before commenting on them. As a relatively new academic discipline, palaeontology developed slowly during the nineteenth century from the biological, geological and archaeological sciences. It took the study of the past to a new plane, and as Charles Darwin's theories of evolution began to circulate in various scientific establishments, the hunt was on to find the link in the chain of evolution between upright standing mammals and humans, especially as he had predicted that Africa might be the place. The first human fossil to be discovered (part of a skull and some limb bones) was by the German J.C. Fuhlrott in 1856. It was in the Neander Valley in Germany, and was subsequently dubbed the 'Neanderthal Man'. But no accurate date of the age of these remains could be established. Thirty-five years later the Dutch scientist, Eugene Dubois, found parts of a skull and a leg bone in Java. It was estimated to have been around half a million years old, but this date was not accepted by the larger scientific community. These two discoveries preceded Raymond Dart's find in 1924 of a child's skull in Taung, South Africa, which he estimated was one million years old, as the link in the chain.

When Dart shared his views with the establishment figures in this field back in London, England, Sir Arthur Keith, Sir Grafton Elliot Smith, Sir Arthur Smith Woodward, and Dr W.H. Duckworth, in their journal *Nature*, they dismissed it as too far fetched. However what they did not tell Dart was that they were trying to promote their own English fossil (a skull) found near Piltdown in Sussex as the 'missing link'. In 1927 more human fossils were discovered in the Choukoutien Cave just outside Peking in China by Davidson Black. These were dated to be around half a million years old. The English establishment figures mentioned above were not willing to accept this discovery either, and continued to work on their own home discovery. It was later proven by the end of the 1950s that this 'Piltdown Man' was a red herring. By this time, however, Robert Broom, C.K. Brain and J.T. Robinson had joined Dart, and they established four other sites: Sterkfontien, Makapangast, Kromdraai and Swartkrans, in all South Africa. As three (Sterkfontien, Kromdraai and Swartkrans) were located within three miles of one another, this was compelling evidence that the cradle of human civilisation was indeed in Africa. Furthermore, the Neander-Java-Peking discoveries were scattered over great distances, which did not work in their favour.

By this time the research had moved to East Africa with the work of Louis and Mary Leaky, Clark Howell, John Napa and Philip Tobias (Dart's student). Sites like Laetoli, Lake Natron, and Olduvai Gorge in Tanzania; Fort Ternan, Lothagam and Kanapoi in Kenya; and Koobi Fora in Lake Turkana on the border of Kenya and Ethiopia were well established by the end of the 1970s.

The discovery at Olduvai Gorge in Tanzania by Louis and Mary Leakey of the complete skull of one of these first human ancestors in 1959 made all the difference. Prior to their discovery, it was believed that the human remains found in Java and Peking were the oldest. But no accurate and consistent form of dating acceptable to the international scientific community had been established. However, at Olduvai Gorge at last a solid date was established. After complex tests were carried out, using the chemical potassium-argon method, the remains of this skull were dated as one million years old. A decade and a half later, older human remains dating around three and a half million years were discovered by Donald Johanson and his team. He was from the Museum of Natural History in Cleveland Ohio.

This discovery was made on 30 November 1974 at Hadar in the Afar Triangle, roughly two hundred miles north-east of Addis Ababa in Ethiopia. Johanson and his team decided to call the fossil

'Lucy' because the Beatles' song 'Lucy In The Sky With Diamonds' was playing on their radio at the time. Among Ethiopians Lucy is known as Dinkenish.

The following year (September–December 1975) Johanson and his team returned to the region and discovered the fossils of the first human family, consisting of thirteen individuals. A comprehensive discussion of these discoveries can now be found in the book Johanson co-authored with Maitland Edy: *Lucy: The Beginnings of Humankind*, published by Penguin books in 1981.

Nine years later, research by eleven scientists from the University of Oxford was published in an essay supporting the claim of the Great Rift Valley of Africa as the origin of human civilisation, which is also an important source. The essay that furnishes this information is entitled 'Evolutionary Relationships of Human Populations, from an Analysis of Nuclear DNA Polymorphisms'. It can be found in the magazine *Nature*, vol. 319, dated 6 February 1986. This team of scientists in their conclusion on page 493 state:

> The earliest fossils of the anatomically modern human race have been found in Africa at Omo in Ethiopia, the Border cave, and at the Klasies River mouth in South Africa. The data from the last site suggest that humans were present in South Africa more than 100,000 years ago. An adult from the Border Cave has been dated about 90,000 years before our present age. Hence, it has been argued that the evolution of the modern human race took place in Africa. Our data are consistent with such a scheme, in which a founder population migrated from Africa and subsequently gave rise to all non-African populations.

*

For my teachers, the theological and historical emphasis of this entire discussion was more important than filling our heads with all the technical language these palaeontologists had developed to describe the various species of fossils like Homo Erectus, Homo Habilis, Australopithecus Africanus, Australopithecus Robustus, etc. From a historical point of view their emphasis was as follows.

Prior to these human fossil discoveries all along the Great Rift Valley the big debating point was not whether the human race originated in Africa. That was a fact established by the end of the 1960s when many African universities in independent African nations were already in existence. Those Europeans who argued against the position of the African origins of humankind were trying to establish a multiple or plural origin of humanity.

They were arguing that although the human race was born in Africa, these first humans migrated to Europe and Asia at a low-level of development, where they evolved into a more advanced stage.

As more and more fossils were discovered during the decade of the 1960s, European scholars either abandoned or changed their theories. However, they did not change their foundation position of a backward group of African ancestors developing in Europe and Asia into the human types that now inhabit the earth. However, with the new scientific evidence available, it has been proved that while earlier types of African ancestors might have migrated out of Africa to populate other continents. They made the necessary adaptations according to the places they chose to live.

Building upon these fossil discoveries of our early human ancestors discussed earlier, a team led by Dr Berhane Asfaw of the Ethiopian Ministry of Culture, Professors T. White and D. Clark of the University of California at Berkeley, and Professor Gen Suwa of Tokyo University published essays in the science magazine *Nature*, 22 September 1994, which give a record of the latest fossil discoveries made in Aramis, Ethiopia. They explain how this new discovery of the fossilised remains of the skull and teeth of seventeen individuals could be dated at 4.4 million years ago. This new information tells us that this human ancestral group died fifty thousand generations before the fossil called 'Lucy' discovered by Dr Johanson and his team in the Afar Triangle in 1974. This one was dated at 3.6 million years BCE.

Daily newspapers such as the *Daily Telegraph* and the *Guardian* gave prominent space on their front pages to these fossil discoveries.

From a theological standpoint the discovery of these human

fossils along the Great Rift Valley, between one and three and a half million years before our time, not only challenged other scientists and historians who have tried to locate the origins of the human race elsewhere. It also now challenged the biblical chronologies of certain circles of biblical scholars who were prone to treat the first few chapters of the book of Genesis as precise historical narratives establishing the origin and growth of the first human communities.

(B) Theological History

After this interlude with the discovery of human fossils, our studies had a more traditional theological and historical character. Our teachers described it for us. We would have to focus on the parts of north-east Africa, north-west Asia and the islands in the Mediterranean Sea which had received early exposure to the gospel of our Lord Jesus Christ, through the journeys of the Apostles and Disciples of Christ, in order to show that the first Christian communities and centres of learning had been established in these regions before the faith of Christ was properly established on the European mainland.

Next we would go into the history of the Oriental Orthodox Churches in Egypt, Syria, Armenia and India who, together with the Ethiopian Orthodox Church, formed one family of ancient Apostolic Churches in full Sacramental communion with each other.

These ancient Oriental Orthodox Churches had a tradition of theological thinking that had developed terminologies and phrases to explain the mysteries of the Christian faith, with at least three full centuries behind it. In contrast, for the Orthodox Churches in the Byzantine Empire and for the Roman Catholic Church in mainland Europe, theological discourse was just emerging during the fourth and fifth centuries. These Oriental Orthodox Churches did not accept the teachings of the Council of Chalcedon on the union of the divine and human natures in the One Lord Jesus Christ, because from a close examination of the Council's proceedings, clear evidence emerged of domination by the Imperial Byzantine Commissioners. Together with the leader of Pope Leo's delegation, Paschasinus, the bishop of Lilybaeum in

Sicily, these Byzantine Imperial commissioners unjustly deposed the aged Archmandrite Eutyches, and also the Patriarch of Alexandria, St Dioscorus, without a full examination of their beliefs and ideas.

The other main objection to this Council by this family of Churches was the manner in which the Council reinstated three bishops who had been deposed because their understanding of the union of the divine and human natures in the One Lord Jesus Christ was not considered to be sound and healthy, after intense examination by the second Council of Ephesus in AD 449.

This Council was held from 8 October to 1 November AD 451, at the Church of St Euphemia, in Chalcedon (present-day Kadikoy, Turkey) by the order of the Byzantine Emperor Marcian and his wife Pulcheria. There are many other reasons why the Oriental Orthodox Churches did not accept this Council, which is without any doubt one of the most controversial Church Councils ever held. But these reasons will be discussed in complete detail later.

The other Orthodox Churches within the Byzantine Empire outside of Turkey accepted the Chalcedonian formula because they had received their Christian heritage through Byzantine missionaries. This tied them very closely with the royal and religious courts of the Byzantine aristocracy of Constantinople (present-day Istanbul) until AD 1453 when the Ottoman Turks overran it.

Today the majority of these Orthodox Churches are fully independent Churches with the right of self-determination to elect their own Patriarchs, archbishops and bishops. They are found in mainland Greece, Russia, Ukraine, Georgia, and other areas of the now dissolved Soviet Union and Yugoslavia, Serbia, Bulgaria, Romania, and other nations of Eastern Europe.

The Orthodox Churches, whose origins go back to the time of the Byzantine Empire, have during this century established branches in Western Europe, North and South America, Africa, China, Australia and Asian mainlands using the same Byzantine canonical and liturgical tradition. However, while preserving their independence, most of them are still connected in a traditional sense with the Ecumenical Patriarchate in Istanbul (former

Constantinople), Turkey, and they regard the Ecumenical Patriarch as their chief spiritual shepherd. The present one is Patriarch Bartholomeis.

The most recent independent Orthodox Church of this tradition to come into existence is the 'Orthodox Church of America' which was granted autocephaly from the Moscow Patriarchate in 1970.

★

Abba Petros also told us that in the course of our studies we would have to go into the designs and plans of the Roman Catholic Church to subject the Ethiopian Orthodox Church to its authority from the twelfth century onwards, and more recently during the Italian-Ethiopian war of 1935–1941. We would have to study as well how the Ethiopian Orthodox Church came to establish the parishes of the Diocese of North America and the Caribbean; the coming of the Ethiopian Revolution in 1974, and its effects on the contemporary life of the faithful; and the Ethiopian Orthodox Church's involvement in the work of the World Council of Churches, the All Africa Council of Churches, and the Caribbean Council of Churches.

All of these studies would be independent of our work on the whole of the Old and New Testament; the history of Church doctrine; the administration and performance of the Sacraments, and the Divine Liturgy; the Art of Preaching; Pastoral care and Counselling, etc.

★

Another one of our teachers, Kes Zereyhun Termesgen, told us in his induction session we were the second class in this unique position and all those who would teach us had the full support of the older generation of priests and bishops in Ethiopia, who were now deposed or murdered because of their resistance to Mengistu Haile Mariam's persecution of our Church inside Ethiopia during the time that his government was in power (February 1975–May 1991). These bishops and priests had resisted Mengistu's government because it was still keeping His Majesty Haile Selassie's grandchildren in prison without any trial by any court of law (from 1974 to 1990).

Kes Zereyhun told us that as far as he was aware, the young candidates who started studying for leadership roles in the Church in Ethiopia after the Revolution of September 1974 were only being taught the history of the Church up to the time of the Patriarch, His Holiness, Abuna Basilos, who died on 12 October 1970. They were not taught about the administration of the Patriarch, Abuna Theophilos, because his reign was caught up in and witnessed the coming of the Ethiopian Revolution between February and September 1974. As a result, full knowledge of his life and theological vision was pushed into the background.

This grieved him, as well as Abba Petros, Abba Mandefro (now Abuna Yesehaq), and also Fr Simon of our sister Church of India, who was the Dean of the Theological Seminary of Addis Ababa in the late 1950s and early 1960s. What had caused these four even more sorrow was to see how all of Ethiopia's biblical references (thirty-nine in all for the use of the name 'Ethiopia'; the name 'Cush', which was another biblical name for Ethiopia, and its cognates appear nineteen times) and the work of the older generation of the Church's scholars were now considered as irrelevant in the teaching and recording of Mengistu's government with its scholars and their project to rewrite the history of Ethiopian civilisation.

In the Church's educational circles during Mengistu's time in power, every one of Ethiopia's Old Testament references was passed over in silence, except for scanty references to the legacy of the Queen of Sheba Mekada, and King Solomon's son, Menelik, found in the book of 1 Kings 10. This son of Makeda and Solomon was the one who established the Solomonic throne in Ethiopia, of which Emperor Haile Selassie I and Empress Menen were the 225th descendants. For the New Testament, the reference to the Baptism of Queen Candace's Treasurer by St Philip mentioned in the New Testament book Acts of the Apostles 8:26–39 is only briefly stated.

In the eyes of the new scholars, the real history of Ethiopian Orthodoxy does not start until AD 330 with the ordination of St

Frumentius as Abba Selama the first Archbishop of Ethiopia, by St Athanasius, the Patriarch of Alexandria from AD 326 to 373.

Even after establishing the narrative from the book of the *Acts of the Apostles* as evidence of the introduction of Christianity into Ethiopia, these scholars are silent about the next three hundred year old Christian presence in the nation. When they pick up the thread of their narrative again, they then proceed to explain and write about Ethiopian Orthodoxy as a main chapter in the history of the expansion of the Coptic Orthodox Church of Egypt, because all the archbishops of Ethiopia came from Egypt, from the fourth century until June 1959, when His Holiness, Abuna Basilos, became the first Ethiopian-born Patriarch of the Ethiopian Orthodox Church.

To counteract this 'Marxist-Leninist captivity' of the entire heritage of Ethiopian Orthodoxy by Mengistu Haile Mariam's military government, its scholars and cadres who had now risen to positions of power in the Church, we were taught all the biblical references to Ethiopia and the work of those African scholars and historians who proved the antiquity of Ethiopian civilisation.

(C) African Studies

In this regard Abba Petros told us that the life and work of the great and distinguished African scholar, Cheikh Anta Diop (1923–1986) of Senegal, West Africa, held a special place in his heart and mind. He spent three ninety-minute classes a week during the winter months of 1978–1979 reading and discussing with us Diop's work, especially his book *The African Origins of Civilization: Myth or Reality*. This book was first published in an English translation from the French original in February 1974 by Professor Mercer Cook of Harvard University.

In this book Cheikh Anta Diop called for a complete reassessment of the role that African peoples and their descendants have played in the world's history. It also called for a reappraisal of the central role its populations held in the establishment of all ancient societies and institutions. Diop's main concern is therefore to replace Africa's ancient history in its proper place. He also challenges in this book certain European and European-American scholarship on the role of ancient Africans in the development of the world's civilisation.

Abba Petros pointed out to us that the original French outline of this book had been Cheikh Anta's doctoral thesis which was rejected by the faculty of the University of Paris (where he had been studying since 1946) in 1954. In this thesis Cheikh Anta had presented a meticulously documented piece of historical writing on ancient Egypt, its civilisation and its population.

Diop showed that ancient Egypt was the centre of an enormous intersection that connected together many strands of Africa's major cultures and languages (including his own Wolof language of Senegal). He said in it that the creators of the civilisation of ancient Egypt were none other than black-skinned, woolly-haired Africans. Cheikh Anta also showed in this dissertation that ancient Greece, the mother of all European civilisation, was nourished by the Africans of ancient Egypt, who were themselves nourished by the Africans of ancient Ethiopia.

Abba Petros then told us how in this line of reasoning Cheikh Anta Diop himself was only building upon the work of other great twentieth-century African historians. He pointed out that in Professor Chancellor Williams' book *The Destruction of the Black Civilization*, chapter 2 is called 'Ethiopia's Oldest Daughter: Egypt'. Other African historians like T. Obenga of Zaire and J. Ki-Zerbo of Burkina Faso had developed similar themes in their work.

Then there was the distinguished Ghanaian historian J.B. Danquah who in his introduction to the book called *United West Africa at the Bar of the Family of Nations* written by Ladipo Solanke said something similar. A part of this introduction read:

By the time Alexander the Great was sweeping the civilised world with conquest after conquest from Chaerona to Gaza, from Babylon to Cabul; by the time the first Aryan conquerors were learning the rudiments of war and government at the feet of the philosopher Aristotle; by the time Athens was laying the foundations of European civilisation, the earliest and greatest Ethiopian culture had already flourished and influenced the civilised world for over four centuries and a half. Ancient Ethiopia annexed

Egypt and established the 25th dynasty, and for a century and a half, the seat of civilisation in the known world was held by these ancestors of modern black Africans, maintaining and defending it against the Assyrian and Persian Empires of the East.

Here in this quotation J.B. Danquah, like Cheikh Anta Diop, is showing that ancient African history is the foundation of world history.

In Cheikh Anta's first major book on history, *Black Nations and Culture*, he writes in the introduction:

The general problem confronting African history is this: how to reorganise effectively, through meaningful research, all the fragments of the past into a single ancient epoch, a common origin which will re-establish African continuity... if the ancients were not victims of a mirage, it should be easy enough to draw upon another series of arguments and proof, for the union of the history of Ethiopian and Egyptian societies with the rest of Africa. Thus combined, these histories would lead to a properly patterned past, in which it would be seen that ancient Ghana rose up in the interior of the continent (West Africa) at the moment of Egyptian decline, just as the European Empires were born with the decline of Rome.

Abba Petros told us also that Cheikh Anta Diop's books were well received by the older generation of Ethiopian historians who knew him, for while using Africa as the vantage point from which to link up to the origins of human civilisations, like Diop, these historians do not neglect the broader dimensions of world history.

John Hendrick-Clarke, the African-American historian and Emeritus Professor of African and Black Studies at Hunter College on E68th and Park Avenue in the Lennox Hill section of Manhattan, had also pointed this out in an article he wrote on Cheikh Anta Diop in 1974:

Roman history is both Greek and Roman, and both Greek

and Roman history have their origins in Egypt, because the entire Mediterranean was civilised by the North African territories of Egypt. Egypt in turn was nourished by other parts of Africa, especially Ethiopia.

If the Ethiopian/African origins of all ancient civilisations are still a puzzle to most Africans within the continent, together with those of African descent in other places, it is because of the whole legacy of the European slavery and the colonial age that dates roughly from the seventeenth century, but became more intense from the 1880s to the outbreak of the Second World War in 1939, when Africa and the majority of her peoples were under direct domination of European Nations, except Liberia and Ethiopia.

During this time European and European-American writers distorted the recording of African history and established the foundation of what they have called 'Western Civilisation' on the false idea that the ancient Africans in Egypt and Ethiopia were the forerunners of modern Europeanised people.

In chapter 1, 'Who Were The Egyptians?', of his book *The African Origins of Civilization: Myth or Reality*, Cheikh Anta Diop describes the origin, rise and decline of Egyptian civilisation from its Ethiopian foundations to the invasion from Western Asia by the Hykos (or Shepherd Kings). Further proof of the Southern African origin of Egyptian civilisation is to be found in the British Museum, London.

In this museum you will find a document there called *The Papyrus of Hunefer*. If you are in the USA a copy of this same document can be consulted in the library of Syracuse University in New York State. In *The Papyrus of Hunefer*, a work dating from the time of the eighteenth Pharaonic dynasty, the Africans of Egypt emphasise their southern African origins:

> We came from the beginning of the Nile, where the God
> Hapi dwells, at the foothills of the mountains of the moon.

The 'we' of this passage refers, of course, to the Africans living in Egypt. They state that they came to dwell in Egypt from locations at the beginning of the River Nile. Now this river, as you may know, is the longest water system in the world, covering 4,100 miles (6,670 kilometres) and has two sources. The furthest point of the White Nile is in Uganda, while the source of the Blue Nile is in the highlands of Ethiopia. Both merge into each other at Khartoum; and where is Khartoum located? It is in Sudan. The Nile flows through Sudan and merges again with the Atbarta River before continuing its journey north through what was the ancient Empire of Meroe. From there it flows through the region of north-eastern Sudan, that the Romans called 'Nubia', until it reaches Egypt. Flowing through Egypt, it ends up in the Sea of Sais (today's Mediterranean Sea).

The mountains of the moon that *The Papyrus of Hunefer* speaks of as the place that the Africans of Egypt came from have to be the mountains of northern and central Ethiopia; Mt Kilimanjaro, between Kenya and Tanzania; and the Rwenzori mountains in Uganda. These are the mountain ranges of the Nile valley.

According to the distinguished African-American historian Professor Ben-Jocannan, the Africans who probably inhabited this vast Nile valley region were definitely black-skinned and were indigenous to the region. He points out that their early societies developed around the clan organisation, where the 'incest taboo' was its foundation and marked the beginning of civilisation. For within the clan, men and women were no longer simple biological animals. Cheikh Anta Diop supports the point, and even develops it with his meticulous scholarship in chapter 5 of part II of his latest translated book, *Civilization and Barbarism*. In this chapter he states that as a result of the formation of the clan based on the 'incest taboo' these early Africans began to regulate their sexual and social relations by observing strict rules of conduct. As a consequence very precise concepts of the role of parenthood, property ownership, ritual worship, and inheritance laws developed.

*

Because of the taboo on incestuous relationships, these early African men and women had to marry outside the clan which in turn produced relationships with two or three neighbouring clans.

This led to tribal structures that expanded and developed monarchies and priesthoods to govern them. Having reached this level of development, these tribes started migrating to the central, south-eastern and south-western parts of the continent.

Once in southern Africa the Nile valley tribes began inter-marrying with the original Africans here called the Grimaldi, who were known for their travels up and down the western coast of Africa, from Namibia to Morocco, before crossing the Straits of Gibraltar and going up into present-day Spain. Some even went as far as present-day Austria. This history of the Grimaldi can be traced step by step by visiting the Museum of Natural History in Manhattan, New York. So these original Nile valley Africans moved around the entire continent, from north to south, from east to west.

Of the archaeological artefacts found in the small settlements and villages that they built, the most recurring are the symbols of the sacred cross, the triangle, the square and the circle. These ancient sacred symbols were brought with them to Egypt. And from Egypt, the Greeks and Romans brought them into the Mediterranean world, where modern-day Europeans discovered them.

These sacred geometrical figures were used by the early African ancestors as different ways of explaining the mystery of God, both as He existed in Himself, and as He was related to the world He created and managed.

Finally, we have to mention the meaning these sacred geometrical figures had for the original inhabitants of the Nile Valley.

The circle represented eternity, or time without beginning or end. The cross represented the union of vertical and horizontal, up and down, left and right, north and south, east and west. The square was the base for the construction of any permanent structure. The triangle was used to explain the mystery of the God who was One in Three, and Three in One.

(D) African Studies and the Bible

The mystical meaning of the triangle is the basis for what would later among the Israelites be accepted as the unity of three Divine Uncreated Persons who was revealed to them as Yahweh,

Yahweh's Word (or Revealed reason/expression) and Yahweh's Living Spirit.

We know from the time of King Solomon's reign that Old Testament scribes who co-edified all the oral traditions collected by Moses in the Torah talked about Yahweh, Yahweh's Word and Yahweh's Spirit as three divine but co-equal persons who share one divine nature. In the New Testament period, the Apostles, who were authors and writers through the mystery of the Incarnation, and the descent of the Holy Spirit on the day of Pentecost, would be inspired to bear oral and written witness and name these three divine uncreated persons who share the same nature as God the Father, God the Son, God the Holy Spirit, who even before the creation of the world and the concept of time. They also go to great lengths to reason about these three divine co-equal persons, who have the same uncreated nature or essence, as the same One God who revealed Himself to the saints of the Old Testament as Yahweh, Yahweh's Word and Yahweh's Spirit.

It is very important to state here that the first use of the terms 'Trinity', 'Tri-une' and 'Trinitarian' to describe the mystery of the God who is One in Three and Three in One is not to be found in any of the original letters and scrolls of the biblical authors and writers, but was the creation of the great second-century North African Christian thinker and writer St Tertullian of Carthage (160–220) near the present-day city of Tunis in Tunisia. We should mention here the African international theological college of Alexandria which gave to the entire Christian Church most of the terminology still used to discuss the mysteries of the Christian faith.

These aspects of the understanding of the mysteries of the Christian faith will be discussed in much more detail later when we come to study the disputes of the third–fifth centuries after the establishment of the Christian Church in the various regions of the then known world. These disputes were really a spiritual battle to find adequate terms to describe the unity of the three uncreated co-equal persons of the Holy Trinity.

The sacred symbols mentioned on page 53 as having their origins among the first inhabitants of the Nile Valley were also used to make the first astronomical and navigational charts known to the human race. There was no doubt that they carried these sacred symbols with them when they migrated north to Egypt and started building pyramids there. If the grandeur of Egypt is its pyramid construction, then one cannot understand how and why they were built there without an understanding of the sacred geometrical symbols of the cross, the square, the triangle or the circle, and their relationship to the thirty-two older pyramids in the Sudan.

★

Another important area of biblical history where the ancient African presence can be felt is in the journey of the seventy ancient Israelites who entered Egypt during the seventeenth century BC and left around four hundred years later, during the time of Moses and Aaron numbering over six hundred thousand. These Israelites had to have acquired from the Africans of Egypt most of the elements of their future religion, science and culture. It is also instructive to remember that their divinely elected leaders, Moses and Aaron, were born on the African continent. Moses, who according to the testimony of *Acts Of The Apostles* chapter 7:22 'was learned in all the religion of the Egyptians, and was mighty in words and deeds' is also identified by two historians of the ancient world, Plutarch and Manethro, under his other name of 'Osarisiph', an elder priest/prophet of the Egyptian priesthood. Together with his older brother Aaron, the Israelites received from these two Africans the concepts of the sacred law and the priesthood for the regulation of the relationship between the divine and the human worlds.

This history of the African link with the world of the Bible does not destroy the concept of Moses receiving of the laws of the Covenant as an act of revelation from the Almighty Living God, as found in the books of the Torah. It only shows that the original revelation first occurred in an African context. As the Apostle Paul would say in the book of Hebrews 1:1, 'long ago God spoke to our ancestors in many and various ways'. So the Living God was revealing Himself time and again, and not only once.

Furthermore, even the language that these Israelites spoke

60

when they made their Exodus from Egypt, that later developed into Hebrew, must have been mostly African/Egyptian, or a form of it.

We know from our own experience of slavery how a language is lost, or assimilated. Our original African parents who were brought to the Caribbean, the Americas and Europe from around the beginning of the seventeenth century AD spoke the language of the region of the African continent from which they were captured. Whereas by the end of the fourth generation of captivity, we who are their descendants speak mainly English, French, Spanish or Portuguese, or a combination of them, depending on how many times our African parents were sold as slaves. In a similar way, it would have been impossible for the Israelites who went out of Egypt in the Exodus not to have been speaking ancient Egyptian, or at least a combination of ancient Egyptian and the earlier language that their ancestors spoke when they entered Egypt around four hundred years before.

★

Finally all these ideas that I have outlined above about the southern African origins of Egyptian civilisation feeding the ancient Israelites and the wider Mediterranean world, as discussed by the African and African-American scholars that I have mentioned, gained international recognition from 28 January to 3 February 1974 by the conference hosted by UNESCO (United Nations Educational, Scientific And Cultural Organisation) in Cairo under the theme 'The Peopling of Ancient Egypt and the Deciphering of the Meroitic Script'.

What is most significant about this conference twenty-one years later is that the two leading African scholars, Cheikh Anta Diop and Theophilos Obenga, who played a leading role at this conference, grounded the Southern African origin of Egyptian civilisation on a solid scientific base by presenting evidence to show that the achievements of the ancient Egyptians in the fields of writing, astronomy, agriculture, physics, navigation, architecture, engineering, mathematics and medicine, all had their origins in other parts of the African continent that was located along the axis of the Great Rift Valley to the south-east and south-west of the borders of Egypt. In its final report the UNESCO document in part says:

> Although the preparatory working paper sent out by UNESCO gave particulars of what was desired, not all participants had prepared communications comparable with the painstakingly researched contributions of Professors Cheikh Anta Diop and Obenga.

Chapter 3
Biblical References
(Old Testament)

I propose to now look at the references to 'Ethiopia/Cush' in the Old Testament in the following manner.

- As a term of identification.
- As a geographical location.
- In the Prophets.
- Ethiopia/Cush in its relations with Judahites.
- In the poetry and wisdom books.

As a Term of Identification

Four times the word 'Cush' appears as the name of a person (*Genesis* 10:6–8, which is duplicated in *1 Chronicles* 1:8–10, and also Psalm 7).

In the first three instances the person is stated to be the first son of Ham, who himself is one of Noah's three children. Ham has been connected as the ancestral father of various peoples of Africa and south-west Asia. More important he is the father of Nimrod, the builder of the first cities in Mesopotamia. In the fourth reference (Psalm 7) it appears as the name of a person from the tribe of Benjamin in the title of the Psalm.

A form of the word 'Cushite' in the King James translation, and 'Ethiopian' in some other English translations, appears twice in *Numbers* 12:1 as the national characteristic of the woman who Moses married. *Exodus* 2:21 gives her name as Zipporah, one of the daughters of Jethro. This double designation is again mentioned in *Jeremiah* 38:7–10, where Ebed-Melech, an officer in King Jehoiakim's court, is described as being Ethiopian, or Cushite, depending on the English language translation one is using. And in *II Samuel* 18:21–32 the name is applied eight times to a courtier in King David's army.

'Cushi' as the name of a person appears once in *Jeremiah* 36:14, where it is given as the name of the great-grandfather of Jehudi, another officer of King Jehoiakim's court. The name appears a second time in *Zephaniah* 1:1 where it states that a person of this name was the father of the prophet and a descendant of Hezekiali, a former King of Judah.

As a Geographical Reference

The name 'Ethiopia/Cush' appears six times as a geographical reference to a place south of Egypt.

In *Genesis* 2:13 it is given as the name of the place through which the River Ghion (ancient name for the Nile) flows. Twice in the book of *Esther* (1:1 and 8:9) the name appears as one of two boundaries of the then Persian Empire.

In *Isaiah* 18:1 reference is made to a land that lies beyond the rivers of Ethiopia, which sends ambassadors by the Nile.

The Prophet Ezekiel pronounces doom upon Egypt that shall reach up to the border of Ethiopia (29:10); and in *II Chronicles* 21:16 an invasion of Judah by Arabians who live near the Ethiopians is reported.

In The Prophets

Ethiopia/Cush is referred to in the prophetic books of *Isaiah, Jeremiah, Ezekiel, Daniel, Amos, Nahum and Zephaniah*. I will deal with these references in the chronological order of the prophets' appearance in the history of the Old Testament, except in the case of two passages in the book of Isaiah, and in the case of Daniel.

• THE BOOK OF AMOS (760–50 BC)

In chapter 9:7 the Prophet compares the Israelites to the Ethiopians, stating that they are equal in God's eyes.

- THE BOOK OF ISAIAH (742–682 BC)

In *Isaiah*, chapter 20, Ethiopia is included with Egypt as the object
of a prophecy of doom. In 43:3 it is included as a message of hope
for Judah. It states that both Ethiopia and Egypt will be given as a
ransom for them. In verse 14 of chapter 45, it appears in a
prophecy that predicts the subservience of Ethiopia, Egypt and the
Sabeans to the restored people of Judah.

- THE BOOK OF ZEPHANIAH (626 BC)

Zephaniah contains two references to Ethiopia: one contains a
prophecy that foresees the destruction of Ethiopia with several
other nations (2:12). The other one refers to the time when the
worshippers of God who live between the rivers of Ethiopia will
bring offerings to Jerusalem (3:10).

- THE BOOK OF JEREMIAH (626–582 BC)

In 13:23 the much quoted proverb is mentioned 'can an Ethiopian
change the colour of his skin, or the leopard its spots'. In 39:15–18
Jeremiah pronounces a blessing upon Ebed-Melech, the Ethiopian official at whose intercession the Prophet was released from
the pit he was thrown into by the King, and also for his trust in
God. In 46:9 the Prophet includes the Ethiopians among the
peoples who had been helpless in giving support to the Chaldeans
in the Battle of Carchemish (605 BC)

- THE BOOK OF NAHUM (612–600 BC)

The one reference to Ethiopia in this book (3:9) includes Ethiopia
as one of the countries that supported the Egyptian city of
Thebes, but were unable to prevent its capture by the Assyrians in
663 BC.

- THE BOOK OF EZEKIEL (593–570 BC)

The prophecy of doom which is pronounced primarily upon
Egypt in chapter 30 includes Ethiopia three times as being also the
object of destruction (verses 4–5,9). In 38:5, Ethiopia is included
among several nations that Ezekiel says will be destroyed.

- THE BOOK OF DANIEL (165–64 BC)

11:43 includes the Ethiopians among those whom Antiochus will conquer.

- THE BOOK OF JOB

29:19 makes reference to the Topaz of Ethiopia.

THE BOOK OF PSALMS

There are two references in the book of Psalms concerning Ethiopia.

Psalm 68:31 is probably one of the most quoted references to Ethiopia in the Bible. In this verse mention is made of Ethiopia hastening to stretch her hands to God.

In Psalm 87:4 Ethiopia is mentioned with several other places of renown.

The Queen of Sheba and Her Son

There is no mistake that Ethiopia's most celebrated Old Testament recorded narrative is that of the Queen of Sheba (Makeda) and her visit to King Solomon's court at Jerusalem 'to prove him with hard questions' as the account of *I Kings* 10:1–13 states. This narrative is also repeated in *I Chronicles* 9:1–9. This must have been a few years after the completion of the Temple that Solomon commissioned and over which he also acted as supervisor when it was being built.

Solomon had replaced his illustrious father David as King of Israel when he was anointed by Zadok, the High Priest. The essential historical components, besides the biblical accounts upon which this narrative is based, are the royal chronicles of the *Kebra Negast* (the glory of the Kings), the *Fetha Negast* (the law of the Kings), and the *Reports of the Ethiopian Institute of Archaeology*. In addition to these written sources there are also oral traditions of the provinces of Begemder and Tegray which have preserved accounts of the Queen of Sheba's visit, and the conception of Menelik 1.

From a close analysis of the two biblical narratives about the Queen of Sheba and her visit to Solomon's court at Jerusalem,

European scholars and historians express doubt concerning the identity of this Queen and the location of her kingdom. That she possessed enormous wealth is clearly stated in *Isaiah* 43:3, where her kingdom, together with those of the Kings of Cush and Egypt, is named among the richest on earth. In 60:6 of the same book, there is another reference to the Queen of Sheba's wealth. Further still, in *Ezekiel* 27:22–33 we hear of the 'merchants of Sheba' who traded in the great markets of Tyre 'in all spices' and in 'precious stones and gold'. Then again in *Jeremiah* 6:20, the land of Sheba is described as being rich 'in incense'. Finally the Messianic Psalm 72:10–11, which is chanted during the Church's midnight Christmas service we hear of 'the Kings of Tarshish and the Iles' who would bring the Infant Messiah presents, and 'the Kings of Sheba and Saba shall offer gifts'. The prophesy is fulfilled with the visit of the three wise men to Bethlehem that St Matthew records in his holy gospel (2:1–12).

At this stage it may be important to point out that in the world of ancient and medieval Palestine and Arabia, it was widely believed that the illustrious Queen of Sheba was an ancient Arabian Queen, named Belkis, and that the Yeminite Kingdom of Himyar was her ancestral home. But when the literary sources that have preserved this account are examined in relation to the Ethiopian sources, one sees very clearly that they have preserved particular details about the dynasty to which the Queen of Sheba belonged; about her parents, her personal history, and above all a very precise record of her visit to King Solomon's court at Jerusalem and its immediate aftermath. Besides these facts, in examining the two sets of historical narratives, one sees that the Ethiopian sources are free of the fictitious events and fabulous inventions which dominate the sources used by Rabbinical and Arabic writers.

The dynasty to which the Queen of Sheba, Mekada, belonged is estimated to have been established in Ethiopia after the flood when Axum was built by a great grandson of Ham called Aksumawi. However, silence reigns about the inhabitants and rulers of ancient Axum until around the year 1370 BC during the era of the Ethiopian Pharaohs of the eighteenth Egyptian dynasty in the reign of Thutmose IV. Its first ruler to have preserved records of his administration is said to have been King Za Besi Angabo who had replaced the last monarch of an older dynasty known as the royal Arwe line.

It is suggested that the rulers of this older dynasty were a mixture of Ethiopian and Egyptian monarchs since some of its kings and queens were worshippers of the serpent, the sun, and the moon, and it was a well-known fact that all three were regarded by Ethiopians and Egyptians as symbols of wisdom and of sacred authority.

In any case this dynasty inaugurated by King Za Besi Angabo maintained its rule for about three hundred and fifty years, during which many kings and queens reigned. The literary and oral traditions however are silent on the actual number or the dates of their reigns.

The Queen of Sheba's grandfather reigned from about 1076 to 1026 BC. His name was Za Sebado. His queen was Ceres. They appear to have had only one child, a daughter, who married her father's chief minister. When King Za Sebado died, this son-in-law became Ethiopia's king and reigned from about 1026 to 1005 BC. To him and his wife, Queen Ismenie, were born two children: a son, called Prince Noural, and a daughter, Princess Makeda, who is said to have been born about 1025 BC. Her brother died while he was still an infant. The tradition relates that while she was still a child, Princess Mekada was attacked by a pet jackal which bit her badly on one foot, leaving her with some scars. (The injury received at this time is supposed to have been responsible for the Arabian tradition which states that one of the Queen's limbs was deformed, and resembled that of a donkey. However the Ethiopian sources state nothing about this.)

When her father died in 1005 BC, Princess Makeda, the only heir, ascended the throne and reigned until she died in about 940 BC. The young Queen is said to have been 'very beautiful, full of intelligence and understanding, as well as possessing a very inquisitive mind'. The narratives further state that Princess Makeda inherited all her parents' wealth of gold, silver, finely woven silks, as well as camels and caravans, which were used to transport goods to the sea port of Syene. From here ships would travel as far as India and China.

One of the great royal traders of Ethiopia at this time was Prince Tamrin who owned around four hundred ships, and caravans numbering over five hundred camels for his extensive business operations. The Prince's most illustrious customer was King Solomon, who was receiving large orders of Ethiopia's products, including red gold, sapphires, and a very rare black timber that could not be bored into by worms or other creatures known to attack timber.

During his sojourn in Jerusalem to deliver Solomon's orders (Solomon was in the process of overseeing the building of the Temple of Jerusalem), Prince Tamrin met other traders, sent from King Hiram of Tyre, who also came to deliver goods for the construction of the Temple. Here the Ethiopian Prince had the opportunity to hear at close quarters for himself the wisdom of this noble king, which had spread throughout the known inhabited world at that time. We are told that Prince Tamrin was highly impressed with Solomon's administration, and the great splendour in which he lived.

On his return to Ethiopia, the Prince would always give Queen Makeda eloquent and detailed accounts of all that he saw and learned from this wise king. It was from reports by Prince Tamrin that the inspiration to visit King Solomon in his capital at Jerusalem grew in Queen Makeda.

After several of these 'business journeys' by Prince Tamrin to deliver materials for the construction of the Temple in Jerusalem, Queen Makeda now discussed with her chief advisers the feasibility of visiting King Solomon in Jerusalem.

She gained their approval and named the Prince as the captain of the royal party who would make the journey with her. The size of the caravan he decided to use consisted of about eight hundred camels, and four hundred mules and donkeys.

Now that all was ready, Queen Makeda, with her score of attendants, set out for Jerusalem to learn at first hand the wisdom of Solomon. Her arrival is the episode that the narratives of I Kings 10:1–13 and 2 Chronicles 9:19 describe.

When she arrived, Solomon gave her and her royal party a cordial welcoming feast and accommodation in his huge palace complex. He then assigned some of his chefs to cater to the

Queen of Ethiopia and her entourage and provide whatever they desired to eat during their sojourn in Jerusalem. Her visit lasted about six months during which time she and Solomon and held many discussions. Religion appears to have been one of the principal topics which often claimed their attention.

In these exchanges Solomon no doubt explained to Makeda about the power and uncreated glory of the One true Living God, who was the creator of the universe, and whom Israelites worshipped as Yahweh, the God of his ancestors Abraham and Sarah, Isaac and Rebecca, Jacob and Rachel. Apparently Queen Makeda was so convinced that she resolved to re-convert her kingdom in Ethiopia, which had given up the worship of the One true Living God, and worshipped the sun, the moon and the serpent.

When the time was drawing close for Makeda to return home to Ethiopia, the narrative of the *Kebra Negast* states that Solomon asked her to stay a little while longer so that he might 'complete her instruction in the divine wisdom of the fathers of his father, King David'. She accepted his invitation in innocence only to discover in due time that Solomon desired her for himself. Being at this time still a virgin, Makeda tried as best she could to safeguard her virginity, but her efforts in due time failed. Chapters 29–32 of the *Kebra Negast* describe the seduction of Queen Makeda and the birth of Menelik I.

Following a farewell dinner at which highly seasoned food was consumed, Solomon invited Makeda to spend the night in his quarters of the palace. She agreed on the condition that he would not try to take her virginity. Solomon agreed with a condition of his own: that Makeda would not take anything that belonged to him. Having reached this mutual agreement, two beds were spread on either side of the royal bed-chamber, and they retired for the night. The Queen slept a little, but awoke during the night because the spicy food she had eaten had made her throat dry.

Now Solomon had told his servants to set a jar of water in the centre of the room. The Queen looked at it and was filled with the longing to drink a little. Thinking that Solomon was asleep, she crept out of her bed and put her hand to the jar. But Solomon had not been asleep, and he seized her arm and said, 'You have broken the oath that you swore not to take anything by force that is in my palace.' Makeda protested that the oath did not apply to water, but Solomon replied that there was nothing more precious than water. She now admitted that she was wrong, but begged that she might have a drink. So Solomon was released from his oath and worked his will on her, and they slept together.

As he slept, the King dreamed a dream in which he saw the sun descending on the land of Judah and shining upon it very brightly; then it was removed and went to Ethiopia and shone there. It came back a second time to the land of Judah, but the native inhabitants of Judah hated it, and plotted to put out its light. It then departed to the land of Ethiopia and Rome.

Early the next morning Makeda resolved to return to her Kingdom of Ethiopia. This time Solomon did not try to prevent her but instead gave her many rich presents, including a ring for the son he hoped she would give birth to. So Makeda began the long arduous journey from Jerusalem back to Ethiopia. As time elapsed on the journey home she realised that she was pregnant and just before she arrived back in Ethiopia she gave birth to a male child whom she called Ebna Hakim (the son of the wise man).

Although she maintained a residence at Axum, the capital of her kingdom appears to have been further south (hence one of her titles 'Queen of the South') near the Red Sea coast around the port of Assab (or Asabe or Saba, as this port was called in the language of Ethiopia at this time).

In Tegrinya she is known as 'Eteye Azeb' (meaning ruler of the South) following the passage of the New Testament (*Matthew* 12:42) when Our Lord Jesus Christ speaks of the Queen of the South to the crowds who followed him.

The Queen of the South shall rise up in the judgement with this generation, and shall condemn it. For she came from the uttermost parts of the earth to hear the wisdom of Solomon: and behold a greater than Solomon is here.

It is also worth noting here that in 1939 the Austrian explorer, Byron De Prorok Khun, discovered in the southern part of

Somalia, about one hundred miles from the Red Sea port of Afars, remains of several ruined buildings and ancient tombs which he later dated to the age in which the Queen of Sheba lived. This discovery was later verified by the Ethiopian Institute of Archaeology which was established in 1952.

When Prince Ebria Hakim became a young man, he himself, together with the ageing Prince Tamrin, his Mother's Minister of State, went to Jerusalem to visit his father Solomon. Chapters 33–34 of the *Kebra Negast* record this part of the history. They state that Solomon was overjoyed to see his son whose identity was proved when he presented the ring Solomon had given to his mother. In response Solomon said, 'What need is there of a ring? without a sign I know that you are my son.' Prince Tamrin now delivered the message that his Queen had given to him, that Solomon should anoint Ebna Hakim with the oil of kingship.

At first Solomon tried to persuade Ebna Hakim to remain in Jerusalem to become his successor as Rehoboam, Solomon's only other son at this time, was 'ample in foolishness and lacking in understanding' as was written in the book *I Kings*. Nevertheless the Ethiopian Prince insisted that he must return to his mother to help her govern and convert those Ethiopians who still worshipped the sun, the moon and the serpent to the worship of the One true Living God. Solomon did not pursue the matter, but anointed him with the oil of kingship and arranged for Zadok, the High Priest, to teach him all the laws of Moses contained in the scrolls of the law. Prince Ebna Hakim (in obedience to a wish of his mother) asked his father and Zadok in an audience for a piece of the cloth that was used to cover the Ark of the Covenant, which rested on the Altar within the Holy of Holies.

This was to convince the Ethiopians when he returned that they had visible contact with the God of Israel who was now identified as the one true God. Both Solomon and Zadok promised to grant his request. Moreover, Solomon summoned his counsellors and officers and said to them, 'I am sending my first-born son to rule Ethiopia. Gather the first-born sons from Levi, Dan and Gad to be his counsellors and officers'. And they obeyed the King's command.

When the time came for them to leave, the first-born from

these tribes grew sad and secretly reviled Solomon.

★

Their greatest sorrow was that they had to leave Jerusalem where
the Ark of the Covenant's resting place was located. Azariah, the
son of Zadok the High Priest, thought of a plan, and binding the
others to silence he revealed it to them. They each gave him ten
silver coins, and he went to one of the carpenters in the court, and
said to him: 'Build me a raft because we are going to journey
across the sea, and if the ship sinks, we can be saved in the raft.'
He now gave to the carpenter the measurements of the Ark of the
Covenant.

The night before they were to depart, Azariah took the raft,
which was in the form of the Ark of the Covenant, and went into
the Temple and entered the Holy of Holies (the Archangel Uriel
opened the doors for him) and he uncovered the Ark of the
Covenant, took it from the Altar, put in its place the raft and
covered it up with three cloths that were covering the Ark so that
no one could see the change. The next day Solomon asked Zadok
to take the outer cloth that covered the Ark and bring it to him.
Solomon gave it to Ebna Hakim who rejoiced in the gift. Now
together with the Levites, the Gadites and the Danites they set out
in a great train of wagons for Ethiopia.

When they arrived in Egypt, Azariah revealed to Ebna Hakim
how they had brought the Ark of the Covenant and copies of the
book of the laws and rituals for worship with him and the rest of
his court in Ethiopia. Upon hearing this news Ebna Hakim was
filled with joy. Finally they arrived in Ethiopia.

Now that his son had departed, Solomon was sad and he told
Zadok of the dream that he had had the night before he slept with
Queen Makeda of Ethiopia. Zadok became worried and said to
the King, 'I wish that you had told me this dream before.' He now
went to the Temple and entered the Holy of Holies and took off
the two remaining cloths that covered the Ark of the Covenant.

He saw instead of the Ark the raft of planks which Azariah his
son had asked one of the court carpenters to build. He then
returned to the palace and informed Solomon. The King now

73

mobilised his army and marched to Egypt where he questioned the Egyptians concerning what time the Ethiopian caravan had passed. They answered that it was many days ago. In his despair a holy spirit sent by the Holy God Yahweh comforted him saying: 'The Ark has not been given to an alien, but to your first-born son.'

When he returned to Jerusalem, Solomon commanded that a replica should be made, and ordered all his counsellors and officers to keep secret that the Ark of the Covenant was now in Ethiopia.

★

Queen Makeda lived many years after her son returned, and finally died about 940 BC.

Upon ascending the throne Prince Ebna Hakim took the name Menelik and established the Solomonic dynasty in Ethiopia. In the course of his reign he moved the capital from Assab in the South to Axum where his mother's tomb was located. The two main reasons for this appear to relate to Axum's great altitude. The climate was milder than the previous capital. The other reason was that its height above sea level made it harder for foreign forces to invade.

Some Essential Aspect's of Ethiopia's Old Testament Faith

One can say that from the time of Menelik's return from Jerusalem with Azariah, priests from the tribe of Levi, and nobles from the tribes of Gad and Dan, with the Ark of the Covenant, the essence of Ethiopia's Old Testament faith in God is summed up in a quotation from Psalm 27:8–9:

Hear, O Lord, when I cry aloud, be gracious to me and answer me! Come, says my heart, seek His face! Your face, Lord, do I seek, do not hide your face from me. Do not turn your servant away in anger, you have been my help.

Do not cast me off, do not forsake me, O God of my salvation.

Included in the book of devotion for worship in the Temple built at Axum, this prayer found its way into the Preparatory Service of the Liturgy of the Ethiopian Orthodox Church.

It helps to capture the inner essence of the Ethiopian Old Testament religious soul. Seeking to behold the face of God; doing everything in one's power to live in God's presence; attempting to mould one's entire life on the pattern of the holy life revealed by the Holy Life of the Living God. Striving to live constantly in the presence of God, straining to cultivate a life of holiness that is associated with sacred space and time, centred around the Temple and other places of worship that were constructed during Menelik's lifetime.

From the time that Azariah came to dwell in Ethiopia, this prayer from Psalm 27 has won the hearts and minds of Ethiopia's kings and queens, her priests, her prophets, her physicians and healers, her musicians and artists, her monks and nuns, her philosophers and scientists, etc.

This prayer from the Book of Psalms has produced various types of Ethiopian men and women, each with a different outlook to one aspect or another of the spiritual and religious life.

For some Ethiopians, especially the scribes who became attached to Menelik's palace compound, seeking the face of God included carrying out studies about the origins and beginnings of the histories of the twelve tribes which made up the nation of Israel, and out of which the Davidic-Solomonic Kingdom arose. To accomplish this task, they began to search out the oral traditions from the four tribes of Israel, now dwelling among them in Ethiopia, about the other eight.

They knew that each 'individual tribe spirit' was very much alive, as was made abundantly clear from the disintegration of the United Kingdom following Solomon's death.[1]

These scribes of Menelik's administration, with the help of the Levites, Gadites, Danites and Judahites dwelling in Ethiopia,

---

[1] *I Kings* 12.

knew that prior to the establishment of the Israelite monarchy with Saul, the 'official histories' of most of the twelve tribes were kept at its central shrine. Based on oral traditions that later became included in the *Book of Numbers*, chapter 2, which is a description of the Israelites gathered around the Ark of the Covenant for worship, the main tribes seem to have been those of Judah, Reuben, Ephraiam, Dan and Levi. And later Old Testament history confirmed this view, because we know more about these five tribes than the others such as Simeon, Naptali, Asher, Mannaseh, Issachar, etc.

Because each tribe had its central shrine, this is where its members would normally gather, especially on the Sabbath, to worship, and also to learn about the origin and history from one of the elder caretakers who lived there.

This was the case of the shrine of the tribe of Ephraiam at Shiloh,[2] before Saul was anointed King, when the Priest Eli served the Ark of the Covenant there. This same tribe had another shrine at Bethel.[3] This was Ephraiam's central shrine because of its connection with the Patriarch Jacob/Israel.

Another shrine which they studied was the one at Shechem[4] which was connected with the history of Abraham, Jacob/Israel and Joshua. Hebron[5] was another important shrine because it was David's first capital before he captured Jerusalem. As a result Hebron became the main shrine for the tribe of Judah.

When the other twelve tribes settled in Canaan, the tribe of Asher seems to have had its central shrine at Acco, on the Eastern bank of the River Jordan, while Dan and Naptali seem to have had theirs at Kadesh and Hazor, Reuben had its shrine at Bezer; while Benjamin had its own at Gilbeath. Records of the shrines of the other tribes have not come down to us.

For other Ethiopian Old Testament men and women, seeking the face of God included giving financial support to the priests at the central sanctuary in Axum, so that the main feast days of the Old Testament Calendar such the commemoration of the

---

[2] *I Sam* 1:1–3; 3:1–3.
[3] *Gen* 28:10–22; 31:13; 35:1–15.
[4] *Gen* 12:6–7; 33:18–34; 31; *Jos* 24.
[5] *2 Sam* 5:5.

Passover, the Feast of Weeks, the Feast of the New Year, the day of Atonement, the Feast of the Tabernacles, the Feast of Lights, etc.

Still others tried to discover the face of God by seeking the 'inner sanctuary of the heart' of which the central sanctuary at Axum was a physical representation, and they prayed for the 'Shekhinah of Yahweh' (the divine fire of God) which consumed the offerings placed on the Altar to descend into the inner sanctuary within their hearts to consume all their sins and imperfections.

Still others sought the face of God by allowing their thoughts to ascend to different planes, and parts of existence, where mystical knowledge is imparted in highly developed symbolic language, music and paintings.

The ultimate path of seeking the face of God involved trying to relive the journeys of Enoch, as he was transported out of himself, and ascended through all the countless worlds of the holy angels and holy spirits, until he reached the foot of the throne of the Everliving, Uncreated, Creator and Sustainer of all life.

*

What all the different types of Ethiopian religious men and women had in common was a commitment to living a life of holiness. They had a deep faith in the Covenant laws, symbolised by the presence among them of the Ark of the Covenant.

In each generation following the death of Menelik I and Arazaiah, the codes of conduct and doctrines contained in the laws of the Covenant first collected by Moses for the Israelites, were redefined and elaborated by the priests and scribes who lived at the various shrines and sanctuaries within Ethiopia. Schools and centres of learning began to multiply as well. Education began to be transmitted under five main categories:

1. Mystery teachings of Heavenly worlds (astronomy and astrology).
2. Mystery teachings of all inhabited places (geography).
3. Mystery teachings of the depths (geology).

4. Mystery teachings of the secret words (philosophy and theology).
5. Mystery teachings of the King's and Queen's administration (law and communication).

The process of knowledge was not understood as a simple matter of acquiring knowledge for knowledge's sake. It was seen rather as a transforming process, where the learner progressed through different stages of growth, during which they became more Godlike in their thoughts, actions, and feelings.

Until the birth of the Lord Jesus Christ, there were ongoing debates among these priests, teachers and scribes about the education system that was centred around the meaning of the laws of the Covenant, and exactly what it was that made up the inner essence of the Covenant itself. No agreement was ever reached to satisfy all the parties involved.

They agreed on these points, however:

a. Some of the laws of the Covenant when applied to their educational philosophy concerned Ethiopian men and women in their relationship with God.
b. Some were concerned with relationships between themselves.
c. Some were concerned with the performance of rituals and acts of devotion.
d. Others were concerned with moral and ethical issues.

They constantly examined and re-examined these laws of the Covenant because correct forms of speech, actions, bodily behaviour, ideas, rules of prayer, and worship were crucial to the kings and queens, the scribes and teachers, the lawyers and judges. These groups within Ethiopian Old Testament society did everything in their power to ensure that the wider population observed all the laws of the Covenant.

Bodily actions, deeds and behaviour were looked upon as aspects of communication and speech, especially when displayed in the context of worship, prayer and litigation. As a result of this, speeches which embodied symbolic actions were framed in fixed rules for performance. Even to this day Ge'ez and Amharic observe these fixed rules that may have evolved from the Old Testament period. Of course there were developments and changes, but any Solomonic King or Queen, or any priest, or scribe, or judge, or teacher was obligated to begin their public utterance with a confession of their belief in the Oneness of God, the 'Shema' of *Deuteronomy* 6:4: 'Hear O Israel, the Lord our God, the Lord is One' had to be declared loudly with allowance for only one change. 'Israel' was replaced with 'Ethiopia'.

So priests, or teachers, before they began a worship service or a period of instruction, had to proclaim in the presence of all their listeners, 'Hear O Ethiopians, the Lord our God, the Lord is One'. The kings and queens had to recite the same confession before they made any public decree or modification to the laws.

Any official who did not begin his public presentations with a confession of 'Shema' of *Deuteronomy* 6:4 stood to face much opposition. In some cases the person in question was in danger even of being deposed and exiled.

The 'Oneness' of God was given several different meanings. It may be the 'Oneness' of six or seven priests or teachers united in a common venture. Or the 'Oneness' might mean the One Almighty power of God, the Creator of all things seen and unseen; or it might mean the 'Oneness' of Ethiopia and her peoples; or the 'Oneness' of the world, etc.

The Oneness of God contained in the 'Shema' of *Deuteronomy* 6.4 reminded the Ethiopian listeners about the fact that Moses had received the laws of the Covenant through the process of revelation on several occasions, especially on Mt Sinai in the Horeb mountain range of the Arabian Peninsula. This is the account that is recorded in the book of Exodus.

Again among the Old Testament population there existed a wide range of beliefs about the exact nature of the revelation which Moses received on Mt Sinai, just as there existed many different ideas about the precise spot on Mt Sinai where Moses had received the revelation. But despite all the questions the historical event itself was never doubted.

Now because of this revelation by God to Moses on Mt Sinai, mountains began to play a significant role in the Ethiopian religious life. In fact the Christian monks and nuns, who built monasteries and convents on mountain tops, just like the kings and queens who built palaces, churches, and military garrisons on Ethiopia's mountain tops, received this idea from the original inhabitants of the Old Testament period.

New Testament References

What I have written so far has been an introduction to my main history of Christianity in Ethiopia and the Ethiopian Orthodox Tewahedo Church. It will become obvious by the end of the book that I have woven a tapestry setting the main layers of the Ethiopian Orthodox Church's history against a background of the entire history of Ethiopia.

★

The Visit of the Three Wise Men (The Magi)

The people of Ethiopia embraced Christianity right from the outset of the New Testament age which was inaugurated with the Incarnation and Nativity of the Lord Jesus Christ, when the three Wise Men (or Magi), one of whom has always been identified as a black King in European Christian art, came to visit the Infant Messiah shortly after He was born. This is the account that St Matthew records (2:1–12). The problem that has puzzled many scholars for centuries has been his name, along with that of the other two wise men, as St Matthew's gospel does not furnish this information.

Hans Holzer in his book *Star Of The East* names them on page 77, as Jaspar (or Caspar), Melchior and Balthasar. Jaspar he calls the King of Afghanistan, Melchior he names as a ruler of Western Asia, probably Persia, and Balthasar as the King of Ethiopia.

However, William Leo Hansbury and E. Harper Johnson name them as Jaspar the King of Ethiopia, Melchior the King of Nubia, and Balthazar the King of Saba.

Furthermore, the learned Ethiopian historian Aleqa Taye, and also the German linguist August Dillman, solve the problem by furnishing information from the records of the Ethiopian

Institute of Archaeology. These two state that Ethiopians had two or more names, therefore Jaspar (or Caspar) could also have been another name for Bazan or Balthazar, because from the lists of monarchs preserved by the Ethiopian Institute of Archaeology, one of the wise men is identified as King Bazan.

This would indicate that he probably assumed this name on ascending the throne. In European academic circles Bazan seems to have become Balthazar over the centuries. Aleqa Taye, the Ethiopian historian, writes on page 62 in an Amharic text, *Ye Ethiopia Hizb Taric*, published in 1955, 'King Bazan ruled Ethiopia for seventeen years, eight years before and nine years after the birth of Christ.'

Dillman's book, *Royal Ethiopia*, also confirms this view. He lists all the rulers from the Queen of Sheba to King Bazan. King Bazan's (Jaspar's) tomb, together with that of his family, was discovered by the German archaeologist Enno Littmann in Axum in 1904. From this Littmann concluded that Jaspar (Bazan) lived in the first century and is the one of the three wise Kings who went to worship the Infant Messiah Jesus Christ in Jerusalem.

Another account is preserved by Professor Wheeler in his book, *The Golden Legend of Ethiopia*. On page 184 he writes,

> When the line of King Menelik I of Ethiopia (son of Queen Makeda and King Solomon) had sat upon the throne for thirty generations, one of the Royal line, the cousin of the King then reigning and a famed student of the Wisdom of the Stars, by the name Jaspar or Gazpor (in the northern lands he is called Gaspard), beheld the shining of the strange star in the East, and on his dromedary, with his two magi brothers, Melchior and Balthazar, came to Bethlehem to find the Saviour of the World.

*

From these references it is not impossible to believe that all three wise men came from one region. It is also recorded by these scholars that during the time that the Lord Jesus Christ was born, Ethiopia dominated several countries, including Nubia and parts of present-day Sudan and Kenya, South Arabia, and other parts of western Asia including Persia and Afghanistan. This was due to the fact that in this time Axum was inhabited by a powerful race of warriors who subdued these regions.

In St Matthew's account the arrival of these three kings took place after the birth of the Lord. And the Church believes it was probably after the forty-day transition period ('the time of purification', as the Old Testament custom referred to the time from the birth of a male child until his circumcision on the fortieth day).

★

In the New Testament Apocryphal tradition, mention is made in a manuscript lodged in the British Museum (British Museum Ethiopic M.S. Add 16196) to the sojourning in Ethiopia of the Infant Christ, His Mother St Mary, and His earthly guardian St Joseph, for about three and a half years.

There is also an account in the seventh chapter of the *Apocryphal Acts of the Apostles* of St Matthew's visit to King Aeglippus' court at Naddarer. This was a minor king who paid tribute to the powerful Axum kings, and his region was north of Axum in present day Eritrea. St Matthew preaches about the Lord Jesus Christ to this king and his court on his way to India.

The Baptism of the Ethiopian Treasurer by St Philip

But there is no question, however, that Ethiopia's most celebrated New Testament reference is the narrative of the Baptism of Queen Candace's Treasurer by St Philip. I mention this because the other references, such as the dwelling of the Infant Messiah Jesus Christ in the country, and the visit of St Matthew to King Aeglippus' court, occur in manuscripts not contained in the canon of the New Testament when it came to be fixed in the middle of the fourth century AD therefore the authenticity of historical events recorded in them is questioned.

As for the reference of the visit of the three wise men, St Matthew's gospel mentions the event, but the names of the three are not given by him. It is only through the records of the Church and the work of the scholars mentioned earlier that their names and identities have been preserved.

However the narrative of the account of the Baptism of Queen Candace's Treasurer is quite a different case, because the book of *Acts of the Apostles* which was composed by St Luke was contained in the list of the books that made up the canon of the New Testament, and the authenticity of the historical facts presented in it have never been questioned.

★

In the narrative of chapter 8 (26–39) this Ethiopian official is identified as a Eunuch and the Treasurer of Queen Candace. He is returning from Jerusalem in his chariot to Ethiopia and is reading the scroll of *Isaiah* 53:7–8: 'As a sheep is led to the slaughter, or a lamb before its shearer is dumb, so he opens not his mouth. In his humiliation justice was denied him. Who can describe his generation? For his life is taken from the earth.' This Ethiopian Treasurer lacks a proper understanding of this passage that he has been reading, and very mystically, the Holy Spirit orders St Philip who is in the region to go and join this Ethiopian Treasurer's chariot to explain that the meaning of this passage of Isaiah's scroll is a prophecy of the sacrificial death and resurrection of the Incarnate Saviour Jesus Christ.

After St Philip gives this Ethiopian Treasurer the proper understanding, it also appears that he preaches to him the importance of being baptised, and probably also the other sacraments, because as they journey on this desert road from Jerusalem to the city of Gaza, this official asks to be baptised as they pass a pool, or a small water-hole in the vicinity.

St Philip tells him that the only condition he must fulfil to be baptised, is that he must confess his faith in the Lord Jesus Christ as the Son and Incarnate Word of God. The Ethiopian Treasurer makes his confession in the Divinity of Christ. St Philip then baptises him.

The narrative ends with their parting at Gaza. St Philip is sent to Azotus by the Holy Spirit, while the Ethiopian Treasurer goes on home to his Queen and the court rejoicing.

★

The city of Gaza, near where the Ethiopian Treasurer was baptised, has been in the news very frequently. It was handed back to the Palestinians by the Israelites in September 1993 and is now the capital of the newly formed Palestinian state whose leader is Yasser Arrafat. As we all know in the last thirty years Gaza was one of the war-torn places of dispute between Israel and the PLO. This city had a long history even before the meeting of St Philip and the Ethiopian Treasurer there.

During the reign of Pharaoh Thutmose III, it served as the base for Egyptian operations in Canaan from about 1469–63 BC Gaza is also mentioned in the el-Amarna and Taanach tablets as an Egyptian administrative centre. The city was allotted to the tribe of Judah (see *Joshua* 15:47 and *Judges* 1:18), but remained in the possession of the Canaanites until the beginning of the twelfth century BC.

At that time, it became the furthest southern city of the Philistine Pentapolis (see *Joshua* 13:3; *I Samuel* 6:7; *Jeremiah* 25–20). The famous Philistine temple of Dagon was located there. In 734 BC the Assyrian King, Tiglath-Pileser, captured Gaza, but it remained a Philistine city, and the short-lived conquest of Hezekiah (see *II Kings* 18:8) did not alter its status.

Pharaoh Necho II occupied Gaza briefly in 609 BC. Under the Persians, Gaza became an important royal fortress. It was called Kadytis by the Greek historian Herodotus. In 332 BC it was the only city in Palestine to oppose Alexander the Great who besieged it and sold its people into slavery. In the Hellenistic period, Gaza was the outpost of the Ptolemies until its capture by Antiochus III in 198 BC. The city was attacked by Jonathan, the Hasmonaen, in 145 BC (see *I Maccabees* 11:61–62) but was only taken by Alexander Jannaeus in 96 BC after a long siege. The 'wilderness of Gaza', as the road that leads from Jerusalem to this city is called in our text, was given this name because of its destruction by Jannaeus.

It was restored by Pompey and rebuilt by Gabinius in 57 BC. King Herod held it for a short time. After his death the city was under the Roman Proconsul of Syria where it flourished. By the time St Philip baptised the Ethiopian Treasurer there, its famous school of rhetoric was established, but the majority of its citizens were still tied to the worship of the gods of the Roman and Hellenic religious traditions. It boasted temples dedicated to Zeus, Helios, Aphrodite, Apollo, Athene and the local god Tyche. Only by the end of the fifth century did Christianity become fully established there.

★

Now, while the authenticity of this narrative has never been disputed, the problems that it has posed surround the identity of the Treasurer and also of Queen Candace. European biblical scholars, such as Wallis Budge, Edward Ullendorft, David Buxton and Jean Doresse, have made much of the fact that biblical 'Ethiopia/Cush' can mean the entire region of the African continent that lies to the south-east and south-west of present-day Egypt. This means Sudan, Chad, Somalia, Djibouti, Kenya and Uganda. Because of this they state that this Treasurer whose name is not mentioned in the text could have come from any one of these places and not necessarily from Axum.

However, Ethiopian historians such as Taddesse Tamrat, Tekle Tsadik Mekuria and Sifu Zeleke, while stating that this narrative of the book of *Acts of the Apostles* at least proves early African exposure to the gospel of the Lord Jesus Christ, have stated in their work that in the oral traditions of Tegray, Begemder and Eritrea, this Treasurer of Queen Candace who was baptised by St Philip is identified as Djan Darada.

A similar problem surrounds Queen Candace. These same European scholars who have questioned the identity of the Treasurer have stated as well that the name 'Candace' was the title of a Queen Mother of Meroe, who led a military campaign against the Romans of the time that Augustus was the Emperor of Rome. From that time in the first century BC it became a dynastic title of all the Queens of Meroe, Napata and Axum. Again to counter these arguments, the Ethiopian historians mentioned earlier state that the Queen Candace of the narrative of the baptism of the Ethiopian Treasurer was loosely connected to this dynasty and her personal name was Qarsemot, the fourth Axumite Queen with that personal name.

One of the early Church historians, Eusebius of Caesarea, speaks of the Ethiopian Treasurer as one of the first believers to be baptised after the great day of Pentecost. St John Chrysostom even believes that he could have been present together with other Ethiopians in the Jerusalem of the great day of Pentecost itself, which traditionally is marked as the birth of the Universal Christian Church. Furthermore, St Irenaeus wrote that, on his return to Ethiopia, this Treasurer preached the gospel that was taught to him by St Philip to his Queen and the court at Axum.

Job Ludolphus, the seventeenth-century German historian, wrote in his book, *The History of Ethiopia*, that as a result of the baptism of this Treasurer Djan Darada, which took place in around AD 34, he preached and ministered the sacraments to many Ethiopians, and some women even engraved crosses upon their heads to signify their acceptance of the Christian faith.

It is also said that before he died in about AD 55 all the court of Queen Candace was practising the Christian faith and converted an ancient temple believed to have been built during the age of the Queen of Sheba into a Christian church. Other smaller churches and schools were built around this time also. The description of life in this early Christian community of Axum relates that a distinct mood and atmosphere permeated Ethiopia, which to my understanding can best be described as a lifestyle flooded with the expectation of the immediate return of the risen Christ to judge the works of His creation. Therefore the period from the journey of King Jasper up until the end of the third century constitutes the earliest of Ethiopia's Christian existence.

Chapter 4
St Frumentius/Abba Selama (The Ethiopian Orthodox Church's First Archbishop) and his Relationship with the Twin Monarchs Ezana and Shaiazana AD 290–356

The noble Church historian Rufinus of Tyre (AD 350–410) in his writings states that towards the middle of the third century, Metrodore, who is said to have been a philosopher living in Tyre, is reported to have visited the countries of Persia, India and Ethiopia. In the course of his travels he acquired a considerable collection of large pearls and rare and precious stones. A part of his collection is said to have been taken by the King of Persia. When he eventually returned to Tyre, Metrodore related in some detail to a few of his friends the observations and experiences he underwent during the course of his travels. One of his closest friends was a man named Meropius. He is described as a philosopher and a merchant Prince. So impressed was Meropius with Metrodore's account of his travels that he resolved to undertake a similar journey himself.

In about AD 289 Meropius set out for the East accompanied by two young companions named Frumentius and Sidrakos Adesius.

While sailing along the Red Sea, the ship on which they were travelling stopped at the port of Assab to obtain food and water supplies. Although the ship's crew had no knowledge of the fact, relations at that time were very strained between the inhabitants of this Ethiopian sea port and Roman and Greek vessels sailing in the nearby waters.

A few years before Meropius's ship stopped at Assab, this Red Sea port had been visited by Greek trading vessels and a fight had broken out between the ship's crew and some of the inhabitants of the town. As a consequence, the inhabitants not only had broken off trading relations with Greek and Roman merchants, but vowed vengeance on all who could be identified as country-men of those who recently violated the port's hospitality. Therefore when the ship on which Meropius and his two young companions with its Greek and Roman crew and passengers endeavoured to tie up the wharf, the native workers on shore attacked the ship. Meropius and all the others on board this ship were massacred, except Frumentius and Sidrakos Adesius.

Eventually these two young boys were taken to the chief priest of Axum, Anbaram. He now brought them to the palace of the King Ala-Amida and his Queen, Sofya (reigned AD 294–325). The King ordered that Anbaram should take charge of them and provide instruction for them.

So Frumentius and Sidrakos Adesius grew up in the house-hold of Anbaram and learned the faith of the Old Testament plus the customs and lifestyle of Ethiopia which included its language and traditional music.

According to Eusebius of Caesarea (lived AD 260–340, was bishop from 322 until his death), this Ethiopian king had sent messengers to Rome to visit Constantine while these two young men were growing up in the household of Anbaram, for the purpose of congratulating him on his recent conversion to the Christian faith and victory over the Germanic tribe of the Goths. This visit therefore must have been between AD 313 and 325.

After many years of living and being educated both at the royal court and in the household of Anbaram, Frumentius and Sidrakos Adesius were at liberty to leave the country after Ala-Amida died in AD 325. However Queen Sofya, now Queen Regent, urged the two young men to remain as her assistants in the government, and as tutors in charge of the final years in the education of her twin sons Abraha and Asbeha, who would eventually become rulers. This occurred in AD 326. After their coronation Abraha took the throne name Ezana, and his brother Asbeha chose Shaiazana. In all the inscriptions that have come down to us, and which have been published by G.W.B. Huntingford, who was a lecturer at the School of Oriental and African Studies in London from 1948 to 1966, these twin monarchs describe themselves as rulers of Axum and Hemer, and Kasu, and Saba, and Habasat, and Raydan, and Salhe, and Seyamo, and Beja, all regions situated south-east and south-west of Axum.

Some of the first laws that they made were to declare Christianity the official religion of Ethiopia and to provide funds to restore and decorate with icons the places of worship already in existence with scenes about the life of the Lord Jesus Christ, and the Old and New Testament saints, especially the great Church of Axum dedicated to St Mary, which housed the Ark of the Covenant. They also started an evangelisation project of building churches and schools in those regions south of Axum in Begemder, Gojjam, and Wollo among the homelands of the Amhara, the Beja, the Himer, the Kasu, the Saba, the Habasat, the Raydan, the Salhe, the Seyamo and the Keuta tribes with the help of their mother Queen Sofya, Frumentius, Sidrakos Adesius, Anbaram and some of the other leading officials at their court.

As the Christian communities in these areas began to grow, discussion began at the court of Ezana and Shaiazana about the need to have a bishop who could perform the sacrament of ordination to make the other sacraments active again. The *Book of Dogmatic Contentions* of St Tekla Haimanot and the *Fetha Negast* take up the story from here.

When he became a fully grown young man, one day Frumentius expressed to Anbaram how touched he had become to see the zeal and devotion of Ethiopians towards the Christian faith. He said to Anbaram, 'My Lord, I admire the life and culture of the people. You Ethiopians practise Circumcision and confess a deep faith in the Lord Jesus Christ, but you do not practise Baptism, nor Holy Communion.'

To this statement Anbaram replied, 'Our fathers, the Levites, brought us circumcision, and the Finance Minister of Queen Candace was baptised by St Philip in the name of the Father, and the Son and the Holy Spirit, yet we no longer have an apostle or bishop now to administer the sacraments. So could we please arrange for you go to Alexandria and be consecrated for this position?'

At this period in the early part of the fourth century, it is quite possible that the practice of the sacraments which was administered by Djan Darada, the Treasurer of Queen Candace who was baptised by St Philip, had discontinued. This left the Christian community in Axum without a successor. So by the time Frumentius and Sidrakos Adesius came to live in the country, the Axumites had reverted to practising the laws of the Old Testament, because Anbaram was a High Priest, after the Order of the Old Testament High Priests, Aaron and Zadok. So although he was exposed to the New Testament and preached and taught it, he did not know how to administer the sacraments of the Apostolic priesthood.

A little time had passed before Anbaram could arrange a meeting with the brother kings and their chief advisers to discuss this possibility of sending Frumentius to Alexandria.

During a pilgrimage to Jerusalem, Frumentius met, among others, Queen Helena, the mother of King Constantine, who was then engaged in overseeing the building and decorating of the Church of the Holy Sepulchre. After he gave her a description of the origin and practice of Christianity in Ethiopia, she gave him the name of the secretary of the Patriarch of Alexandria (a young deacon by the name Athanasius) who was now attending the Council of Nicea together with the Patriarch St Alexander.

When he returned to Axum he met with Anbaram, and the royal court of Ezana and Shaiazana, who now approved of the move to have Frumentius sent to Alexandria to meet with the Patriarch and his synod to be consecrated as the Archbishop of Axum. So he made his way first to Alexandria where he met some of the bishops, before going to Nicea in Bithynia, where the Council of Nicea was still in session examining the teaching of Arius, who had inflamed the Christian world with his teaching that the Lord Jesus Christ was only a human being born of St Mary, his mother.

The Patriarch of Alexandria, St Alexandria, died shortly after the Council ended and was replaced by St Athanasius in AD 326. The Synod of Alexandria now considered the proposal with considerable care but concluded that instead of sending a delegation to Axum to investigate the matter, Frumentius himself should remain in Egypt to study the New Testament Apostolic priesthood before being ordained as archbishop and sent back to Axum. He wrote back to the twin kings, Ezana and Shaiazana, informing them of this decision. He was ordained as archbishop in AD 330, but did not return to Axum until about AD 334.

In his possession Frumentius (now called Abba Selama) brought back copies of the Greek Old and New Testament, the eighty-five Apostolic Canons, the Apostolic Tradition, the Didascalia, the Didache, the books of St Pantaenus, St Clement, St Origen, St Dionysius, St Didymus, St Alexander and St Athanasius. Not too long after he returned, he ordained Anbaram first to the deaconhood and then to the priesthood. As Archbishop, Abba Selama also gave him the new name Hezbe Kades. This meant he now had the spiritual gift of performing all the sacraments except ordination. Later Anbaram was made a bishop under the jurisdiction of Abba Selama. Both now preached and taught the gospel and baptised thousands of men and women in the Christian faith.

When news of Abba Selama's ordination as Archbishop of Ethiopia reached the new Roman Emperor Constants II (reigned 341–68) who had adopted the doctrine of Arius, Constants wrote to Ezana and Shaiazana requesting that Abba Selama be sent back to Alexandria for the new Patriarch named George (Constants had supported the deposition of St Athanasius and replaced him with this new one) to decide whether or not Abba Selama was worthy of being Archbishop of Ethiopia.

Unfortunately we do not possess the letters that might have revealed the reaction of the brother kings. However although inter-state relations may have forced them to maintain friendly contact with Constants II, it would seem that they did not comply with his wish.

All the Church's historical sources affirm that Abba Selama carried out his episcopal duties to the end of his life. The *Synaxarium* (a book of the biography of the saints) which describes his administration ends with these words:

He (Frumentius) arrived in the land of Ethiopia during the life of Ala-Amida, and Abraha and Asbeha. He preached and administered the sacraments and teachings of our Lord Jesus Christ throughout the country. This is why he is called Abba Selama. After leading many people to the faith of Christ, he died in the peace of Christ.

Abba Selama's Account of his Years in Egypt

Visiting and sojourning in Egypt during those critical years (326–334) and becoming closely attached to St Athanasius, the Patriarch of Alexandria, Abba Selama was in a position at a key stage in the history of the Coptic Orthodox Church of Egypt to receive first-hand information not only about the Holy Family's flight and sojourn in Egypt, but also the history concerning the work of St Mark and the Cathedral School of Alexandria during the reign of Patriarch Demetrius I (188–230), and the origins of the Arian theology which led to the convening of the first Ecumenical Council in Nicea in 325 which produced the creed or prayer of faith still recited today.

*

Abba Selama learned that the flight of St Mary, the Holy Theotokos, and St Joseph with the Infant-Messiah Jesus Christ from Bethlehem to the furthest point of their journey in Upper Egypt is the most celebrated event in the Coptic Orthodox Church's early Christian history. Coptic Church historians will never grow tired of describing the history of all the shrines which mark the places where the Holy Family stopped to rest. They stress that the group must have crossed the Sinai Peninsula by the northern caravan route alongside the Mediterranean coastline from Gaza to Raphia, and then followed the frontier brook known as the River of Egypt before coming to Rhinocolura (present-day al-Arish). From there they went to Ostrakini, later the diocesan capital of Bishop Abraham who participated in the third Ecumenical Council of Ephesus in AD 431. Their last stop was Pelusium (present-day al-Farama) which at the time of the flight of the Lord Jesus Christ was the key city in north-eastern

Egypt. Professor O.E.A. Meinardus' study, *In the Steps of the Holy Family from Bethlehem to Upper Egypt*, published in Cairo in 1963, states that the Holy Family must have passed and stayed a little time in the ancient city of Bubastis, the capital of Egypt during the reign of the Pharaohs of the twenty-second dynasty which the famous Greek historian Herodotus visited in the fifth century BC, and old Cairo where a convent dedicated to St Mary, the Holy Theotokos at Haret Zwayla was erected.

After the history of the sojourn of the Holy Family in Egypt, the next most celebrated New Testament testimony of early Coptic Christianity that Abba Selama learned about was the history of St Mark, one of the four Evangelists and author of the oldest canonical gospel, which the Holy Spirit allowed the other three Evangelists St Luke, St Matthew and St John, to use in the composition of their gospels. *The History of the Patriarchs of the Coptic Church of Alexandria* begins with a very detailed account of the life of St Mark, the Evangelist and first Patriarch of Alexandria.

St Mark's parents were both Jews who had lived in Cyrenaica in North Africa until they were attacked and had their property raided by the Berber tribes. As a result they decided to move to Jerusalem, where St Mark is said to have been born shortly after the nativity of the Lord Jesus Christ. He was given a good education and was able to speak Greek, Latin, Hebrew and Coptic fluently.

Furthermore, he received his Christian initiation from his older cousin St Barnabas who knew the Apostles, St Peter and St Paul, very well. In fact St Barnabas later became their travel companion. This same cousin introduced St Mark to St Peter, and so St Mark became associated with the Lord Jesus Christ, who visited his home more than once and later chose him as one of the seventy disciples. Even after the Lord's ascension the disciples used to meet at St Mark's home; and it was from there that the Holy Spirit descended upon all the faithful on the great day of Pentecost (ten days after the ascension of Christ) before St Peter and the other Apostles went out to preach to all the faithful who had gathered in Jerusalem on that great day as recorded in *Acts of the Apostles*, chapter 2. The upper room of St Mark's house therefore became one of the first Christian places of worship in history. Being one of the closest witnesses to our Lord's earthly life, together with his relationship with the Apostles, St Peter and St Paul, had given him the best preparation for the composition of the holy gospel which bears his name. St Athanasius told Abba Selama that St Mark's gospel was first composed in Alexandria in Greek (the international language at that time) between the years AD 43 and 45, later it was translated into Hebrew and Latin.

After the great day of Pentecost St Mark travelled with St Paul, and his cousin St Barnabas, to Antioch in Syria and Cyprus before returning to Jerusalem. He then travelled with St Peter to Rome.

But St Mark's real mission was reserved for Africa. First he crossed the Mediterranean to Cyrenaica where his parents were born. It was now colonised by the Greeks, and included many Jews among the crowds to whom he preached and in whose presence he performed many miracles which helped to establish the Christian faith there. He next went to Alexandria through Old Cairo. At this time this city stood second to Rome in its importance in the maintenance of the Roman Empire, but was still tied to the African religious heritage of the age of Pharaohs. The task therefore of establishing a strong Christian community here would be the greatest challenge that St Mark would face.

The narrative of *The History of the Patriarchs of the Coptic Church* states that on entering the city by the eastern gate, St Mark broke the strap of his shoe. So he went to find a cobbler to mend it. When the cobbler took up one of his tools to begin working on the shoe, he accidentally pierced his hand and cried out, 'God is One.' St Mark rejoiced at this statement and, after miraculously hearing the cobbler's wounded hand, he began to preach to him about Jesus Christ. This cobbler, who was a Jew, was converted and became a disciple following the path of the gospel of the Lord Jesus Christ. He happened to be Ananius, St Mark's successor as the second Patriarch of Alexandria.

Ananius invited St Mark to his home to preach to his family who in time were baptised. With this act the word began to spread throughout the neighbourhood, and in time many more families accepted our Lord Jesus Christ and were baptised and started the Christian life. This community of Alexandria began to grow rapidly and St Mark began to be sought everywhere. Sensing danger he ordained Ananius a bishop, with three priests and seven deacons to watch over the congregation, in case anything should happen to him.

After these ordinations St Mark undertook two voyages. First he sailed to Rome, where he met the Apostles Peter and Paul to inform them of his work in Cyrenaica and Alexandria, and left Rome only after their martyrdom in AD 64. He then made a short visit to Aquilea near Venice before his return to Alexandria. Upon finding the Church in peace he decided to visit his parents' native country again where he ordained more bishops and priests. When he returned to Alexandria two years later the congregation had grown to such an extent that they were able to build a church of a considerable size in the suburban part of Baucalis.

The building of this church attracted much attention and the local Egyptian non-Christian population began to feel threatened that their forms of worship would eventually be overtaken by the Christian celebration of the sacraments and the worship of the Holy Trinity. St Mark now became the most wanted man among them. And the end came in AD 68. In that year Easter came on the same day as the festival of their god Seraphis. Crowds of these non-Christians now descended on the church at Baucalis while the Easter celebration of Holy Communion was being conducted. St Mark was seized and bound. Next they dragged him by a rope, which they put around his neck, through the streets. Then they locked him up for the night. The following morning the same ordeal was repeated until he eventually died. His body was badly battered and covered with blood, and it was the plan of these non-Christians to burn his remains. But to prevent this a storm broke out with heavy winds and rain. Everyone had to run for shelter. When the storm subsided a few of the faithful carried his body and buried it in a grave which they had carved in the rock in the Church under the altar.

★

Quite apart from the life and work of St Mark in Alexandria on the African continent, Abba Selama discovered that this city would have secured its place as one of the most illustrious cities in world history. After the fall of Jerusalem to the Babylonians in 587 BC, many citizens of the Kingdom of Judah were exiled to Babylon. However, a good number of them went in different directions. For example in *Jeremiah* chapters 40–44 we read how a certain number of Jews (including the Prophet himself) headed towards Egypt and stayed there. And there are clear indications from the testimony of many Jewish and Christian historians that Jews were later found in many cities all over the huge territory of the Roman Empire.

With the emergence and conquests of Alexander the Great in the late fourth century BC, Egypt moved into the orbit of the Greek-speaking world, and Greek became the international language of the Alexander's Empire. In the synagogues, the need began to be urgently felt that the books of the Hebrew bible be translated into Greek so that the majority of the Greek-speaking Jewish faithful would not be deprived of the knowledge of the God of the Hebrew Old Testament.

This urgency led in time to another need, namely that of having a uniform text to prevent the spreading of varieties of translations by various rabbis. Such an effort was achieved in Alexandria, being one of the main cities established by Alexander the Great in 332 BC.

Under the Ptolemies, the successors of Alexander who ruled Egypt, Alexandria grew into one of the three major cities of the Roman Empire. Indeed it was the Roman Emperor's headquarters in Africa. The other cities were Rome, and Antioch in Syria, which was established in 300 BC by Seleucids I and named after his father Antiochus. Antioch was the capital of the Seleucids, the successors of Alexander who ruled in Syria. However, it was Alexandria, based in north-east Africa, which became the intellectual and cultural capital of the Roman Empire. Moreover, it probably had the largest concentration of Jews at that time.

With this combination of factors it was precisely in Alexandria that the translation of the Hebrew Old Testament into Greek took place, starting in the middle of the third century BC.

Since at that time the concept of a uniform scriptural canon was not yet formed, this translation included all the main Hebrew scrolls that were honoured among the Jews, as well as some other Jewish books that were written directly in Greek. It was no wonder then that such a translation became widespread in the synagogues in those areas of the Empire where Greek was the language of the colonial masters, who imposed it upon the indigenous people whom they ruled. Nor should it be considered strange that the Apostles, as well as other New Testament authors, used Greek in their preaching and writing, together with their native languages Aramaic and Hebrew.

The actual process of the translation is recorded to have taken place like this: King Ptolemy II Philadelphus (283–246 BC), the famous patron of education and the builder of the great Alexandrian libraries, wanted a copy of all the sacred books of the Hebrews for his own personal library. He therefore sent seventy-two elder-scribes (six from each tribe) to Alexandria. From Alexandria they were sent to the island of Pharos and placed in seventy-two separate locations from where they produced identical translations. The number of these elder-scribes was the origin of the name given to this translation, namely 'the Septuagint'.

The two biggest libraries established by Ptolemy II in Alexandria together contained 540,000 volumes. This was the largest collection of books in the world at that time. The larger of the two was built in the Bruchem district and had nearly half a million volumes. This was the one destroyed by Julius Caesar. The smaller one was built in the serapeum quarter of the city. The Patriarchal library that Frumentius (Abba Selama) came to know when he sojourned in Alexandria was this smaller one. Of course we know that by the time Abba Selama came to study in Alexandria, this library contained the works of the illustrious heads of the cathedral school of Alexandria, St Origen, St Clement and St Pantaenus, besides those of the Patriarchs before St Athanasius, and other outstanding teachers from other parts of the Christian world.

*

The head of the cathedral school during Frumentius' (Abba

Selama's) sojourn in Egypt was St Didymus the Blind. The actual establishment of the school has been a source of lively debate among the Coptic Orthodox Church's historians and theologians. Some even suggest that it was established during the lifetime of St Mark. If this is the case then the names of the Deans have been lost, because it is only from the reign of St Pantaenus (168–190) that we possess any accurate knowledge of the syllabus of the school. It included the humanities, biology, chemistry, physics and mathematics, besides the study of the Old and New Testaments, and the early Apostolic history and theology.

There is no doubt that St Pantaenus and his staff were the ones responsible for the formulation of the first systematic outlines of theology and the monumental works of biblical analysis. Apart from being a great teacher, St Pantaenus is also credited as being one of the early pioneers of the adoption of the Greek alphabet in the old Coptic script. He was also assigned by St Demetrius I to go on a mission to India before his death in 190.

Following his death his successor was St Clement who was born in Athens in 150, but moved to Alexandria as a young man and became a pupil at the school in about 172. He reigned from St Pantaenus' death until 215. Like his contemporaries St Irenaeus and St Tertullian of Cartage, St Clement had made an exhaustive study of newly growing Gnostic Movement, with its emphasis being on the possession of secret doctrines originating from newly discovered scrolls of the Apostles Peter and Matthias. These secret doctrines could lead the believer to the path of salvation independent of the sacramental life and discipline of the Church. Through his written work St Clement attacked the two most prominent Gnostic philosophers in Alexandria, Valentius and Basilides, and to counter them he began to promote a more Orthodox approach of attending Church services and living the Church's life as a more sound way of understanding the mysteries of the Christian faith.

St Clement wrote an abundance, though much has been lost. Of the books that have survived the most important ones are *An Exhortation to the Greeks*, *The Pedagous*, and a work on the Christian virtues and ethics, *The Stromateis*.

After St Clement died, the cathedral school was taken over by one of the most famous and distinguished saints of Alexandria, St Origen (155–254). As a biblical scholar, spiritual director, student of medicine and theologian, St Origen was an omnivorous reader and collector of manuscripts. This made his literary output and creativity colossal.

While I was still studying for the priesthood, I was fortunate to have been an observer of a very lively debate by two Coptic Orthodox priests in New York in 1978 concerning the actual number of books that St Origen had written in his lifetime. One speaker was defending the traditional number of six hundred, while the other one was saying it was nearer seven hundred. This debate did not reach a conclusion, and after three hours it was adjourned. In any case I thought, whatever the actual number of books published by St Origen, there was no doubting that he was one of the most prolific writers of any age, even if the actual number was six hundred.

St Origen's life and personality have never been free of controversy. As a young man he became extremely attracted towards the ascetic and monastic life, and observed the most rigorous fasts and vigils. He even castrated himself, taking the passage of *St Matthew* 19:12, 'There are Eunuchs who make themselves Eunuchs for the sake of the Kingdom of Heaven's sake', in its most literal sense. This action of the young Origen aroused the anger of Patriarch Demetrius I against him.

He later studied Greek philosophy and literature under the illustrious Ammonius Saccas (174–242) the establisher of philosophy of Neo-Platonism and teacher of Plotinus of Alexandria at the Ptolemic school. He travelled widely and knew the most eminent scholars and bishops of his lifetime. His journeys extended from Arabia, Palestine and Syria to Greece and Rome.

Possessing an enigmatic personality, St Origen was one of those refined and highly educated Christians whom one either loved, or loved to hate. He fell into trouble again with Patriarch Demetrius during his first visit to Palestine in 217 when he was invited by the Bishop of Aelia and Caesarea to preach in his Diocese. For the Patriarch St Demetrius and other Coptic and Ethiopian Christians at that time, it was unthinkable that a layman could preach in the presence of bishops, so St Origen was at once recalled to Alexandria before Easter 218. He forbade Origen to do any more preaching, and so he involved himself with writing and teaching for the next twelve years. In these years Synods met to discuss and analyse his theological output. His year of deliverance came in 230 when he fled back to Palestine. Origen was here honoured by being ordained to the priesthood. But as everyone expected this action was not received well by the Patriarch who wrote nullifying his ordination and permanently excommunicated him by dismissing him as the head of the cathedral school.

St Origen now became an exile, and in 231 he settled in Caesarea. A new school now arose around him which some of the most distinguished leaders of the second half of the third century attended. During the great persecution of 250, he suffered imprisonment and torture. Though he survived these horrors and regained his freedom, his health began to decline, and he died in the city of Tyre in 254 at the age of sixty-eight.

After his death his personality and massive theological output became even more controversial than during his lifetime. The term 'Origenism' was now attached to his theological universe. His defenders became 'Origenists' and his opponents 'Anti-Origenists' in the struggle to untangle his thinking. One merely has to look at the history of the period after his death to see the names of distinguished bishops who joined the contest for or against St Origen. Defending him or parts of his works were St Pamphylius, St Athanasius, St Basil, St Gregory Nazianzen and St Didymus the Blind. In the hostile camp were Lucian of Antioch, Paul of Samosata, St Epiphanisus of Cyprus, St Jerome and St Theophilos. Later in the fifth century Byzantine officials called Church councils solely to discuss St Origen's massive theological output; and finally he was condemned two centuries after his death at two councils held at Constantinople in 542 and 553 at the bidding of the Byzantine Emperor Justinian.

★

After St Origen's flight to Palestine and his dismissal as head of the cathedral school, Abba Selama learned that his successor was St Heraclas who later followed St Demetrius as Patriarch of

Alexandria from 230 to 246. With him the school came directly under Patriarchal authority. One of the first acts of St Heraclas when he became Patriarch in 230 was to lift St Demetrius' sentence of excommunication over St Origen, and to try to persuade him to return to his native Egypt. But his efforts were in vain.

The next head of the school was another famous pupil of Origen, St Dionysis of Alexandria, who was noted for his powerful preaching voice. He occupied the post from 246 to 264 when he became Patriarch.

St Dionysis' lifetime was full of trouble. In 250 the Decian persecution was conducted by the Roman Emperor Valerian. The whole of Egypt was invaded from the south by non-Christian African tribes. In Alexandria, Emilianus, the Roman Prefect of Egypt, declared himself Emperor and civil war broke out which ended in his capture by General Theodosus who sent him in chains to Rome to face trial and execution. This war devastated Alexandria and its population. And making matters worse was the announcement of a plague and a famine. At the end of the persecution Patriarch Dionysis was faced with the problem of defectors. But he seemed broad-minded enough and readmitted them to the sacramental life of the Church after they went through periods of penance.

Abba Selama's Account of the Origins of Arianism Prior to the Opening of the Council of Nicea in 325

According to Abba Selama, Arius's early biography appears quite sketchy. Apparently he was born in 250 in Libya, North Africa. Abba Selama wrote that this fact of his birth place was preserved by Patriarch Alexander of Alexandria (reigned from 313 to 326) who himself stated this in his book, *The History of Arianism*.

Because Arius was a native of Libya, after the Council of Nicea was closed he received support from Secundus and Theonas, the Bishops of Ptolemais and Marmarica, the chief cities of upper and lower Libya at the time. He was received by these two Libyan bishops because they themselves were resisting the canonical rule over their episcopal districts by the throne of St Mark here in Alexandria.

These points are further established in a letter from Emperor Constantine to Arius written around 333 in which he states how Arius returned to his native country of Libya in 327 with support from Bishop Secundus.

★

Arius was ordained to the priesthood by Bishop Achillas and then seems to have gone to Antioch in Syria where he became a student of Lucian, the establisher of the theological school of Antioch in 260. Lucian himself had contacts with the Bishop of Antioch, Paul, who originally came from Samosata. This same Paul was deposed as Bishop of Antioch in 269.

Lucian was full of jealousy towards the theological school at Alexandria, and especially the fame and massive theological output of St Origen. He boasted to his students that Antioch had a history just as illustrious as that of Alexandria, if not more than this African city itself. Was it not the greatest trading city located in the valley of Orontes, at the crossroads of the river Euphrates and the Mediterranean sea? Was not Antioch the place where Asia and Palestine met? Did not African, Syrian, other Asian and Greek merchants trade in its great markets?

Was not Antioch the Syrian headquarters of St Peter and St Barnabas as witnessed in *Acts of the Apostles* 11:19–27; 14:21–26; 15:22–23, 30–35; 18:22? Was not the first Christian community established there by St Peter long before St Mark went to Alexandria and Rome? These and many more are some of the arguments that Lucian employed in his efforts to discredit Alexandria and promote Antioch, and Arius was part of his circle when these attacks were being made.

★

A prominent biblical scholar in his own right, Lucian wanted to show Arius and his other students, as well as all of Syria, that he was on an equal standing with St Origen as far as biblical scholarship was concerned. He therefore continued the work that St Origen had begun on the Greek biblical text. To complete this work Lucian used the Hebrew Old Testament and some ancient Syrian manuscripts. To gain wider recognition he consulted and worked with Macarius of Edessa, another prominent biblical scholar of Asia. When they finished, their corrections of the *Septuagint* received general recognition in almost all the Churches of western Asia.

Lucian introduced Arius and his other students to the theological discipline of exegesis (the art of analysing the biblical text). He opposed St Origen at every point and heavily criticised his fourfold method (the historical, the spiritual, the allegorical and the mystical) of biblical interpretation and instead established a straightforward historical and grammatical approach. But while parting ways with St Origen as a biblical scholar, Lucian could not help recognising St Origen's greatness as a master of the ascetic life, as a director of spirituality, and as possessing the most refined theological mind of the first half of the third century.

Lucian came under a ban in 264 when Paul, the Bishop of Antioch was condemned by the Patriarch of Alexandria, St Dionysis, for his views concerning the mystery of the Incarnation of the Divine Son and Word of God. He therefore had to stop teaching. Five years later in 269, the decision of 264 was upheld at a council held in Antioch.

Coming from a poor family, Paul had amassed great wealth which it was said he used to raise himself to the office of Bishop of Antioch. His enemies said this because of his well-known contacts with Zenobia, the Queen of Palmyra, whom he had taught in her youth. But Paul was deposed mainly for his doctrine that Christ was only a mere man upon whom the Holy Spirit had descended. The other main charge against him was that he denied the divine personality of the Son and the Holy Spirit. Consequently he refused to confess our Lord Jesus Christ as 'One of the Holy trinity in the flesh'. This was the core of the matter for St Dionysis, the Patriarch of Alexandria. For Paul, the Lord Jesus Christ was merely a chosen human being to whom God the Father and God the Holy Spirit communicated in a manner similar to the chosen saints of the Old Testament. Lucian had accepted these ideas of Paul. Nevertheless Lucian died a martyr in 312 and his name was entered in the Syrian Church's calendar of martyrs.

Although Arius was a student of Lucian, he did not simply adopt his doctrine from Lucian and Paul, and the independence of his ideas was stressed first by St Alexander, and then by St Athanasius. While in Antioch, Arius also apparently developed the skills of an orator, a poet and a singer.

By about 310, Arius was back in Egypt and established at the college of Alexandria. Shortly after St Alexander's elevation to the Patriarchal throne, Arius was appointed parish priest of the famous Church of Baucalis. By this time he had become a popular preacher with a reputation for asceticism. Patriarch Alexander did not realise the seriousness of Arius's theological outlook until Arius began to make the faithful of the Church of Baucalis confused with his strange teaching about the person of our Lord Jesus Christ. These teachings came to the attention of the Patriarch when the faithful began to complain to him, and some of the other bishops of Egypt, about Arius's beliefs concerning the mystery of the Incarnation (how the Eternal Word and Son of God the Father came to be united with the human nature He took from the Holy Theotokos, St Mary, through the grace and power of the Holy Spirit). But the sparks did not start to fly until around 320 when Arius was permanently excommunicated and deposed by an Alexandrian synod attended by one hundred Coptic Orthodox bishops. Taking no notice of this, Arius immediately appealed to Eusebius, the Bishop of Nicomedia, and also his namesake in Caesarea, together with the bishops in Bithynia.

In the meantime, Arius began to set his theology to poetic meter, and composed hymns known as 'Thalia'. These were successful, and the uneducated Christian population sang the Arian theology everywhere in Egypt.

Eusebius of Nicomedia now involved the Emperor Constantine who was his friend and whom he would later baptise. Together with his namesake in Caesarea, and the Bishops of Bithynia, a campaign was mounted for Arius's reinstatement. St

Alexander in a series of letters set out the problem of Arius's theology. The Emperor Constantine now commissioned Hosius of Cordova to mediate, but the situation was unsolvable and Constantine was left with no choice but to yield to the recommendations of both St Alexander and Hosius to convene an Ecumenical Council to meet in Nicea in Bithynia in the summer of 325. With the convening of this Council, representative bishops from the entire Christian world numbering three hundred and eighteen met to settle all the outstanding doctrinal and canonical problems that Arius and his theology presented to the Church.

Arius and his Theology

Abba Selama in his account of Arius's theology starts by saying that in his ideas concerning the concept of God, Arius considers God to be a perfect unity, or a self-contained monad (from the word 'mono' meaning one), following the Old Testament, and also some Egyptian philosophers. For Arius this divine monad was God the Father. Everything else that was in existence was radically different from the inner nature of God the Father. The complete and whole nature of the divine being of the Father excluded any possibility for him that the Father might impart or give His inner nature to someone else. For this reason the Word and Son of God the Father, as a living person, or as a truly existing being, was definitely and totally different from the being of the Father. The Son for Arius comes into being as a mediator between the Father and the creation for the main purpose of fashioning and designing the created world and its different orders of life. This is why according to the logic of Arius's reasoning, there had to be a certain 'interval' separating the Father from the Son.

This is also why, for Arius, the Word and Son could not be co-eternal and co-equal with the Father. If they were equal and had the same divine nature, this would mean for him that we would have to accept the notion of two 'uncreated beings', or 'two origins' at the foundation of existence, which would mean a rejection of the truth of the Oneness of God. Therefore to preserve the Oneness of God, in Arius's own words, 'There was a time when the Word and Son did not exist.' For Arius there must have been a time when the Son came into existence. And if the Son came into existence, He had to be a created work of the Father. For this reason the Son's nature had the potential for change like every other created object of life that came into existence. Divine glory was somehow imparted to Him by the 'grace' of the Father. Such in general terms was Arius's doctrine concerning the Incarnation of the Son and Word of God, Abba Selama wrote in so far as the fragments of his ideas and sermons were preserved by St Alexander and St Athanasius.

Arius's teaching essentially denied the mystery of the eternal uncreated relationships of the Holy God in Trinity: the God who is Three in One, and One in Three. For Arius the mystery of the Holy God in Trinity meant something generated, with this genesis separated by 'intervals of time'.

As St Gregory of Nazianzen later in the fourth century observed, 'For Arius the mystery of the Holy God in Trinity was a diminished Trinity, a kind of union, or a society of three unlike beings.'

Abba Selama had also seen this aspect of the problem. To his way of thinking, Arius was before all else very African in his philosophical leanings. He had studied Plotinus' philosophy, as well as some of the ancient Greeks such as Pythagoras, Zeno, Plato, Socrates and Aristotle. In this philosophical tradition, the being of the world and the being of God formed an unbreakable unity. In his theology Arius was still saturated with the Old Testament concept of the Oneness of God.

Therefore, for him the idea of a Holy God who lives eternally in a Holy Trinity of uncreated relationships could never be one God, as only the Father was God. The Eternal Son/Word and the Holy Spirit did not share the same divine nature as the Father, but were the first creations of the Father's will, to be mediators between Himself and all the twenty-two different created orders of existence recorded in *Genesis*, chapter 1.

With this line of reasoning Abba Selama showed how this aspect of Arius's ideas was almost a repetition of Paul of Samosata's reasoning. This for him was why Arius was able to gain so much support in Libya, besides Antioch, Bithynia and

Palestine.

Therefore, the crucial theological problem this immediately posed first to St Alexander, then to St Athanasius as the Patriarch of Alexandria in the middle of the dispute, as well as to Abba Selama as the Archbishop of Ethiopia, was first to find concepts and phrases to describe the eternal uncreated inner relationships between the Father, the Son and the Holy Spirit in the unity of the Holy Trinity; and then to find another set of concepts and terms to describe the relationship between these three divine co-equal persons of the Holy Trinity and the created world.

Abba Selama stressed the close ties that existed between (a) Arius's theology of God in Trinity and the concept of time; (b) the question of the creation; and (c) the question of the origin of the world. These were the basic questions that all three of our Church fathers set out to answer when they engaged Arius's theological universe.

Because the act of creating meant for Arius the coming into existence of something that never existed before, he could not distinguish the eternal uncreated birth of the Son from the being of the Father, from the creation of the world. Both had the same meaning for him. To be born for Arius was the same as to be generated, or to begin to be.

St Athanasius was the first one, Abba Selama pointed out, who stressed to Arius and his followers that the concept of 'birth' or 'origin' could have two meanings. First of all it could mean the base, or the source of a living being; or secondly it could mean a moment in time. For Arius and his followers these two meanings were blurred.

This is why they passionately defended the 'created' nature of the Son. For if the Son is from the Father, then He is derived from the will, and not from the inner divine nature, of the Father.

Abba Selama wrote that, on his return from Alexandria to Axum to take up his episcopal duties, he clearly saw that Arius's theology presented the sacramental and worshipping life of Church with a theological consciousness that rested upon an ancient African philosophical foundation, upon which later the Israelites, and then the Greek philosophical tradition built their ideas. In exposing Arius's ideas to the scrutiny of the sacramental life of the Church, he states how St Alexander, and then St Athanasius, reasoned mostly about the different modes of time. St Alexander started from the idea of the divine co-equal inter-relationships of the Holy God in Trinity, and stressed the complete indivisibility of the Father, the Son and the Holy Spirit. 'The Father is always,' St Alexander had written in one of his letters to Arius, 'the son is always, the Holy Spirit is always. The Son, and the Holy Spirit were always together with the Father.' By these phrases any idea of 'intervals of time' in the being of the Holy Trinity is excluded. St Alexander further wrote in the same letter, 'Not for the shortest moment did the Father anticipate the coming into being of the Son and the Holy Spirit.'

The main achievement of the three hundred and eighteen bishops who met at Council of Nicea in the summer of 325 was the composition of the creed (or prayer of faith) on 19 June. This creed, which is the most widely used symbol of the Christian faith (it was lager expanded at the second Ecumenical Council in 381 at Constantinople), revealed above all else that Christians are, first and foremost, worshippers of the Heavenly Father, through the Incarnate Son/Word, the Lord Jesus Christ, in the power of the Holy Spirit. It also revealed that this understanding of the mystery of the unity of the three divine persons of the Holy Trinity grew out of the sacramental and worshipping life of the Church, which itself was grounded on the witness of the holy scriptures.

For the three hundred and eighteen bishops at Nicea in 325 the sacraments and worship of the Church came first, and the creed implicitly hinted at this. Arius and his followers, by declaring that there was a time that God the Son and God the Holy Spirit did not exist made the celebration of the sacraments and worship all too human, without any dynamic between the idea of immanence and transcendence.

By operating with select proof texts from the scriptures they tended to ignore this dimension of the sacraments and worship in the life of the Church. For the bishops these came first. The doctrines and spiritual principles encased in the creed grew out of this experience and defined the inner structure of the life of the Church.

As bishops, this sacramental worshipping experience revealed something very important to them, which would have an enormous impact on the future life of the Church: that the nature and being of God could only be known through personal relationships, based on the foundation of love, in a community of believers. The uncreated nature and being of God gave life to the created world and revealed God as a being that existed in eternal personal relationships. However, while being totally different from the being of the created world, with its different orders of existence, God could have contact and communicate with the creation.

Without these two concepts (communication and contact) it is not possible to talk of the eternal relationships of the Father to the Son and to the Holy Spirit. In terms of later theology of the Holy Trinity, what the Nicean dogma established was this: a distinction must be maintained between the eternal inner relationships of Father, Son and Holy Spirit and their relationships through the Incarnation to the created world, especially the human world.

For the three hundred and eighteen bishops who met at Nicea (whose liturgical Anaphora the Ethiopian Orthodox Church has preserved and uses to this very day) it was unthinkable to speak of 'One God' without also speaking of the God who, in an eternal uncreated manner, existed in three inter-personal relationships in the unity of the Holy Trinity.

The mystery of the Holy God in Trinity was for them a crucial theological tool, received from the heritage of the scriptures preserved by the holy Apostles, and not some philosophical notion added to the divine essence, as would later be the case with the dogmatic textbooks of the Latin-speaking Christian world, which first discussed the concept of the 'One God' before proceeding to discuss the concept of the 'Holy Trinity'.

It is remarkable how the only real non-biblical terms of the creed of Nicea were the three key terms used to describe the inter-relationships between the Father, the Son and the Holy Spirit. These terms were of course 'Consubstantial', 'Of one essence' and 'Hypostasis'. And for the remainder of the fourth century St Athanasius of Alexandria, St Frumentius (Abba Selama) of Axum, St Basil of Caesarea, St Gregory of Nyssa, St Gregory of Nazianzen and St Cyril of Jerusalem laboured to establish once and for ever the Church's belief in the mystery of the Holy God in Trinity, in the face of much opposition from Arius and his powerful followers.

Chapter 5
The Orthodox Christian City of Axum from the Fourth to the Ninth Centuries

(A) The Origins of its structure

The layer of beliefs and the institutions that were established in Axum through the lives of the brother kings Ezana and Shaiazana have been confirmed by the archaeological investigations carried out in 1905–10, during the time of Emperor Menelik II, by a group of Ethiopian and German scholars under the direction of Enno Littmann. They discovered ancient stelae, the subterranean mausoleum of Emperor Ethiopis (the great ancient Emperor after whom the country was named) and of Menelik I. In this mausoleum they discovered some remains of the head of this great ancient African king still wearing a crown of gold. Of more importance was the discovery of a genealogical table where Menelik I traces the history of his ancestors and the origins of the city of Axum. This table states 'Shem begat Kam' (named Ham in the book of *Genesis*), 'Kam begat Kush, Kush begat Ethiopis, Ethiopis begat Aksumawi, Aksumawi begat Malakya Aksum, who begat six sons known as the fathers of the city of Aksum: Sum or Malakya, Nafas, Bagio, Kuduki, Akhoro and Farheba'.

This Ethiopian-German archaeological team also discovered the foundations of the palace Enda Mikael (reigned at the beginning of the sixth century), later transformed into a church, the tombs of Emperor Kaleb (lived in the mid-sixth century) and Gabre Masqal (late sixth century), the site of the original cathedral of St Mary of Zion, and the remains of the palace of Emperor

Tekla Mariam.

Again in 1954–55 further archaeological investigations were carried out by the Archaeological Section of the Ethiopian National Library created by H.I.M. Emperor Haile Selassie I. These investigations uncovered more information of the earlier sites, plus tombs, stelae and carved monolithic towers previously uncovered. These discoveries of the ancient kingdom of Axum have given both the Ethiopian Orthodox Church and the nation unquestioned proof of Ethiopia's role as one of the most advanced nations of the world of antiquity. So the layer of beliefs and institutions that were established in Axum at the time of Ezana and Shaiazana, together with the growing influence of monasticism, as well as the life and episcopal ministry of St Frumentius (Abba Selama) as Ethiopia's first Archbishop, extended right down to the revolution that shook Ethiopia between February and September 1974. ('The creeping Revolution' as it is otherwise known.)

This layer constitutes a second distinct mode of existence whose most visible characteristic is the intimate union of the Solomonic-Orthodox Christian dynasty with the Apostolic throne of St Philip, plus Ethiopia's relationship with the throne of St Mark of Alexandria. The Roman Christian Empire with its seats of government in Rome (312–476) and Constantinople (330–1453) manifested a similar outward form. In this world the visible and invisible worlds are always in union with each other. The supreme Creator and Sustainer of it is the Holy Co-Equal Trinity. Good and evil invisible spirits manifest themselves in the visible world as healthy and unhealthy energies and influences which the head of the Church and the senior Church officials, the King, the court officials, the monks and nuns, the builders, craftsmen, artists, teachers, and the entire Orthodox Christian population had to distinguish.

Through the monastic spirituality of St Anthony, St Pachomius and St Amonas, a method was developed for identifying and casting out evil demonic spirits, while the righteous angelic spirits had to be received according to the power and guidance they brought from the Holy Trinity for the building up of the Christian commonwealth. However, the final responsibility for all plans for growth and development was entrusted to the Archbishop and the King jointly. These two sacred offices, together with those of the monastic fathers, became the most powerful ones within Ethiopia's Orthodox Christian civilisation.

Because of the Church's close affiliation with the venerable Apostolic Throne of St Mark of Alexandria, with the ordination of St Frumentius as Abba Selama, Ethiopia's first Archbishop, by St Athanasius (the Patriarch of Alexandria from 326–373), the holy synod of the Coptic Orthodox Church of Egypt assumed canonical jurisdiction over the Ethiopian Orthodox Church by providing it with its archbishops.

In the mind of the population the office of the archbishop, the priest, deacon and deaconess, that of the Solomonic king and queen together with their ministers, the spiritual rank of the monk and the nun were sacred offices. Some naturally assumed responsibility for the population's spiritual needs, while the others catered for their physical and material ones. In the realm of theology its living model was the union of the body/soul/spirit in each human being.

This understanding obtained classical expression when King Kaleb (reigned 514–542) received from the Byzantine Emperor Justinian (reigned 527–565) a copy of his sixth novella which was dated 16 March 535:

> There are two major gifts which God has given to the human race of His eternal divine glory: the priesthood and the imperial authority. Of these the former is concerned mainly, but not only with things divine, while the latter is conversely concerned in the most part with human affairs and takes care of them. Proceeding from the same source, both adorn human life. Nothing is of greater concern for the emperors as the dignity of the priesthood, so that the priests may in turn pray to God for them to be filled with the Holy Spirit. Now if the holder of one sacred office is in every respect blameless and filled with confidence towards God, and the other one does rightly and properly to maintain in order the commonwealth entrusted to it, there will be a certain fair harmony established which will furnish

113

whatsoever may be needful for Christian families. We are therefore highly concerned for true doctrines inspired by God, and for the dignity of the priesthood. For we are convinced that, if they maintain their dignity, great benefits will be bestowed by God on us; and in addition we shall acquire those things which we have not yet secured. This is the case, when the scared canons are carefully observed, which the glorious Apostles, those sanctified eyewitnesses and servants of the Lord Jesus Christ, have handed down to us, and which our holy fathers and mothers have kept and explained.

After reading this passage, anyone will realise two things. First of all, the Byzantine Emperor Justinian must have recognised and respected Emperor Kaleb of Axum to have sent him a copy of this sixth novella. Secondly, the world that he was describing was already in existence in Ethiopia. He was talking about two different but equal ministries or functions which were established in a united Christian commonwealth.

Both were brought into existence by the divine authority of God Himself. 'Proceeding from the same source' is one of the key phrases of this novella of Justinian. This means that as a divine gift, the power of the royal throne was different from that of the sacred priesthood. Both had to work in harmony for the faithful maintenance and transmission of the good news of the holy gospel.

Throughout all of Ethiopia's history after the joint reigns of Ezana and his brother Shaiazana, according to the *Fetha Negast*, the legal status of the King and Queen in the Empire depended on their loyalty to the doctrinal and canonical discipline of the Church. In their coronation oath, both had to confess the Orthodox Christian faith.

Furthermore, only by their loyalty to the purity of the doctrines of the holy gospel and the sacraments preserved in the Church was their special place in the Empire maintained. They had to be very familiar with the history of dogmatics and canons, as they were legally responsible for defending the Orthodox Christian population from aggressive foreign armies.

The position of the Archbishop was just as sacred. He was first of all charged with trying to reflect the living image of the Lord Jesus Christ. In his preaching, teaching, and sacramental ministry, he was obligated to demonstrate the truths which Christ proclaimed for our salvation. He had to be crucified to the fallen corrupt ways of this world and live the life of the sacraments. To the non-Christian he had to try to convert them mainly by the holiness of his life. His task towards the believers was to strengthen and instruct them. And he had to be impartial to all. Before the King and Queen he had to speak the Apostolic faith without fear or shame.

Of course, this was the idealised picture. In the actual course of Ethiopian Orthodox Church history the reality was many times much darker and less clear. But the union of the government of the Church with that of the government of the Solomonic-Orthodox Christian dynasty was kept intact from this time until the 'creeping revolution' between February and September 1974, when it was destroyed by a group of middle-ranking army officers, who proclaimed in their slogans once they seized power, 'Revolutionary Ethiopia or death, there is no other way forward for Ethiopia now.'

The continued growth and spreading of the Christian faith in Ethiopia during the fifth and sixth centuries received a fresh burst of energy from the arrival and sojourn of nine churchmen whom all the traditional texts describe as 'Tsad-kan' (just), or 'Tesseaton Ki-ddussan' (nine saints). Their arrival was accomplished through the help of the Alexandrian Archbishop of Axum and Ala-Amida IV who reigned in the late fifth century. These nine monks came from Constantinople and other areas of Western Asia. They did not accept the teachings of the Council of Chalcedon held in 451 concerning the union of the divine and human natures in the one Lord Jesus Christ.

After the Council had concluded its deliberations, the Byzantine Emperor Marcian, his wife Empress Pulcheria, Pope Leo of Rome, and their successors had made life unbearable for those bishops, priests and monks who would not accept the Chalcedonian dogma concerning the person of the Lord Jesus Christ. In this atmosphere many had to flee to Palestine, Egypt, Nubia,

Arabia, Armenia and Persia, besides Ethiopia, to escape.

The arrival of the nine saints at Axum gave the Ethiopian Orthodox Church a first-class library and direct knowledge of the theological disputes current at that time in the Byzantine Empire and in Rome. These nine Church fathers were Abba Aregawi, Abba Pantelewon, Abba Gerima and Abba Likanos who all came from Constantinople. Abba Gubba came from Cilicia, Abba Afese came from Asia Minor, Abba Tsehma came from Antioch, Abba Alef came from Caesarea and Abba Yemata came from Cooz. After their arrival they made a very significant contribution to the growth of the Church by introducing some of the Anaphoras that the Church uses to this day.

These nine saints also made more translations of scrolls and books from Greek, Hebrew, Aramaic, Syraic and Latin, mainly into Ge'ez, the classical language of the Ethiopian Orthodox Church. They also made a few copies into Amharic, Tegreniya, Gallina and some other Ethiopian languages. But the bulk of the translation was done in Ge'ez.

Abba Aregawi went up to Debra Damo, where the cult of the worship of the python had followers among the local population, and started a monastic community there. Abba Gerima settled at Mettera near Senafe, and Abba Afese went to Yeha, where there was a temple dedicated to the local Ethiopian fertility god Almuqah. Abba Pantelewon and Abba Likanos remained in Axum. Abba Alef and Abba Tsehma went to Bhzan and Tseden Tsedeninya. Abba Yemata and Abba Gubba settled in the region of Guerealta. In all these places they established, with the initiative of the Church faithful, monasteries, schools and churches.

(B) The Council of Chalcedon Revisited

As I mentioned earlier, with the arrival of nine monks in Ethiopia in the last decades of the fifth century, the Ethiopian Orthodox Church received a first-class library of the Council of Chalcedon, its minutes and proceedings. These have all been preserved until this day.

In May 1988 I was fortunate enough to visit St Euphemia's

Church at Chalcedon (now called Kadikoy), where the Council met as part of a ten-day consultation hosted by the International Religious Foundation under the theme 'Christians and the Wider Ecumenism'. The consultation was centred at the Etap Marmara Hotel in Istanbul, but we visited other historical sites in Istanbul as well, for instance the headquarters of the Ecumenical Patriarchate where we met the Ecumenical Patriarch, Father Demetrius. We also visited the site of the first Ecumenical Council at Nicea, now called Ismir, and the site at St Sophia Church, the remains of the palace of the Byzantine Emperors, and the city of Bursa. Most of this chapter is based on what I shared with Professor Durwood Foster of the Pacific School of Religion in Berkeley, California, and Professor Savas Argorites, the distinguished Greek Orthodox theologian of the University of Athens. Both showed interest in trying to find out how the Council of Chalcedon was received by the Ethiopian Orthodox Church.

I told them that it is difficult for me to reflect on the historical problems of the Council of Chalcedon as it is viewed from the minutes of its proceedings. [For this reconstructed account of my discussion with both I am going to use notes I made from Schwartz's *Acta Conciliorum*, A.C.O., vol. II, published in Berlin between 1932 and 1938, while I was still a candidate for the priesthood. However, when I was discussing the reception of this Council by the Ethiopian Orthodox Church with these two theological educators I relied purely on my memory.] This stems from the simple reason that I was not born Ethiopian Orthodox and, in the history of the Ethiopian Orthodox Church, this Council is known by the very derogatory term as 'the Council of the Byzantine and Roman dogs', an attitude that I did not want to adopt blindly.

I first learned about the Council of Chalcedon when I was growing up in Roman Catholic Church schools. In teaching manuals and books by writers such as K.J. Hefele, A. Grillmeier and C. Moeller, Chalcedon was a victory for Pope Leo, in that his Tome to Flavian, the Patriarch of Constantinople, describing the mystery of the Incarnation was the first theological document accepted as an official document of the faith of the universal Church by a Pope.

For Rome, Chalcedon also stripped the Alexandrian Patriarchate of its leading role in theological debate, which it had in the Christian world at the time because of the legacy of its famous theological school. For Rome also, Chalcedon neutralised the influence of the Antiochian theological tradition.

When I became exposed to the theological heritage of Ethiopian Orthodoxy and began reading critical accounts by Ethiopian and other Oriental Orthodox writers of the Roman Catholic Church's histories of this Council, this only made my difficulties increase.

I couldn't agree either with the other Orthodox Churches of the Byzantine theological and liturgical tradition of Russia, Greece, Eastern Europe and their analysis of Chalcedon, as their leading writers, such as Fathers Florovsky and Myendoff, Professors J. Coman and J.S. Romanides, appeared only to be concerned with the final Chalcedonian formulation, and not the actual conduct of the proceedings over its sixteen sessions.

I thought that the reason for this could lie in the fact the theological tradition of the Constantinoplian Patriarchate was only about one hundred years old by the time that this Council took place and, to be faithful to their theological heritage, these writers had to assert Constantinople's leadership role as both the imperial and religious capital of the Byzantine world.

Other writers of the European theological tradition such as R.V. Sellers, G.L. Prestige, A. Fortescue and E.R. Hardy seemed to me to follow the lines of discussion opened up by the Roman Catholic Church scholars and historians without adding anything new to their analysis.

Even without going into a full account of the Council's proceedings session by session, one sees that this Council did a number of astonishing things. For example, it ignored the decisions of the Second Council of Ephesus in 449, without examining them against the background of their doctrinal origins. It began from the outset by considering the aged Archmandrite Eutyches, the popular leader of the monks of the imperial capital of Constantinople and godfather to the powerful Chrysaphius, who was in the service of Emperor Theodosius II, and close friend of St Dioscorus of Alexandria, a confirmed heretic, showing no concern for a confession of his beliefs he had submitted.

Chalcedon exonerated Flavian, the Patriarch of Constantinople, and Eusebius of Dorylaeum, the president of the Synod of 448 and the accuser of Eutyches, without examining the grounds on which they had been condemned by the Council of 449.

Chalcedon passed sentence of deposition against St Dioscorus, the Patriarch of Egypt, Ethiopia, and all the other districts of north-east Africa under his jurisdiction, by a small section of the delegates, without bringing a definite doctrinal charge of heresy against him.

Chalcedon adopted a definition of the faith concerning the union of the divine and human natures of the Lord Jesus Christ that He existed from the moment of the conception in the womb of St Mary 'in two natures' despite determined opposition from a large majority of the Council's delegates, including Patriarch Anatolius of Constantinople.

Chalcedon acquitted Theodoret of Cyrus and Ibas of Edessa, both of whom were highly suspicious figures who were keeping alive the teachings of Nestorius, who himself had been condemned by the third Ecumenical Council held at Ephesus in 431.

These two men were reinstated, without the controllers of the Council even examining whether there were any grounds at all for the charges that had been levelled against them by the Council of Ephesus in 449.

In any study of the Council of Chalcedon these events can on no account be ignored, and these are the problems to this day that Ethiopian Orthodox Church writers like myself have had with studying Roman Catholic and Byzantine Orthodox accounts of this Council, in spite of the series of meetings which have taken place through the auspices of the World Council of Churches Faith and Order Commission from the 1960s onwards. This is why I find it necessary to look at its minutes in close detail. The main purpose is to show why it was rejected for centuries by the Ethiopian Orthodox Church and the other Orthodox Churches of the Oriental Orthodox Church family.

Events Before Chalcedon

Any impartial reader who examines the minutes of the Synod of Constantinople in 448, the Council of Ephesus 449, and the Council of Chalcedon 451 will see that there was a fundamental difference in procedure between the first two assemblies on the one hand and the third assembly on the other. The Constantinoplian Synod of 448 had a theological issue to resolve, namely the position and teaching of Eutyches who had come under attack in 447 when Theodoret of Cyrus published a volume called 'Eranistes' which took the form of a debate between an orthodox Christian (which was Theodoret himself) and a heretic (which was Eutyches). From this work he became known as 'Eutyches the monophysite heretic'. By this phrase Theodoret wanted everyone to believe that Eutyches essentially denied the reality of the Lord's human nature. The response of Eutyches and the monks of Constantinople was not long in coming. In a letter to pope Leo, Eutyches complained that the condemned ideas of Nestorius were gaining popularity in Constantinople again through Theodoret.

Eutyches also appealed to the Emperor Theodosius II who issued a ruling against the Nestorians and Irenaeus of Tyre. Theodoret of Cyrus, the author of the piece against Eutyches, was attacked, as Flavian, the Patriarch of the capital, showed no desire to intervene in this fresh dispute between Alexandrian and Antiochian theological schools.

This was the background that led to the Synod meeting of November 448, and the bishops examined the questions before them in their own way, using their own methods.

The same is also true of the Council of Ephesus in 449. However, the Council of Chalcedon of 451 met at a time when there were very serious theological disputes between Antioch and Alexandria concerning the union of the divine and human natures of the Lord Jesus Christ which demanded a solution to prevent splitting the unity of the faith and the Church, but this Council ignored these disputes.

Both the Constantinoplian Synod of 448 and the Council of Ephesus of 449 began their respective examination of the matters before them by first clarifying the accepted nature of the Church's faith. To accomplish this the Synod of 448 had the Creed of Nicea, the Second letter of St Cyril to Nestorius, and the Reunion formula signed in 433 between Cyril of Alexandria and John of Antioch, read.

All the participants acknowledged that they accepted the doctrines contained in these documents. The Council of Ephesus in 449 also adopted a similar procedure. Soon after the assembly was called to order, the imperial statements describing the purpose of the meeting were read, and the bishops affirmed their acceptance of the Church's faith in the Creed of Nicea, as it had been accepted also by the third Ecumenical Council of Ephesus held in 431. Following these procedures, both of these assemblies took up the specific issue before them.

The Synod of 448 then went on to hear the nature of the accusation brought against Archmandrite Eutyches by Eusebius of Dorylaeum, to the effect that the old monk would not admit that the Lord Jesus Christ was 'two natures after the humanisation', nor that Christ was born in and possessed the same human nature as we do, except for the condition of sin. On this basis, Eusebius concluded that Eutyches denied the Lord's human birth at Bethlehem, despite Eutyches himself stating that this was not his understanding. As to this Synod itself, I have to admit that there was an investigation of the two questions that were causing the problem, however one-sided it really was. And the investigation was one-sided because Flavian, the Patriarch of Constantinople, who was one of the presiding officers, refused to take as evidence a confession of faith composed by Eutyches himself, without giving any reason for his refusal. In the end the old monk was asked to accept two propositions of Eusebius and to condemn all who would not accept them. Since Eutyches refused to do this he was condemned as a heretic.

The Second Council of Ephesus of 449 took up for further examination an appeal made by Eutyches which incorporated his confession of faith, which the Council fathers declared to be sound and orthodox. Since this appeal was against his condemnation by the Synod of Constantinople the previous year, the bishops now read the Synod's minutes. When coming upon the phrase 'in two natures after the union' in the minutes of this

Synod to describe the mystery of the Incarnation of the Divine Word/Son of God, a good number of the assembled bishops spoke in very strong terms against this phrase. They were surprised at its appearance. The final judgement reached by them was that the condemnation of Eutyches by this Synod meeting could not be allowed to stand. But it meant bad news for Flavian, the Patriarch of Constantinople, who was the president of the Synod, as well as for Eutyches' accuser, Eusebius of Dorylaeum. Both were now condemned.

While it appears that the decisions of both the Constantinoplian Synod of 448 and the second Council of Ephesus of 449 were one-sided, it is a fact that on both occasions the bishops present made serious attempts to examine the issues before them. The Council of Chalcedon of 451 on the other hand, never even tried to face the raging disputes between the bishops and theologians of Alexandria, Antioch, Constantinople and Rome before arriving at its final formulations.

Some Key Facts About the Council of Chalcedon

(A) HOW IT WAS CONVENED

This Council began on 8 October 451 and finished on 1 November. It held sixteen sessions. It was the original plan of the Byzantine authorities to convene it in the same location in Nicea where the first Ecumenical Council was held in the summer of 325, because of the very high regard that Nicea held in the Christian world. However at the issuing of an imperial mandate from the Byzantine court, the delegates were asked to go to Chalcedon instead. For the student of Church history, especially the history of the Ecumenical Councils, this showed the interest the Byzantine imperial court took in this Council from the very beginning.

Furthermore, the Emperor Marcian and his close advisers wanted to take every precaution to ensure that the Council that they had convened would receive as much historical fame as the first Ecumenical Council of Nicea itself. There was also the concern for the safety and peace of the Council, as the threat of are invasion of Illyricum by the fierce tribe of the Huns was thought possible. This is why the Emperor Marcian felt the need for holding the Council in a place close enough to be in touch with its proceedings, as well as to conduct a speedy defence of the Empire should the need arise. Constantinople itself was not chosen, because as the Church historian Trevor Jalland records, Marcian had fears that the monastic communities of Constantinople which held the old monk Eutyches in very high regard might create trouble.

(B) THE SEATING ARRANGEMENT

About five hundred and twenty delegates assembled in the Church of St Euphemia on 8 October 451 when the Council was formally declared open. From the outset the issue of who was in control was never in dispute. Marcian and his wife Pulcheria appointed eighteen high-ranking Byzantine government officials as the presiding officers, who no doubt were the sharpest legal and constitutional minds within their Empire at the time. No Church Council before or after had state officials appointed to preside over it. It was usually the bishops who elected a group of their peers for this function. The role of the emperors was only to convene the Council and make its final decisions law throughout the Empire.

The Byzantine commissioners had their seats fixed across the enclosed Altar Sanctuary of St Euphemia, and the delegates were seated on the other side. On the left sat in order the Roman Catholic delegates of Pope Leo, then Anatolius, the Patriarch of Constantinople, then Maximus of Antioch, then Thalassius of Caesarea in Cappadocia, Stephen of Ephesus, followed by the other delegates from the Orient, Pontus, Asia, Trace. They had already signed Pope Leo's Tome and had made their peace with Rome.

To the right sat St Dioscorus, the Patriarch of Alexandria and its surrounding areas in north-east Africa, then Juvenal of Jerusalem, then the bishop representing Anastasius of Thessalonica, then Peter of Corinth, and then the other delegates from Africa, Illyricum and Palestine. By the seating arrangements these official delegates were divided into two parties, those who had expressed their agreement with Pope Leo of Rome and those who did not. The leader of this second group was none other than the Patriarch of Alexandria, St Dioscorus.

As soon as the delegates took their seats, an astonishing thing happened. Paschasinus, the Bishop of Lilybaeum in Sicily and head of the Roman Catholic delegation, insisted that St Dioscorus should be removed from the Council by the order of Pope Leo of Rome. When asked by the imperial commissioners to list any charges against St Dioscorus, he couldn't. After a little hesitation, Lucentius, another member of the Roman Catholic delegation, said that St Dioscorus was charged on the grounds that 'he had seized the office of judge and dared to conduct a Council without authorisation from the Apostolic See of Rome, a thing that has never happened before and which ought not to happen in future.' After expressing their reservation in this matter, the imperial commissioners now asked St Dioscorus to move from his seat in the assembly. He was now shown a seat reserved for people on trial.

One should pay particular attention to the nature of this allegation by Lucentius against St Dioscorus. He stated that the Patriarch of Alexandria dared to conduct a Council without Rome's authorisation. This was the second Council of Ephesus of 449 over which St Dioscorus was the presiding officer. The fact is Rome had sent a delegation to that Council, so Lucentius' claim did not have a solid base in historical facts, but in the papal government of the universal Church, which a few Church scholars suggest saw its origin with the papacy of Pope Leo.

As soon as St Dioscorus took his new seat, Eusebius of Dorylaeum brought forward a document which charged the Patriarch of Alexandria with two ecclesiastical crimes. He told the Council that St Dioscorus had, on the one hand, tried to establish the heresy of Eutyches as sound and orthodox through the Council of Ephesus of 449, which he had dominated through the agency of a disorderly mob and money. The other charge was that St Dioscorus had deposed him and Flavian, the previous Patriarch of Constantinople, neither of whom had stepped outside of the boundaries of the faith with regard to their administration of their sacramental responsibilities. After presenting the two charges Eusebius made it clear that they could be proved by an examination of the Council's minutes.

In this move, it was plain that Eusebius of Dorylaeum was following up the opening made by both Paschasinus and Lucentius. And this is one of the problems with this Council.

If Church scholars (whether Roman Catholic or not, whether Byzantine Orthodox or not) who only love to praise the final Chalcedonian formulation, and quote it on every occasion, were to be totally honest, they would have said long ago that the Roman delegates and Eusebius were all united in the working out a plan of action which they had already decided upon before the Council opened. Furthermore, it is a fact that, the charges against St Dioscorus which they raised were charges against the Council of 449. They should have been dealt with by examining that Council's decisions against their historical and theological background. Yet this is precisely what Chalcedon failed to do. The Roman delegates and Eusebius instead proceeded by declaring the decisions of Ephesus 449 indefensible without an examination of the nature of how that Council reached final decisions. What is even worse, they then put the entire responsibility on the shoulders of the Patriarch of Alexandria.

Procedures like this one, which was embraced by men who controlled the Council of Chalcedon, probably had the intention of frightening the other bishops from Africa and other parts of the Christian world who supported St Dioscorus and held the theological tradition of Alexandria in high regard. Furthermore, not one of the Roman legates or Eusebius showed any knowledge on this occasion that they were going against the injunction of Pope Leo himself, who had said on 13 April 451 in a letter to Anatolius of Constantinople that the men responsible for the decisions of the Council of Ephesus 449 were St Dioscorus, Juvenal of Jerusalem and Eustathius of Berytus. Leo wanted their names removed from the liturgical calendar, thereby showing Anatolius that he was excommunicating them on his own authority and judgement.

When St Dioscorus was finally given an opportunity to answer the charges against him, he began by saying that the Council of Ephesus of 449 had been convened by Emperor Theodosius II himself; it reached its decisions after examining the proceedings of the Constantinoplian Synod of 448; and that the minutes of its proceedings should be read. Because Eusebius had also made the same request when he began to present his case against St Dioscorus, the imperial commissioners yielded to his request. However, he first asked for the accepted faith of the Church that was inherited from the time of the Apostles to be read out before the minutes of Ephesus 449 was examined. The imperial commissioners denied this request on the grounds that the personal charges against him had to be investigated first.

Now the importance of St Dioscorus' request must not be overlooked. As I have already outlined earlier, the bishops of the Constantinoplian Synod of 448, as well as the ones of the Council of Ephesus of 449, had taken up the issues before them only after having the accepted nature of the faith of the Church publicly stated. This was so that the accepted faith inherited from the time of the Apostles could act as a measuring rod when considering any deviations.

Here at Chalcedon, in the face of the allegation that the theological position of Ephesus 449 was nothing but that of the teaching of Eutyches (at least as Eusebius had understood this Council's final decisions), it was perfectly legitimate on the part of St Dioscorus, who had been accused, to ask the presiding officers for a clarification of the accepted faith that the Church had inherited from the time of the Apostles, if they were going to make a judgement on the decisions reached at Ephesus in 449. The answer of the imperial commissioners showed that as the controllers of the Council of Chalcedon they decided not to open up and face the real issues before them at all.

(D) THE AFFAIR OF THE BLANK PAPERS AND THE USE OF VIOLENCE

This request of St Dioscorus was indeed a challenge to the Council, and it had to be met. The delegates who were sitting on the left tried to meet it by referring to the case of the blank papers, as well as of the use of force to extract signatures from delegates who were unwilling to accept the decisions.

This occurred after a rather interesting incident. The reading of the minutes of the second Council of Ephesus 449 began with the mandates of Emperor Theodosius II which had been issued to convene the Council. When the first of them, which was a mandate addressed to St Dioscorus containing the injunction disallowing the participation of Theodoret of Cyrus in the Council, the imperial commissioners ordered the Bishop of Cyrus to enter the present Chalcedonian Council as a full member on the grounds that he had been rehabilitated to his episcopal rank by Pope Leo and that the imperial authority had given the necessary permission. Although the delegates who supported St Dioscorus expressed their disapproval on the grounds that Theodoret was a well-known promoter of Nestorius's Christology, which was condemned at the third Ecumenical Council of Ephesus in 431, the Bishop of Cyrus remained in the assembly.

When the reading of the minutes of the Council of Ephesus of 449 was over, St Dioscorus then made a very powerful observation. This Council of 449, he said, was presided over by himself, Juvenal of Jerusalem and Thalassius of Caesarea in Cappadocia. Furthermore, the Council's decisions had been reached with the full approval of all the delegates concerned. How then could he alone be set apart for trial, he asked. This was indeed a serious challenge to the gathered delegates at Chalcedon, and the bishops seated on the left side now cried out that the decisions were not of the Council, because they had been forced to sign blank papers.

The bishops seated on the right side responded, 'They are ones who had signed first. Why do the clergy shout now? The Synod is of bishops, not of the clergy. Those who are not of the Synod, send them out. May those who signed come forward to the middle; it is with you that we signed.' We see here a division. While the bishops on the side of the Roman delegates referred to the case of the blank papers and spoke of violence, the bishops on the other side challenged these so-called allegations in very strong terms. The delegates on the right even showed that the second Ephesian Council of 449 did not suffer more from any disturbance created by an unruly crowd than did the present Council of

Chalcedon.

Stephen of Ephesus and Theodore of Claudiopolis in Isaurea were the two bishops who supported the story of the blank papers. It is therefore important to see what exactly they said. Stephen told the assembly that the imperial commissioners at Ephesus 449, Elpidius and Eulogius, came to his residence with soldiers and monks who supported Eutyches and by threats forced him to sign the decisions already arrived at by St Dioscorus, Juvenal, Thalassius and the other bishops.

Theodore also complained that force and threats had been used to get consent from the delegates to the decisions already reached by the same three. This last account was a total distortion of the truth, because St Dioscorus and Juvenal were two of the three presidents of the Council, so if they wanted to distribute blank papers, they had other less high-profile persons to carry out this task. Now the two men who gave the damaging report against St Dioscorus and the Council of 449 were answered by the bishops on the right side, as well as St Dioscorus himself. When they tried to pressurise St Dioscorus again, he asked that the copy of the minutes in the possession of Stephen himself should be read to see if they were the same as the copy he and the other delegates had, so that they could prove the basis of the story once and for all.

The bishops on the left side who spoke of violence and blank papers were forced on a later occasion by the imperial commissioners to admit that the story of the blank papers was made up. And when Basil of Seleucia supported the phrase 'two natures after the union' to describe how the divine and human was united in the Lord Jesus Christ, in contradiction to his own statements at Ephesus in 449, the imperial commissioners now asked him how Flavian could then have been condemned, seeing that he did not subscribe to this phrase. Now the bishops on the left cried out, 'We have all sinned. We ask for forgiveness.'

The commissioners responded, 'Do you not complain that you were forced to sign the condemnation of Flavian on blank papers?'

Again the bishops said, 'We all have sinned. We ask for pardon.'

From this context it is clear that the second apology was done to soften the anger of the commissioners as it had no base as historical facts. Stephen of Ephesus, who had an array of damaging reports to give about the second Council of Ephesus 449, was one of the leading bishops at that Council. He had occupied the sixth place among the delegates. After Juvenal, he spoke in favour of the reading of the minutes of the Constantinoplian Synod of 448 before reading Leo's Tome. He had also spoken for acquitting Eutyches and for the removal of Flavian and Eusebius.

Furthermore, he was the fourth one to sign the decisions of the first session of this second Council of Ephesus of 449. The order was Dioscorus, Juvenal, Domnus and Stephen. Therefore his signature was one of the early ones mentioned by Theodore of Claudiopolis.

If an episode such as this one had happened with reference to any other Council, then I am sure that Church historians and scholars would have emphasised the fact that the men in control of Chalcedon used untrustworthy characters to mock a churchman who had the moral and physical courage to defend his convictions.

As for the case of the blank papers, the following facts should be remembered.

a. Two years had elapsed between the second Council of Ephesus and the Council of Chalcedon. During this time no one, including Eusebius of Dorylaeum himself, who was present at the Ephesus 449, ever made this point against the Council.

b. The Bishop of Dorylaeum who mentioned the story in his second presentation against St Dioscorus on 13 October did not refer to it in his first one on 8 October. This shows that as a bishop who was present at that Council, he had to wait over two years to hear the story for the first time from the group opposed to the Patriarch of Alexandria at the Council of Chalcedon.

c. In spite of all these reasons, even if we grant for the sake of argument that the story is based on solid fact, it should be remembered that no one at Chalcedon 451 accused St

Dioscorus alone of having committed the crime.

Therefore the efforts of the Roman Catholic delegates to single out St Dioscorus as the man solely responsible for the misgivings of Ephesus in 449 were based on very fragile grounds. But they and their allies were determined to see their plans through to the end. Exploiting the silence of the imperial commissioners who were themselves opposed to the Patriarch of Alexandria, they met separately without the bishops on the right side and the imperial commissioners to enforce their plans against the Patriarch of Alexandria for crimes which I have shown above had no basis as historical facts.

(E) CHALCEDON APPROVES THE CONDEMNATION OF EUTYCHES

We come now to the case of Eutyches and his unjust condemnation. As we have already shown earlier when we began to look at this Council in greater depth, Archmandrite Eutyches had been acquitted by the Council of 449 at Ephesus on two grounds. This Council declared that his confession of faith as contained in his appeal against the charge of monophysicism was sound and orthodox. He was also acquitted because most of the bishops present said that the Constantinoplian Synod of November 448 had betrayed the Church's faith in the mystery of the Incarnation, when it insisted that the Lord Jesus Christ existed 'in two natures after the union' which took place in the womb of St Mary, the Holy Theotokos, through the power and grace of the Holy Spirit.

Now the issue before Chalcedon as regards Eutyches was this. The Constantinoplian Synod in 448 had condemned Eutyches as a heretic because he refused to admit to the formula that the Lord existed in two natures after the union of His divine and human natures in the womb of St Mary, the Holy Theotokos, through the power and grace of the Holy Spirit. This Synod also condemned him because he hesitated to affirm that Christ was of the same human nature as us, except for the condition of sin. However in reaching this conclusion, the Synod paid no attention either to Eutyches' own verbal statements or to the confession of faith which he submitted. Therefore, the decision was one-sided. Ephesus 449 reacted very strongly against this ruling by declaring that the phrase 'in two natures after the union' as an acceptable description of the mystery of the Incarnation was totally contrary to the already established faith of the Church on this matter.

After reading Eutyches' confession and his verbal statements they overruled his condemnation as this was the proper course of action to take. But the Council of Chalcedon, contrary to what one would normally expect from a Church Council, proceeded from the beginning assuming that Eutyches was a confirmed heretic, and what is worse is that this was done in the absence of Eutyches himself. This conduct by the presiding officers of Chalcedon can on no account be justified. Equally unjustifiable was the assumption that the phrase 'in two natures after the union' to describe the mystery of the Incarnation was the accepted faith of the Church. This fact should be stressed both from a historical and from a theological standpoint. The way in which Chalcedon handled Eutyches' confession of the faith was indeed unacceptable, especially when one considers that it contained the following sentences:

> For He who is the Word of God came down from heaven without flesh and was made man from the very flesh of the Virgin unchangeably, and inconvertibly, in a way He Himself knew and willed. And He who is always perfect God before the ages was made man in the end of days for us and for our salvation.

Now if these sentences do not clearly state that Christ's human nature was the same as ours, except for the condition of sin, then I do not know how much plainer one could express it. At Chalcedon these sentences were not read. As the appeal of Eutyches was being made from the minutes of Ephesus 449, when the reading came to where Eutyches had registered his rejection of the sentence 'those who say that the flesh of our Lord Jesus Christ came down from heaven', Eusebius, the Bishop of Dorylaeum, his main accuser, interrupted and made the comment that Eutyches avoided the phrase 'from heaven, but did not say from where'.

We have already seen that from the beginning Eusebius, the Bishop of Dorylaeum, had been accusing the old monk of denying a real human birth of the Lord. He stressed time and again that for Eutyches, the body of our Lord came down from Heaven. But from the passages of his confession that we have quoted above, the old monk made it plain that this was not his position. Since this passage of his confession contradicted the charge against him as stated by Eusebius, the attention of the assembly was skilfully moved from the real issue.

Before the next part of Eutyches' confession was presented which contained thoroughly orthodox answers to Eusebius' questions, the bishops started to raise a series of questions of their own about the ideas of the old monk, and when the reading of the minutes resumed the sentences quoted above were left out. Therefore the Council of Chalcedon did not even undertake an examination of the beliefs of Eutyches and, in assuming that he was a heretic, did not base its decisions on solid facts.

(F) CHALCEDON OVERTURNS THE CONDEMNATION OF FLAVIAN AND EUSEBIUS

We come now to the matter of the exoneration of Flavian and Eusebius. Two incidents led to this.

In the first incident, while the delegates were engaged in an intense debate about the teaching of Eutyches, Basil, the Bishop of Seleucia, made this statement, 'My affirmation has always been that I worship our Lord Jesus Christ, the Only Son of God, God the Word, as made known to me in two natures after He became Incarnate and was made man.' This remark produced one of the most serious outbursts that Chalcedon would face. The imperial commissioners now asked how, if Basil's position was orthodox, Flavian could be excommunicated. Basil now answered that Flavian had been unjustly condemned.

In the second incident, Chalcedon had a statement of Eustathius of Berytus read to it from the minutes of Ephesus 449. Following the reading of St Cyril's second letter to Nestorius, and the Reunion formula which he also signed with John of Antioch in 433, which had been recorded in the minutes of the Constantinoplian Synod of 448, Eustathius had pleaded that for a correct understanding of St Cyril, his letters addressed to Acacius of Melitene, Valerian of Iconium and Successus of Dio-Caesarea were just as important. According to these letters, Eustathius had insisted, it was unlawful to affirm two natures in the Lord after the union took place in the womb of St Mary, by the grace and power of the Holy Spirit. Instead it should be (to use St Cyril's phrase) 'One Incarnate nature of God the Word'. When these things were read at Chalcedon, the delegates on the left shouted, 'Eutyches says these things! Dioscorus says these things!' Now St Dioscorus intervened: 'When we say One Incarnate nature of God the Word, we do not speak of confusion, neither of division, nor of change. Let those who say change, confusion, or mixture, be anathema.'

Now the imperial commissioners raised the question of whether the position referred to by Eustathius was to be found in the canonical letters of St Cyril to which Eustathius had made reference. Stung by this challenge of believing he was not telling the truth, Eustathius, the Bishop of Berytus, rushed to the middle of the assembly, flung down the letters of St Cyril he had in his possession and said, 'If I stated wrongly, see the work of Cyril. Let that be anathematised.' The bishops on the right supported Eustathius and cried out what he spoke was the truth as they themselves had copies of the letters.

This was a moment of real triumph for them, especially as they all supported the theological tradition of Alexandria and were stunned by the way St Dioscorus was treated. But the situation was spoiled by Eustathius himself. He continued by saying that the letters of St Cyril state the use of this key phrase in this manner:

It is unlawful to speak of two natures after the union. One should say only, One Incarnate nature only. However, if anyone affirms One nature in order to explain away the flesh of Christ which is of the same substance with us, let them be anathema. So anyone who speaks of two natures after the union in order to divide the Son of God, let them be anathema also.

Up to this point Eustathius had clarified the issue very well, and had he stopped here then the exoneration of Flavian and Eusebius would not have been an easy thing to accomplish. But Eustathius went on to say that Flavian had accepted the teachings of St Cyril and had made this known to the Emperor Theodosius II himself in writing. The issue before Chalcedon therefore was not what Flavian, the Patriarch of Constantinople, had presented to Emperor Theodosius II soon after the Synod of 448. The issue was why that Synod of 448 had condemned Eutyches and all those who refused to accept the phrase 'in two natures after the union' to describe the mystery of the Incarnation. In order to come out of this sticky situation the Byzantine imperial commissioners were anxiously waiting for some clue or opening where they could exonerate one of their former Patriarchs as well as Eusebius of Dorylaeum.

So they asked why, if he had been orthodox, Flavian was condemned at all.

'I failed,' responded a nervous Eustathius. The commissioners had now gained their point and straight away required of the delegates to signify whether Flavian and Eusebius were orthodox or not. Seeing no way out a large number of them responded that they were. In this way, without ever raising the real issue, the Byzantine commissioners upheld the condemnation of Eutyches and acquitted Flavian and Eusebius.

However, it should be noted that in declaring Flavian and Eusebius orthodox the delegates did not mean that the insistence of the Synod of 448 on the phrase 'in two natures after the union' to describe the mystery of the Incarnation was orthodox, they only meant that the confession of faith that Flavian had presented to Emperor Theodosius II was orthodox. Since Eusebius held the same position he had to be orthodox as well.

St Dioscorus again raised the real issue, but this had no effect on the assembly which had already signified that Flavian and Eusebius were orthodox.

So the commissioners, as the presiding officers, gave their verdict. They said that the Council of Ephesus in 449 was dominated by evil men who deserved punishment. These evil men they marked as Dioscorus of Alexandria, Juvenal of Jerusalem, Thalassius of Caesarea in Cappadocia, Eusebius of Ancyra, Eustathius of Berytus and Basil of Seleucia. They ordered that these should be deposed.

While this verdict was praised by the Oriental party, the bishops from Egypt and Illyrian asked for a general amnesty. This is clear proof that they did not believe that either St Dioscorus or the other condemned bishops had committed any crime.

Also the verdict of the commissioners was proof that they did not support the Roman delegates and Eusebius of Dorylaeum in their efforts to declare St Dioscorus as being solely responsible for the alleged misdeeds of Ephesus in 449.

(G) THE DEPOSING OF ST DIOSCORUS

The session of the Council which met on 10 October was literally a waste of time. In it the imperial commissioners tried to get the unanimous agreement of all the delegates in having the Tome of Pope Leo to Flavian accepted as a document of the faith of the Church regarding the mystery of the Incarnation. However they did not succeed in their plan. Pressure was mounting because the commissioners had assured Leo that his letter would be approved and adopted as the one of the Council's doctrinal statements. When this move failed they adjourned for five days and gave a specific brief to Anatolius, the Patriarch of the capital, to meet with the delegates who had problems with Pope Leo's Tome to Flavian, so that they could discuss all the outstanding issues regarding it.

However, an extraordinary thing happened. The five-day recess was not kept. On the third day a section of the delegates held a meeting of their own, without the knowledge of the commissioners, to reopen the charges of Eusebius of Dorylaeum against St Dioscorus. It was the same charges, except that it added the affair of the blank papers and the use of force as established facts. St Dioscorus was served with three summonses. And during the period between the second and the third summons four men from Alexandria appeared with petitions of their own against St Dioscorus.

In the end this 'back-room meeting' outside of the reach of the commissioners unanimously decided that St Dioscorus should be deposed for disobedience, and this verdict was passed on. The statement made on the occasion by the Roman delegates,

and the verdict of the commissioners when the Council recon-
vened, deserves special attention, especially with the accepted
viewpoint of all those belonging to the Chalcedonian position that
St Dioscorus was a monophysite heretic, that he was arrogant and
prone to fits of violence, and other statements of the kind.

The charge of disobedience against him was a very strange
one, especially when one sees that he answered the summonses
brought to him. He said that when he was served the first one, he
was ready to go to, but was kept in custody. And by the time the
deputies of the commissioners came to bring him to the assembly,
he was told by these same deputies that there was a fresh charge
against him brought by Eusebius. Realising now that a plot was
being hatched against him by his enemies, St Dioscorus insisted
that the commissioners should be present at the meeting to
discuss the issues once again. Later when the second summons
was delivered to him, he asked whether the other churchmen
condemned with him were going to be there at the meeting. He
was told that they would not be. To this reply St Dioscorus stated
in strong terms that he would attend the meeting only if the
commissioners and the other churchmen condemned along with
him were going to be present. Now this demand of his was in my
opinion quite fair and just. But it was denied to him by those
presenting the summons.

Can this action on the part of the deputies be vindicated in any
way? Let us look into the statement of the Roman delegation
which contained five charges against St Dioscorus, the Patriarch
of Alexandria responsible for all the Churches in north-east
Africa.

The charges are as follows:

1. That he admitted to communion Eutyches after he had been
    deposed by the Synod of 448, and before he was reinstated by
    the Council of Ephesus 449.
2. That even after the other bishops who had taken part in the
    Council of 449 had made their peace with the holy See in
    Rome, he remained in rebellion.
3. That he did not permit the reading of Pope Leo's Tome to
    Flavian at the Council of 449, thereby causing the Church of

Rome to be greatly scandalised.

4. That he overstepped the bounds of his authority by excommunicating Pope Leo of Rome, an act which passed the limits of forgiveness.

5. That he did not obey the canonical summons presented to him.

I am not going to go into every point in these five charges. But I have to make some comments on them nevertheless.

Regarding the charge that he admitted Eutyches to communion. If by 'communion' they meant the sacrament of holy communion, it is a fact that nobody else, including the bishops of Egypt or the neighbouring in districts in North Africa, ever made. In any case even if he did, can this be considered a worse error than Leo's own, when he restored Theodoret of Cyrus to his episcopal chair on his own personal authority?

As for the second charge, that even after the other bishops who had taken part in the Council of 449 had done so without Leo's consent had now made their peace with him, except for St Dioscorus. I think that I can leave this to one side.

The third charge is more substantial. The minutes of 449 do not show that St Dioscorus ever prevented the presentation of Leo's Tome to the assembled Church fathers. Moreover, the reading of this document at Chalcedon, and its declaration as a document of the faith of the Church regarding the mystery of the Incarnation, only served to drive a wedge in the Church community which we in the twentieth century have inherited and are trying to heal.

As for the fourth charge, not one of the delegates at Chalcedon had ever heard of an excommunication order by St Dioscorus, the Patriarch of Alexandria to Leo, the Pope of Rome before the story was told by a certain Deacon Theodore from Alexandria on 13 October 451. Even granting that St Dioscorus had issued one, can it be considered a worse crime than that of Leo himself, who had excommunicated the Patriarch of Alexandria, Juvenal, the Bishop of Jerusalem and Eustathius, the Bishop of Berytus, exactly six months earlier to the day when the Romans made this charge against St Dioscorus?

The assembly had no more satisfactory grounds for passing its sentence of deposition against St Dioscorus. So their verdict said:

> On account of contempt for the sacred canons and your contumacy towards this holy Ecumenical Council, whereby, in addition to other offences of which you have been convicted, you did not respond to the third summons of this holy and great Council which were administered to you in accordance with divine canons, and answer the charges made against you: Know, then, that you have been deposed on the 13th day of the present month of October by the holy and Ecumenical Synod from your episcopate and deprived of all ecclesiastical rank.

In such terms then did Chalcedon handle the case of St Dioscorus. It should be remembered, however, that the men who constituted this so-called 'holy and great Ecumenical Council' which made the decision were only about half of the entire delegates present.

In the history of the Church, the Council of Chalcedon is not the only assembly which condemned a churchman in his absence, and if I must be fair and honest, St Dioscorus was not the only one to be treated like this. Paul of Samosata and Nestorius had been condemned in this way as well. But the Councils which took up their cases made every attempt to examine all available evidence and witnesses before arriving at their decisions.

The few powerful men who controlled Chalcedon did not see the need for this same fair treatment towards a Patriarch of the north-east African nation of Egypt. And since over the centuries this fact has become much too sensitive and delicate to admit, those who were persuaded to defend Chalcedon and its final formulations had to invent a heresy and attach it on to an African Church father whom the Council of 451 could not accuse formally of any heresy whatsoever.

The charges of the Roman legates are open evidence that they had no justifiable foundation for adopting the attitude of hatred and jealousy towards St Dioscorus that they did, except perhaps for the fact that he belonged to an African Apostolic tradition which went back to the sojourning of the Holy Family (the Lord Jesus Christ, His mother, St Mary, and St Joseph, His earthly guardian) in Egypt. This tradition was also linked with the venerable memory of St Mark, and a theological school which made Alexandria the leader in matters of theological argumentation that was preventing Rome from promoting itself.

(H) THE COUNCIL COMPOSES ITS DEFINITION OF THE FAITH

We move now to considering how this Council came to compose its definition of the faith in the mystery of the Incarnation.

After the episodes on 13 October, the third official session convened on the 17th. In this session Pope Leo got what he wanted: namely his Tome to Flavian was formally declared a document of the faith of the Church concerning the mystery of the Incarnation. On that day when it was approved there was hardly anyone present to oppose it.

If this kind of thing had happened in another Council, writers of Church history and theology would have surmised that the bishops who accepted the African theological tradition of Alexandria had endorsed Leo's Tome not really because they approved Leo's theology, but so as to avoid trouble for themselves. And to show that this is not a cynical conclusion on my part, when we read the statement of the Illyrian bishops, this mood comes across quite clearly in the way they formulated their views: 'We hold the saving faith of the three hundred and eighteen fathers' (referring to the Nicean bishops of the Ecumenical Council in 325) 'which was confirmed by the one hundred and fifty fathers' (referring to the bishops of the second Ecumenical Council in 381 at Constantinople). 'The same faith was ratified by the Council of Ephesus.' (Referring to the third Ecumenical Council in 431.)

'Regarding the Tome of Leo our doubts have been cleared by Paschasinus and Lucentius when we met with Anatolius. Concerning Jesus Christ, we believe that from the Holy Virgin Theotokos, Godhead and Manhood were united in Him, without confusion, change and division. Seeing that the Tome agrees with this faith, we subscribe to it.'

On 22 October when, as we shall see, the Eastern delegates

insisted that their draft definition should be adopted by the Council, the same Illyrian bishops said that those who were unwilling to accept their own draft were Nestorians, and that they would do well by joining the Nestorian camp of Leo at Rome.

So, following the adoption of Pope Leo's Tome by the Council, the five other men condemned with St Dioscorus who had already signed the Tome were admitted back into the Council, and the deposition of Patriarch of Alexandria was formally made official because he refused to appear when summoned.

It was also on 22 October that the subject of the composition of a definition of the faith was taken up. Two weeks earlier on the 10th, the commissioners had proposed that the delegates prepare themselves for this task. But when it was made, almost all had opposed the proposal. Now on the 22nd the Eastern bishops, under the leadership of Anatolius, the Patriarch of Constantinople, had come to the Council with a draft composition. Although it does not appear that this draft was preserved, it is clear from the record of the ongoing debates that it did not contain the two highly controversial phrases to describe the mystery of the Incarnation 'in two natures', or 'two natures after the union' of the Synod of 448, but only the phrase of St Dioscorus 'from two natures'.

More important is the fact that these Eastern delegates had to struggle very hard to have this draft composition accepted with the addition of the doctrinal title of the Holy Virgin Mary, 'the Holy Theotokos', to protect the mystery of the union of Godhead and Manhood in the Lord Jesus Christ. The other delegates would not accept this draft, and it was only after long periods of heated and bitter exchanges that they agreed that another draft should be composed. They did so on the power of the line of reasoning advanced by the commissioners representing the Byzantine Throne that the phrase 'from two natures' was the position of St Dioscorus regarding his understanding of the mystery of the Incarnation. The commissioners said that St Dioscorus was now condemned, and all the delegates had accepted that decision. Whereas the phrase 'in two natures' to describe the mystery of the Incarnation was the teaching of Pope Leo, the leader of the Church in Rome whose Tome they had already declared a document of the faith of the Church regarding the Lord Jesus Christ. Therefore these Eastern bishops had to choose between these two churchmen, Leo or Dioscorus.

In the course of this almighty struggle Anatolius, the head of the Church in the Byzantine Empire, had made a point of stressing to the commissioners and the Roman legates that St Dioscorus had not been condemned on a question of the doctrinal faith of the Church. This statement of Anatolius was not challenged at all. Therefore, bearing these facts in mind, I think it is perfectly sound and fair to say that the majority of the bishops held the same position as St Dioscorus concerning the understanding of the mystery of the Incarnation. However, after doing their best to have him restored, they had to leave their appeal to one side, because they realised that the bond of Rome and Constantinople which controlled Chalcedon was far too strong for them to oppose.

To show this hostility on the part of the controllers of Chalcedon and probably another reason why the bishops backed down in their attempt to have St Dioscorus restored, I think that I need to say a few words about the widely circulated story from the end of the second Council of Ephesus 449, that Flavian, the previous Patriarch of Constantinople, soon after this second Council of Ephesus had closed, died as a result of ill-treatment which he had received from the so-called disorderly mob of monks under the control of St Dioscorus, one of the presiding officers of that Council.

This story has been repeated by some modern writers, but I must stress that not one of the churchmen who attended both Councils, including Eusebius of Dorylaeum, the Roman legates, and even the bishops of the Eastern regions under Antioch, ever reported anything of this kind in an official capacity in any of the sessions of Chalcedon, although no one is willing to swear for what was said behind closed doors.

There is evidence from another source that Flavian died not too long after Ephesus 449. Nestorius refers to this in his book, *Bazaar of Heracleides*. In this work he says that Flavian had died in prison on the fourth day after he was put into custody. This happened, so Nestorius reports, on account of both the mental and physical agony meted out to him by the soldiers who were guarding him. However, Nestorius in this work does not accuse any of the presiding officers of the Council of letting monks or anybody else inflict this kind of treatment to Flavian. He only said that the soldiers who took Flavian into custody and were guarding him brutalised him on account of his beliefs.

From an impartial historical standpoint of the written sources that have come down to us, it is therefore plain that the story of the ill-treatment of Flavian by the Council of 449, of which St Dioscorus was one of the presiding officers, is also a creation that started circulation between the end of the second Council of Ephesus 449 and the Council of Chalcedon 451; just as was the affair of the blank papers being presented to some bishops, as well as the use of violence to get their signatures to add strength to St Dioscorus' position were also a creation. But sometimes in the history of the Christian Church, fictitious creations have proved just as powerful as the revealed truth is in influencing the minds and outlooks of the Church faithful of future generations.

(I) THE CASE OF THEODORET AND IBAS

Finally, we come to consider the way in which the Council's controllers restored Theodoret and Ibas to their episcopal duties. Theodoret had, as we have already seen, been invited back into the first session of the Council of Chalcedon by the imperial commissioners in the atmosphere of an uproar by most of the delegates. Now on 26 October his case was taken up again. Most of the bishops, ignoring the actions of Pope Leo, who had already restored him to his episcopal seat on his own authority, shouted when he entered the assembly, 'Theodoret is still under Excommunication, isn't he?'

The Bishop of Cyrus responded by saying that he had submitted an appeal to the Emperor and also to the Roman legates, and that, if they wished, they could read it themselves. The commissioners blocked this move and asked him simply to condemn Nestorius and his teachings in clear and plain terms in the hearing of all those present.

Theodoret began by trying to convince the gathered delegates that he was always orthodox in his beliefs, but the bishops were not convinced and demanded that he should openly condemn Nestorius and his teachings. Finally, he said, 'Anathema to Nestorius.' This serves to prove that up until then he still had not excommunicated Nestorius.

Now without implying that Nestorius, or anybody else, should have been condemned, I should point out that Pope Leo himself, together with his legates and the imperial commissioners, who were all claiming to be opposed to Nestorius and his teachings, had been supporting Theodoret without publicly clarifying their own position on the matter.

This is what made the bishops, especially those from Egypt, uneasy, as they could only understand this action to mean that Pope Leo and the Byzantine authorities were trying to discredit the Council of Ephesus in 431 in which Nestorius and his teachings were condemned. What is more, they all knew that Theodoret had had close contacts with Nestorius even after he was condemned.

Furthermore, the way in which Ibas, the Bishop of Edessa, was reinstated also supported this view of the Egyptian bishops. One of the grounds on which Ibas was condemned by the Ephesian Council of 449 was his letter to Maris of Persia (otherwise known as Dadiso, the Catholics of Seleucia-Ctesiphon). In this letter Ibas insisted several times that St Cyril, the Patriarch of Alexandria before St Dioscorus, had fallen into the heresy of Apollinarius, and that the second Ecumenical Council held in Ephesus in 431 had made an error in approving St Cyril's third letter to Nestorius which included twelve anathemas.

At Chalcedon, when the question of Ibas's reinstatement was opened up, the Roman Catholic legates stated that, after having read his letter to Maris, they had no problem with the beliefs of Ibas. The other delegates were shocked as this meant that these legates of Pope Leo were showing no respect either for the theology of St Cyril or, even more importantly, for the third Ecumenical Council of 431.

★

Conclusion

It should now be clear, after this close examination of the minutes, that not one of the decisions of the Council of Chalcedon held in October 451 was reached after a proper examination of all the issues involved in each question that was before it.

What is very telling is the testimony of Pope Leo's legates in the case of St Dioscorus. They had all decided to depose him in advance of the opening session, and all the bishops who came to the Council were made to accept their decision. This meant that Church fathers who had a good understanding of the Alexandrine theological tradition, and who had taken it upon themselves for the twenty years between the second Ecumenical Council at Ephesus 431 and Chalcedon 451 to defend the decisions of that Council against the Nestorian beliefs about the mystery of the union of Godhead and Manhood in the Lord Jesus Christ were now defeated. For try as they might at Chalcedon, they could not oppose the alliance of Pope Leo's chief legates and the Byzantine imperial authority to have their own way.

(C) Major Events from the Sixth to the Ninth Century Decline

Axum and South Arabia

It is an established fact among Ethiopian Orthodox Church historians that from Old Testament times groups of peoples of Semitic origin crossed the Red Sea from South Arabia and settled in Axum and its surrounding areas. Native Ethiopians also went to Arabia. The migration of the inhabitants of Arabia was probably to seek more fertile and richer soils for farming than their own desert lands. Upon arriving some of these newcomers entered into armed conflict with the indigenous population controlled by the Axumite state, which in some cases resulted in them taking over the palace compound and establishing urban centres outside Axum itself, in Adulis (Axum's port town), Yeha, Matara, and Asmara in present-day Eritrea.

Those natives who crossed the Red Sea from Arabia became more and more powerful, to the point that Axum became a world power. Bringing with them their own religious beliefs, they built temples, palace compounds and covered markets which displayed circles and crescents symbolising their gods, Mahrem and Almuqah.

In the time of Asbeha and Abraha's reign in the fourth century AD there is evidence of Ethiopian communities in South Yemen, Nagran, parts of the Straits of Babal, Mandab and Himyar. These communities show that migration was not a one-way affair. In fact this is confirmed by the appearance of the names of these places on inscriptions of these brother kings of the fourth century. And they clearly show that they were under the dominion of the Axumite throne. Cosmas Indicopleustes, an Egyptian shipbuilder and navigator who later became a monk, arrived in Axum around the year 522 during the reign of Emperor Kaleb and wrote in his *Christian Topography* that the Axumite state at this time had fully established international commercial and diplomatic relationships with Palestine, Phoenicia, Syria, South Arabia, Constantinople, India, Persia and Sri Lanka (formerly Ceylon). He writes on pages 365–66 of his work:

Axum and Adulis towns were overwhelmed with commerce and swarmed with merchants of every nationality, Greeks, Syrians, Indians, Persians and Armenians.

It was probably in the midst of all these activities that Christian communities began to grow in South Arabia from the missionary work of monks and wealthy Orthodox Christians from Axum. However, on the evidence provided by the Ethiopian historian Tekle Tsadik Mecuria in his work, *Ye Ethiopia Tarik, Nubia, Axum and Zaguwe*, published in 1951, he states on page 340 that it was through a Syrian-born preacher, Famiwon, that Christianity was first introduced into Arabia.

The Struggle Between Christians and Jews

Other groups on this South Arabian peninsula who practised the worship of the Old Testament God, the Holy Yahweh, according to laws of Moses, had also been living in this region since the destruction of Jerusalem by Nebuchadnezzar in 587 BC and its occupation by the Lagidae. Their numbers increased greatly after the third destruction of Jerusalem by the Roman Emperor Titus in AD 70, when Jews persecuted by the Romans received a welcome from their compatriots in South Arabia. Furthermore, many Christians left the Byzantine Empire in the decades after the Council of Chalcedon and sought refuge in Arabia. In time, with the help of the archbishops and the kings of Axum, Christian communities were established. From Syria another migration of Orthodox Christians headed for Hira (present-day Najaf in Iraq) and from this location they eventually reached and settled in Nagran. Mingling between these Christians and Jews was a large native Arab population. Among them were Yemenites, Catabans and Hadramuts who clung to their traditional cult of moon worship. Islam as an independent religion was not yet established, so these three religious communities lived side by side in periods of conflict and peace. The Christian community, with massive support from the archbishops and kings of Axum, increased in number, developing and organising many churches, schools and monasteries. Nagran and Zafar (or Tafar as some books have it) became great religious and cultural centres and trading posts. The Jews too, with the skills and gifts they usually possessed in many fields, formed powerful communities in Saba and Himyar from which they controlled their trade. Sharp rivalry therefore developed between these Christians and Jews. The Christians considered the Jews infidels destined to burn in the fires of hell for refusing to recognise Christ as the Incarnate Saviour, while the Jews outraged the Christians by labelling them 'idol worshippers' because they adored the Lord Jesus (who for the Jews was merely the preacher and miracle-worker from Nazareth) as the Christ, and prayed to him to forgive them their sins, and also to grant them eternal life.

The Massacre of the Christians of Nagran and Zafar by the Jews

While Emperor Kaleb (reigned 514–42) ruled Axum, Justin I (reigned 518–27) was the Emperor of the Byzantine Empire. It was at this time that the Jews, with the help of the Himyarites, massacred the Christians of Nagran and Zafar. Besides the Ge'ez text, this event is recorded by two Byzantine church historians of the period, Pocopius and Sergius. In their texts Emperor Kaleb is given the Greek name Hellesthaios. In certain passages his name changes again to Elle Atsbaha. In a similar fashion, the Jewish King of Himyar, who is known as Zurah or Masruc, is identified as Yussuf, the name he assumed when he came to power. Among Arab historians he is known as Dhu-Nuwas. In the Ge'ez texts which tell the story of the massacres he has the name Finhas.

The actual course of the event as recorded in the Ge'ez text is this. Finhas, the King of the Himyarites, persecuted and burned in pits of fire the three hundred and forty Christians of Nagran, with the support of Jews and other non-Christians. Upon receiving this news, the Archbishop of Axum, Thomas, went to Emperor Kaleb to seek aid and found it. The Emperor called for one of his generals, Haywana, to organise an army to travel to Nagran to attack Finhas and those responsible for the massacre. This army of General Haywana set sail on the Red Sea and arrived in the naval base of Boulikas where it disembarked and set out for Nagran. When Finhas saw its strength, he realised that he and his army would not be able to engage such a powerful force, and he therefore signed a peace treaty with the Axumite general. Thinking that everything was now settled, Haywana left a small part of his army behind and returned to Axum to report to Emperor Kaleb. Knowing that the main body of this Ethiopian army had returned to Axum, Finhas now turned savagely upon the Christian community of Zafar, and burned all their churches, together with the three hundred soldiers Haywana left behind as a garrison. But the worst massacre took place in 532 at Nagran, the most developed of the Christian communities of South Arabia.

St Yared, in his famous book of *Mazqaba Degwa* recorded the massacre of the Christians of Nagran in this way:

Peace be unto you, O Great land of Nagran,
The land of thunder, the land of God.
You are called the land of the blood of
paradise because of your martyrs,
Their blood flowed as water in a river stream,
Their thunderous voice ascended to the sky:
Peace be unto you, O great land of Nagran,
Your stars are bright, your trees are joyful,
Your clergy are scholars, your deacons are messengers,
And your faithful are members of the holy Orthodox
  Christian Church.

Like paradise you are, joyful land of Nagran, clear and
  bright,
Bishops, priests, deacons, men, women, and children are
  born of you, and are called children of God.
You promised them eternal life prepared by the Son of
  God.
Crowned like the tree of life, you are holy land of Nagran,
  land of conquerors and martyrs.
Your mountains curdle their blood into the milk of para-
  dise,
Your stones upon which their feet walked are precious as
  diamonds,
Your trees are sweet, anointed as they are with the blood of
  Christ.

Emperor Kaleb's Expedition

After the initial massacres of 523 at Zafar and Nagran, a nobleman
named Umayyah managed to get back to Axum, and told the
Archbishop of Axum, Thomas, and Emperor Kaleb how these
two communities were destroyed by Finhas and his army. A few
others who escaped made their way to Constantinople to inform
the Byzantine Emperor Justin. While this was happening, Kaleb
sent a letter to him through the Patriarch of Alexandria, Timothy,
telling him of his plans to avenge the bloodshed of the Christians
in South Arabia. Justin sent him support in the form of soldiers

and warships. Kaleb now assembled an army of about 120,000 soldiers and sixty warships. Setting out towards the end of May 525 Emperor Kaleb headed for South Arabia. In fact when he arrived with his army they found the enemy port of Zafar blocked by chains and guarded by Finhas's soldiers who were ready to defend themselves. Fighting broke out and one of Finhas's family was captured by the Ethiopians. He was forced to tell them where they could disembark without facing any more resistance. This now enabled Kaleb and his army to advance inland to Zafar and Nagran. On their way there, they defeated Finhas's regiments whenever they met up with them. Finally, when they arrived at the outskirts of the city of Zafar, they met the main body of Finhas's army. He and several of his high ranking officers fell into Emperor Kaleb's hands, and Kaleb, wishing to avenge the death of all the Christians who had been slaughtered, slew Finhas.

When the major battles ended, the Ethiopian army, under the leadership of the Emperor Kaleb, moved upon the population of both cities who were still loyal to Finhas. They now began a systematic and controlled seek and destroy campaign of those who resisted surrender. During the slaughter, Christians who could not speak the Ethiopian soldiers' language drew the sign of the cross on their hands to show that they confessed the Lord Jesus Christ as the Incarnate Messiah, and their lives were spared. Finally, before he returned to Axum, Kaleb had a monument erected at Marib, so that his name might be remembered by future generations. He then presided over a ceremony to unveil it. Before he returned to Axum he left a certain Sumyapha Awsa to watch over both Zafar and Nagran, under the authority of Ariat, who was appointed Governor of South Arabia and left with a force of 10,000 men as a permanent garrison to keep order.

News of the campaign was followed closely by the Churches of Western Asia (Constantinople, Antioch and Jerusalem) as well as by the Patriarch of Alexandria. Therefore Kaleb's victory was greeted with relief. As a result the Patriarch of Alexandria met with Emperor Kaleb, and they agreed to send a bishop from Egypt to establish a diocese of South Arabia with his seat at Nagran, which was also the residence of the Governor.

After a while a power struggle arose for Ariat's leadership. A certain man named Abraha was encouraged to lead the revolt. When news of this reached Emperor Kaleb, he tried to quell this power struggle by the means of armed intervention on more than one occasion. Eventually a war erupted between the supporters of Ariat and those of Abraha. Ariat was slain and Abraha was installed King of South Arabia and now manoeuvred to become totally independent of Axum.

Amidst all these activities Kaleb decided in 542 to take monastic vows and retired from his position as Emperor. It is estimated that the population of Axum at that time was around 450,000 to 500,000. In a spectacular move which was received with mixed emotions by the population of Axum, Kaleb sent his coronation crown to Archbishop John of Jerusalem, requesting that it be placed near the tomb of the Lord Jesus Christ. He now moved to the monastery of Abba Pantelewon which stood on one of the highest mountains just outside of Axum. He died roughly two years later on 20 May 537 (544 according to the European calendar). He was later canonised as a saint not only by the Ethiopian Orthodox Church, but by some of the Eastern Orthodox Churches as well. In the Roman Catholic Church he is honoured on 27 October.

The Life of St Yared (505–571)

There is no question about the fact that St Yared is one of the greatest and most loved saints of the Ethiopian Orthodox Church. His influence has been so enormous since his death in 571 that the music with its accompanying texts which he composed for the Church is still used without much change even to this day. It is definitely one of the unique characteristics of the tradition of Ethiopian Orthodoxy.

The son of a wealthy Axumite couple, Abyud and Christina, St Yared was born at Axum in AD 505. In 512, when he was seven years old, his father died, and he went to live with his paternal uncle Gedewon, who at that time was the Treasurer of the Great Church of St Mary of Zion in Axum. This was the famous

Church where the Ark of the Covenant was kept. Besides being an accountant, his uncle Gedewon possessed an encyclopaedic knowledge of theology, philosophy, the history of Ethiopia's natural world, and music, which he passed on to his nephew, Yared, over the next twenty-five years. During this time Yared was appointed a professor of biblical studies in the school attached to the famous Church of St Mary of Zion at Axum.

When his uncle died in 537, Yared took over the office of Treasurer of this church. In addition to this, he was appointed Dean of its theological school. A few years later, Yared was ordained to the deaconhood before marrying and entering the priesthood.

In fact St Yared has left us with a very vivid description of how the sacrament of ordination was performed during the sixth century at Axum, through the episcopal ministry of the Coptic Archbishop. This description of ordination remained intact in its basic form, right up until this century, when the Ethiopian Orthodox Church gained the freedom to elect its own bishops and archbishops from the Holy Synod of the Coptic Orthodox Church. The description has been preserved by the Ethiopian canon law historian, Paulos Tsadua, in the *Fetha Negast*. The dogmatic manual, *Haymanot Abew*, also contains a description of ordination. This description was shared with us by our teachers when we were studying for the priesthood.

A huge white tent was usually pitched in a field behind the Great Church of St Mary of Zion. All the candidates for ordination who had been studying for three to seven years would stand with their teachers. These have in their possession a copy of each one's record of study. The archbishop makes his appearance in a horse carriage, or sometimes on horse-back, accompanied by many elder priests and monks. When he reaches the front opening of the huge tent he stops and without dismounting, he makes a speech in his native Arabic, which one of the priests or monks translates.

The main theme is an outline of the duties and responsibilities of the deaconhoods and priesthoods into which most of the candidates will enter. When he has finished, the archbishop dismounts and heads for his chair which had been placed in front of the tent.

Three priests, each with a book to take the name of each candidate sit on either side of him. Each candidate is now led forward by his teacher to be examined in their knowledge of the Old and New Testaments; and also the Church's history, worship, theology and canons.

As they approach the archbishop, the record of their studies is presented by their teachers for him to examine. Sometimes this could take the entire day as there could be as many as five hundred candidates, and the examination process begins early in the morning. The archbishop is usually very thorough and takes his time with each, as he will probably never see many of them again.

When this personal examination is finished, the archbishop retires, and the next morning he makes his way to the portable altar which has been erected in the huge tent, which has two doors. The candidates who have passed his examination form a line. When all are ready they are commanded by the senior priests to approach the altar in the tent to be ordained into their appropriate rank. This is accomplished by the laying on of the archbishop's hand on them, the administering of vows, the distribution of frankincense over each, and the anointing with the holy oil of ordination. Finally, in the last part of the process, the archbishop uses his hand and makes the sign of the cross three times over them to seal the vows they have just taken for entry into the deaconhood or the priesthood. When all candidates have received their ordination, the service of the sacrament of Holy Communion commences.

St Yared also had communication with the nine saints who were now dwelling in Ethiopia. He became especially close to Abba Pantelewon, who had remained in Axum. In their conversations, and then later in his life, St Yared acquired much information about the Council of Chalcedon, the efforts of the Byzantine Emperors, Leo I, Zeno, Anastasius, Justinian, as well as theologians living in the imperial city of Constantinople in the sixth century like John Maxentios, John the Grammarian, Anastasius of Antioch, Leontius of Jerusalem and Theodore of Raithu to try to reconcile the deep wounds caused by the aftermath and the reception of the Council of Chalcedon. The Emperor Justinian in particular did much to try to heal these wounds, and wrote a long letter in 542 to the monks in Alexandria about Chalcedon's interpretation of St Cyril's theology. Nine years later in 551 he published his 'Edict on the True Faith'. Finally Justinian convened the fifth Ecumenical Council in May–June 553 and tried to deal with all the unsolved problems of Chalcedon, but the wounds caused to the Church in the Holy Land, Egypt, Ethiopia, Syria and Armenia were already too deep, and no lasting reconciliation was formed. St Yared apparently acquired such an abundance of information that he even visited Constantinople twice.

However, the labour of love for which he is particularly remembered by devout Ethiopian men and women is his composition of the bulk of the Church's music and hymns, some of which he received from his uncle Gedewon. This showed that the art of music and singing existed in Ethiopia long before his birth. Some of the music that he received from his uncle is even said to have had its origins in Old Testament Ethiopia. Other parts of St Yared's musical compositions came into existence by direct inspiration from the Holy Spirit. These were used in the performance of every sacrament and type of worship service, whether private or public. Even the monks and nuns, in communities where the life of silence was not lived, sung and chanted St Yared's music.

In fact outside of the sacramental, worshipping and praying life of the Church and its faithful (a life which was built on a solid biblical foundation), St Yared's music cannot really be fully appreciated. The texts of the entire collection of his music contain references to the Holy Trinity's work of creation of the various levels of life, including animal, plant, bird, angelic and human life. It refers to Adam and Eve's existence before and after they transgressed the Creator's commandment; Noah and his sons preparing the Ark for the flood; Melchedecek, the mystical High

Priest; Abraham and Sarah; Jacob's life before and after his name changes; Moses, Aaron and their sister Miriam; the history of Makeda, Menelik, and the coming of the Ark of the Covenant into Ethiopia.

The texts of his work contain references to the Israelite monarchy starting with King Saul, then David and Solomon; the civil war following Solomon's death, and the creation of the two independent kingdoms of Israel and Judah; the prophets Isahiah, Jeremiah, Ezekiel, etc. In fact the text is almost a musical history of the entire Old Testament. His understanding of the New Testament starts with the gospel fact that there was only one person in the Lord Jesus Christ. This person was the pre-existing Logos (or Word) of God, the second person of the Holy Trinity who became Incarnate, by the power of the Holy Spirit, in the womb of St Mary. And he traces the Incarnate Saviour's earthly life from His birth at Bethlehem to the Cross, the Resurrection, the Ascension, and the descent of the Holy Spirit on the great day of Pentecost from this aspect. In his musical compositions of the New Testament, St Yared also refers to the life of St Mary, and the Apostles and disciples.

It was during the reign of Emperor Gabre Masqal (550–64) that Yared compiled the massive collection of music called *Mazqaba Degwa* (Treasury of Hymns). In terms of its composition it has three main tone structures: 'Ge'ez' is the first tone structure, and is mainly for use on non-feast days. 'Is'le' has a more measured beat and is usually performed at funerals and sad occasions. Finally 'A'ra-ray' is a lighter, freer mood suitable for festivals, marriages feasts and happy occasions. Stylistically it is divided into four parts which characterise the four seasons of the year, 'Messow' (autumn), 'Hagie' (summer), 'Tseday' (spring) and 'Kiramt' (winter). In analysing the texts of the *Mazqaba Degwa* one again sees how strongly the world of the bible was alive in St Yared's mind and heart. He quotes the biblical texts directly, or makes some reference to the early church fathers' allusion, or interpretation of the biblical passage he is trying to compose music for. The pieces are arranged according to the rules of poetic meter in a verse by verse manner (the first line is usually written in red). There is a verse for each monthly and annual feast or fast.

When the *Mazqaba Degwa* comes to the section of music and chanting used in the performance of the divine liturgy, there is a distinction between the chanting used in the 'Preparatory Service', the 'Anaphora', and the period after Holy Communion. These have four basic cadences which symbolise the four heavenly animals around the throne of God found in the book of *Revelation* 4:6. The chanting and instructions for the musicians and choir leaders are divided in such a manner that the same text can be chanted and performed by soloists and choirs accompanied by musicians in several different ways.

I will briefly give an idea of these four cadences:

(1): KUM-ZEMA: This is the basic cadence, in its simplest form.

(2): ZEMANE: (The melody moves back and forth like a pendulum swinging.) This style has the longest notes where the melody of the music moves back and forth. When performed with a choir, the three leaders of the choir (Ethiopian Orthodox Church choirs usually have three sections each with their leaders. One stands in the centre and has the title Meriga-Getta. One stands on the left and has the title Ghera-Getta. The other one stands on the right and has the title Keggne-Getta). These three have long batons which they hold in their right hand waving and twisting it in controlled directions. They try to move their bodies in harmony with their batons and the melody of their voice.

(3): MEREGDE: (up and down). The style of the chanting and music here is much faster than Kum-Zema and Zemane. The leaders of each section of the choir hold their batons in their left hand, sometimes they lean on it. With their right hand they hold a small percussion instrument called a sistrum which is made of gold or silver iron. Each leader shakes the sistrum in an up and down movement. There are also drummers with various sizes of drums who accompany their leader with his sistrum in the regular rhythm of the melody.

(4): TSFAT: (hand-clapping). This style has the quickest cadence, and the verses are repeated several times to the accompaniment of the sistrums. Towards the end it is followed by a solo chanted by the member of the choir with the most melodic voice. The rest of the choir listen before joining him in a chorus that goes from chanting and clapping in a moderate speed, to a faster one, to the fastest. Usually by this time the drummers are on their feet, as they have fastened the drums around their necks with a chain or cord. They strike their drums very hard while holding the beat very tightly, everyone now chants and claps as loudly as they can before reaching a grand finish.

The *Mazqaba Degwa* was composed in honour of the churches at Debra Damo and St Mary of Zion at Axum. When he finished it, accompanied by Emperor Gabre Masqal and Abba Aragawi, who were close friends, St Yared travelled throughout Tegray. They also travelled through Begemder together, until they came to Lake Tana. After spending two years at Lake Tana, they went to Gaient and there commissioned the building of the Church of St Mary at Zur Amba. While watching the building of this church over the next three years, St Yared also created a school, which became the principal centre for learning his music. After three years in Gaient, St Yared returned to Axum and dwelled at Medebay-tabir where he now composed the music for the Anaphoras. Having finished this work he went to Telemt where he composed the music for the book of Psalms. In his last years he travelled again to Wagara and Agaw, where he attracted many students. Finally, he died on 11 May 571 at the age of sixty-six.

St Yared's sacred works were continued by his students and disciples in following centuries beginning with Sawiros, Sandros, Beldados, Keffa, Gabru, Abba Gera, and Abba Georgis who was the teacher of Lisane Eferat, the distinguished Debtera of Bethlehem in Begemder during the time of Emperor Zera Yacob (1434–68). He wrote a massive book explaining the notation of the *Mazqaba Degwa*. From that time and throughout the reign of Emperors Lebna Dengel and Sartsa Dengel, it was very difficult to obtain any copies of the *Mazqaba Degwa* or other theological books because of the destruction by Ahmed Gran and his army of most of the canonical literature and proprieties of the Ethiopian Orthodox Church. However through the grace of the Holy Spirit one book of the *Mazqaba Degwa* similar to Lisane Eferat's was found at Sede Gagne Georgis, near Bethlehem in Begemder. This discovery made Emperor Sartsa Dengel establish Sede Gagne Georgis as the new centre for the learning of Zema, Degwa, Meeraf and Tsome Degwa.

After Lisane Eferat the list of disciples of St Yared continues with Zekale Ab, Echege Kale Awadi, Hinsa Haimanot, Tetemqe Medhin Wolde Melekot, Sartsa Mariam, Kinfe Mikael, Gabre Egziabher and Gabre Medhin.

Therefore by the end of the eighteenth century the works of St Yared could be found all over Ethiopia. Handwritten manuscripts could be obtained in Wollo at Debre Nagodgad Church; at Atronsa Mariam, Tedbada Mariam, and the monastery of Abba Gerima in Tegray; in Shoa at Debre Libanos monastery; and in Gojjam at Mertula Mariam. From the introduction of the printing press in the last century the works of St Yared can be found in every diocese of the Ethiopian Orthodox Church today, except for those monasteries and convents where the monks and nuns lead the life of silent prayer and adoration.

The Decline of the Axumite Kingdom and its Communities in South Arabia

By the ninth century Axum was in a state of decline, and by the end of the tenth it was completely destroyed. In AD 842, and for the next few decades, at the time that Anbessa Weddem was the monarch, the Orthodox Christian population of Axum suffered a great persecution by the Felasha warrior, Queen Yodit, and her army of Tegray. During this time the Solomonic dynasty was overthrown. Yodit and her Felasha army tried to extinguish the Christian faith and proclaim Judaism in its place. To this end she and her army destroyed most of the royal palaces with their stelae, as well as churches and monasteries, in their rampage of Axum. The royal Solomonic line moved further south to Shoa.

Furthermore, in this period Axum lost all of its communities in South Arabia, mainly as a result of the rise of the Islamic Empire. In a short news item written by Roy Kitezman, from Manam in Bahrain, on the Saudi Arabia peninsula, which was published in the 18 August 1994 edition of *The Ecumenical Press Service*, the author describes the results of excavations carried out by a team from London University's School of Oriental and African Studies under the direction of Geoffrey King. Kitezman writes of the evidence that was made public of the existence of a pre-Islamic Christian community on the peninsula. A site on Sir Bani Yas island, now owned by the United Arab Emirates, was uncovered, revealing the remains of a building with at least one courtyard and no fewer than fifteen rooms, which was used by ancient Christians. Our author further states that Geoffrey King also reveals discoveries made over the last eight years by archaeological societies throughout Saudi Arabia. These discoveries show the extent of several other pre-Islamic Christian communities brought into existence by the Axumite state and later elevated to bishoprics on the eastern shores of Arabia, at Bahrain, Darin (a village on the island of Tarut), Mashmahiq, Qatar and Oman.

What is remarkable about these discoveries is the fact that all the researchers who examined the remains conclude that they began to decline in the eighth century and were extinct by the end of the ninth century. These dates also coincide with the decline of the Axumite state.

From the time of Abraha in the sixth century, the Ethiopian rulers of South Arabia were not very happy about the non-Christian practices in Mecca (where a record of a small Christian community is established from the annals of Emperor Gabre Mesqal) and other areas on the Arabian peninsula. This had caused Abraha when he was in control to become very hostile towards the native population. This is confirmed in the book of the Koran where it states that around the year AD 540 'an expeditionary force was sent by Abraha to attack the shrine at Mecca which was still non-Christian at this time'. However, the expedition was not completely successful.

In retaliation, North Yemen, where Abraha lived, was attacked by Arabs in AD 572. Jean Doresse, who worked for the Ethiopian Archaeological Institute during the 1950s, writes on page 87 of his book, *Ancient Cities and Temples of Ethiopia*, 'This allowed a Persian fleet to penetrate by way of Aden and thus occupy the country without the use of force... the Persians continued to advance and by 602 the entire peninsula was occupied.' Therefore Abraha and his successors were defeated and exploited by this Persian conquest. South Arabia did not stay under the rule of the Persians for it was later controlled by the Arabs. With the advent of Islam, not only was the Axumite state pushed out of the Arabian peninsula, but within a century these Arab followers of the Prophet Muhammad conquered and controlled the vast area from the Pyrenees on the border of France, to the Parmis in Central Asia. Spain, North Africa (including Egypt) and the former colonies of the Byzantine Empire south of the Taurus mountains, as well as the Persian Empire in the east formed the boundaries of this Arab Islamic world.

The Ethiopian Orthodox Church even lost contact with Alexandria for a while. Being now cut off from Egypt and its ties with Constantinople, the leaders at Axum had no other choice but to establish practical ties with Islam. This relationship at first was peaceful as there is evidence from the eighth-century Arab historian Al Tarabi of the small Ethiopian community at Mecca who provided a nursemaid for the Prophet Muhammad (lived 570–632) when he was still an infant. Furthermore at the time of the persecution of his followers in Arabia about 615 by the Quraish, a group of refugees, including the Prophet's daughter, Rukaya, fled from Mecca to Axum and were given protection by Emperor Armah.

Pages 111–112 of the Russian scholar Yuri Kobischanov's book, *Axum*, published in 1979, support the authenticity of this report preserved by Al Tabari. According to both of these scholars, the group of refugees consisted of eleven men and four women.

Furthermore, this refugee group is said by Al Tabari to have arrived in Axum in the month of Rajab 615, and was led by none other than Usman, a nephew of the Prophet. They were later joined by a larger one that consisted of eighty-two men with their children and wives, headed by Ja'far, Muhammad's first chronicler, who was the son of Abu Talib, a cousin of the Prophet.

While dwelling in Axum a few hostile groups in South Arabia tried to have this large refugee group deported, but Emperor Armah paid no attention to their requests. On their eventual return, Jules Leroy, on page 16 of his book, *Ethiopian Painting*, published by Merlin Press in 1967, records that this same chronicler, Ja'far, writes of the splendour of Ethiopian icon painting. Usman and Rukaya are said to have told him of how Ethiopian churches were constructed and decorated. They were especially impressed by 'the beauty of the Cathedral of St Mary of Zion at Axum, and the fine paintings on its walls'.

Ja'far further writes that Muhammad is said to have appreciated this hospitality given to them, and told his followers to leave the Ethiopians in peace. But as Professor Taddesse Tamrat shows on page 31 of his book, *Church and State in Ethiopia 1270–1527*, this injunction was short-lived as Arab Muslims did not stop populating the Ethiopian sections of the Red Sea coastline. Over the next few centuries they established principalities along the coast from Massawa to Adulis and Zeyula, and inland to the highlands of Shoa, where the Mahzumite Sultanate existed from 989 until it was conquered by the Ifat Sultanate in 1285.

★

Between 918 and 1002 the Ethiopian Orthodox Church found it very difficult to secure a bishop from its ancient sister Church in Egypt, due to pressure from the Fatimid dynasty which now controlled the capital, Cairo. However, on pages 666–668 of Burge's translation of *The Ethiopian Synaxarium of March*, we learn that between AD 919 and 931, in the time that Muhammad Tughj was ruler of Egypt and Patriarch Cosmas III was the head of the Coptic Orthodox Church, a bishop by the name of Abuna Petros was sent to Ethiopia.

The new bishop was received with great joy, because the Ethiopian faithful had not seen a Coptic Orthodox bishop for years. But after seven years Abuna Petros came face to face with the trauma of anointing a successor for King Geda Djan, who had died due to old age. This king had two sons (unfortunately we do not know their names) who started struggling for the right of succession. Abuna Petros chose and anointed the younger one.

The older one now became very hostile towards the bishop and waited for an opportunity to attack him. This came in the shape of two Syrian monks, Abba Menas and Abba Fiqitor, who had been dismissed from the monastery of St Anthony in Egypt and made their way to Ethiopia. The two had made an agreement that one of them should become a bishop. Upon arriving in Axum they became friends with the older of the two brothers who was denied the throne by Abuna Petros.

Forged documents bearing the signature and seal of Patriarch Cosmas III from Cairo were presented by these two Syrian monks which explained that Abuna Petros was a false bishop, and that from now Abba Menas should be bishop, with the elder son of Geda Djan being named successor to the throne. This forged document now changed everything. A bitter and violent power struggle now broke out between the two brothers. Menas became bishop, the elder son eventually won and became the new king, while Abuna Petros was sent to prison.

Later the two monks had a dispute between themselves, and Abba Fiqitor departed for Cairo, where he told Patriarch Cosmas III about the entire matter. Abba Menas was now permanently excommunicated and deposed. He was subsequently executed when news of his evil deed reached the elder son of King Geda Djan, who had outmanoeuvred his younger brother in their contest for the throne. The new king wanted to bring Abuna Petros back to assume his episcopal office, but he had already died. He wrote to Patriarch Cosmas to send another bishop but, while this request was supported by the Patriarch, the Synod of the bishops refused it.

Chapter 6
The Church During the Zagwe Dynasty

By AD 980 the Islamic expansion cut off Ethiopia from both the Mediterranean world to the north-west along the course of the Mediterranean Sea; Asia to the east and north-east across the Red Sea; and the rest of Africa to the south-west. By the end of the century the main churches at Axum, and the palaces and homes of the Solomonic monarchs were destroyed. Rulers of a different dynasty known as the Zagwe dynasty moved the capital from Axum further south. However, the leaders of this new dynasty were just as concerned for the preservation and growth of the life of the Church, as were the Solomonic monarchs of Axum. The way in which the new dynasty established itself is as follows.

While Del Na'od was on the throne, Mara Tekle Haimanot (912–25), who was his son-in-law, killed him and captured it for himself. He now moved the kingdom from Axum in Tegray to Wollo. This new monarch had been a soldier at Del Na'od palace before he married Del Na'od's daughter, and was appointed Governor of both Eritrea and Lasta. He was from the line of the ancient Ethiopian Agaw clan and adopted Zagwe as his royal name. At first the people were unhappy with this new ruler. They refused to recognise him until he could convince them of his right to the throne. He did this by stating that his wife was the daughter of Del Na'od, the last Solomonic king of Axum. Furthermore, Mara Tekle Haimanot was able to provide evidence (in the form of genealogy tables) which showed that his family were descendants of the Agaw people, who were of the same blood line as King David and Menelik I. Their ancestral parent was a man named Addel who was the grandson of King David, and son of Ith-reaham (or Yetraham as some pronounce it). Addel and his people came to Ethiopia with Menelik I in the ninth century BC, and Addel was appointed by Menelik to rule Agaw, Lasta and Yejju. Being satisfied with this explanation by Tekle Haimanot, the people accepted his rule. This dynasty inaugurated by him ruled for approximately three hundred and thirty-three years. The Ethiopian historian Le'qe Tebebt Ak'lile Brahan, on page 86 of his work, *Mat'sehe'te Amin*, lists the monarchs of this Zagwe dynasty as Tekle Haimanot, Tataw-dem, Jan-Seyoum, Germa Seyoum, Imra-hana Kris'tos, Kiddus Harbey, Lali-bela and Neku-ta La'ab. During the reign of this dynasty the problem of obtaining Orthodox archbishops from Egypt was just as difficult. And while the rulers of this new dynasty concentrated on securing the ties with the Coptic Orthodox Patriarchate, to make sure that the Ethiopian Orthodox Church was not left without the ministry of at least one Coptic archbishop, the majority of the Ethiopian Orthodox population concentrated on the sacramental liturgical worship and ascetic life of the Church through its daily, weekly, monthly and annual calendar of fasting and feasting. As most of them could not read or write, this was the only way they had of keeping their faith in the Holy Trinity alive. The senior celibate priests, monks and nuns, together with icon painters, put all their waking hours into making new illustrated handwritten copies of the Old and New Testament. They also reworked all the manuscripts in the country of the theological works of the Ecumenical Councils, and the great bishops and monastic teachers of the worldwide Church between the fifth and tenth centuries. This meant that all the doctrinal controversies from the Council of Chalcedon which produced such passionate feelings and divisions between the Church in Rome, in the Byzantine Empire, Palestine, Egypt, Syria, Persia and Armenia, were resurrected again in their discussions. This was a different climate than the one that existed before the rise of Islam, and the destruction of the Solomonic-Orthodox Christian heritage of Axum.

★

I shall now give a summary of the fifth, sixth, and seventh Ecumenical Councils, and the origin of the dispute concerning the origin of the existence of the Holy Spirit, that was keenly debated by the Ethiopian Church scholars during the time of Mara Tekle Haimanot, the establisher of the Zagwe dynasty.

The fifth Ecumenical Council (553) tried to heal all the divisions caused by Chalcedon 451, but its success was not long lasting. It took up the question of the way that Theodoret of Cyrus, Ibas of Edessa and Theodore of Mopsuetia (Nestorius' teacher) were rehabilitated at Chalcedon. All their work against St Cyril was condemned. It re-evaluated Leo's Tome in the light of St Cyril's theology. But it said nothing about the unjust deposing of St Dioscorus and Eutyches. This Council also drafted and accepted a series of anathemas against the spirituality of St Origen and St Evagius of Pontus. But these decisions did not restore the sought for unity of the Church.

The same can be said about the sixth Ecumenical Council (680). Before this Council met, the Byzantine Patriarch Sergius (the theological counsellor of the Emperor Heraclius) had worked out a theological formula to try to heal the deep divisions between the Church communities which still refused to accept the Chalcedonian theology of the Incarnation.

He tried to appease the opposers of the Chalcedonian formula in Palestine, Egypt, Ethiopia, Syria and Armenia. The key passage of this Chalcedonian formula had stated that the Lord Jesus Christ existed 'in two natures' after their union in the womb of St Mary, the Holy Theotokos. Sergius hoped these Church communities would accept Chalcedon's terminology if he emphasised that the 'two natures' were united into 'one energy' (mono-energite) and 'one will' (mono-thelite). In an effort to gain support, Sergius wrote to Honorius the Pope of Rome, who replied to him in 634, offering his support for this formula. Now while this new formula enjoyed a limited amount of success in parts of Egypt, Syria and Armenia, it was denounced by the Patriarch of Jerusalem, Sophronius, and Maximus the Confessor, a Church father in the Byzantine Empire.

Heraclius and Constantine IV (the Byzantine Emperors at the time) supported this formula of Sergius known as 'monoenergism' and 'monothelitism'. Constantine IV in 678 triumphed over the Arab Islamic expansion and forced them out of Constantinople. It was against the background of this victory that he felt confident enough to convene the sixth Ecumenical Council in 680 to have this new formula accepted. But at this Council it was not the moderates in Egypt, Syria and Armenia who had accepted it who were condemned, but rather Sergius of Constantinople and Honorius of Rome. Furthermore, the Chalcedonian theological formula of the union of the two natures in the Lord Jesus Christ was again restated: namely that there were two natures in Christ, and each had its own energy or will.

The seventh Ecumenical Council (787) dealt with the thorny theological problem that was ravishing the world of Byzantine Orthodoxy: namely the veneration of icons, and the styles, techniques and materials used in painting them. Fifty years earlier, in 726, Emperor Leo III had forbidden any form of veneration to icons, because he feared that for some among the faithful, the veneration and honour given to them bordered on idol worship, and was not a medium for entering into contemplative communion with the Incarnate Saviour, or the biblical saint or event depicted in the icon. In that case Leo III feared that a violation of the second commandment was being committed. Compounded with this atmosphere of mistrust in this period was the confrontation of Islam by the Byzantines (and in Persia the rise of Persian Zoroastranism). In both religious traditions there was no place in its devotional and worshipping practices for icons. They were considered by these two groups of worshippers as 'idol image worshippers'. At a council held in 754 by Constantine V, the use of icons during prayer and worship was condemned as Nestorian and Monophysite heresy.

This was the decision that was overturned at the seventh Ecumenical Council held at Nicea between 24 September and 23 October 787, and the Iconoclastic group (meaning 'image-breaker' literally, and those opposed to the use of icons within the Council) was defeated. In arriving at this decision the Council (as the Holy Spirit would have it) based its theology mainly on the third book in defence of holy icons by the great Syrian father, St

John of Damascus. In this work, St John lists six kinds of icons, or holy images.

1. Within the life of the Holy God in Trinity, the Son is the perfect and consubstantial image of the Father, just as the Holy Spirit is of the Son.
2. In God's mind there exist eternal plans for the construction of all His creative works, which come into being at a certain time and in a certain location.
3. All human persons are created in the image and likeness of the Holy Trinity. They also exist as beings who are One in Three, and Three in One, in that they possess a body, a soul and a spirit.
4. The imagery that the holy scriptures uses to describe the different levels of life, especially unseen life, reveals to us that in the invisible and immaterial planes of existence relating to God and the angelic world, consciousness and activity exists.
5. In the history of the two covenants, earlier events are images of later ones, like the fire in the burning bush that caught Moses' attention because it was not consumed is a foreshadowing of the union of the divine and human natures in the Lord Jesus Christ.
6. Past events can be relived in our human memory either through the written, or the sung, or the painted image.

These were the main ideas of St John that the Council used to defend its use of icons. It must be said however that in the Church communities in Palestine, Ethiopia, Egypt, Nubia, Syria and Armenia, where the tradition of iconography originated from Old Testament times, this defeat of the Iconoclast group was not designated as the 'triumph of Orthodoxy' as it was in Byzantine Orthodoxy. In fact these African and Asian Church communities shared neither the Byzantine experience of joy in the Council's defence of icons, nor the consequences that would follow. It was even said by some groups in these communities that, once again, it was an Asian or African Church father who provided the Byzantines with a solution and a way out of its difficulties.

Concerning the manuscripts that dealt with the origin of

'Filioque dispute' (the addition to the third article of the Nicean-Constantinoplian Creed of 381 which was the universal prayer of faith). This addition said that the origin of the existence of the Holy Spirit stemmed from both God the Father and God the Son, as from one source. Whereas the creed affirmed that the Holy Spirit's origin was from God the Father alone.

In this dispute Ethiopian Orthodox Church scholars at the time saw that this addition to the Creed made its first appearance in Roman Catholic Spain, where a local Council of Toledo held in the year 589, in denouncing Arianism, added the phrase that the Holy Spirit proceeded from the Father 'and the Son' to the third article of the Nicean-Constantinoplian Creed of 381, to stress the divinity of the Incarnate Son Jesus Christ, and also to show that there was an eternal relationship between the second and third divine persons of the Holy Trinity. From Roman Catholic Spain, this addition spread to France and Germany in the next two centuries (the Frankish Empire as it was called that time). At another local Council of Frankfurt in 794, Emperor Charlemagne and the theologians of his court openly debated its addition, and the emperor was even angry that the Orthodox Churches in the East had not already included it in its reworded Creed. He was also frustrated that while the Roman Catholic Pope Leo III (795–816) accepted its theology, he refused to make its addition to the Creed an official act.

This dispute again re-appeared when Bulgaria accepted the Christian faith (864). As both Rome and Constantinople were competing for canonical control, the leaders of both sees engaged in an intense and heated controversy. A respite was achieved at a Council held in 879–880 at Constantinople between both sides. The legates of Pope John VIII signed an agreement stating that the Creed 'cannot be subtracted from, added to, altered, or distorted in any way'. This settlement would last until the eleventh century when Pope Benedict VIII (1012–1024) allowed its addition to the Latin version of the Creed. From that time it would be one of the main theological problems in the relationship between Rome and Constantinople.

So while these debates were an ongoing affair among many monks, monk-priests, nuns, and married priests and their wives, who knew of these matters, the leaders of the new dynasty were making another request for an archbishop during the time that the Coptic Patriarch Christodolus was the leader of the Church of Egypt (1047–77). However, as I mentioned in the last chapter, because Egypt was under the control of a powerful Muslim aristocracy, everything had to go through them. (At this time it was the Fatimid Sultans who were in control of Egypt.) Furthermore, the episode with Abuna Petros made the Synod of Coptic archbishops very reluctant to send another one of their peers to Ethiopia. Professor Taddesse Tamrat writes on page 46 of his book, *Church and State in Ethiopia 1270–1527*, that these Muslim Sultans 'also interfered in the actual selection of the Egyptian archbishop to be appointed as Archbishop (Metropolitan) of Ethiopia'. Professor Tamrat further writes on page 47 that during this time a self-ordained Egyptian called Abdun arrived in Ethiopia as Archbishop Cyril. Suspicions about his legitimacy arose in the palace and among the senior priests and older faithful, and an Ethiopian delegation was sent to Egypt to secure proof of Abdun's claim. But Abdun was also busy at work, for while the Ethiopian delegation was on its way to Cairo, he sent his own agents to the Fatimid Sultan, Amir Al-Juyush, to command Patriarch Christodolus to confirm his identity and position. Abdun even promised to send wealth in the form of gold and other precious stones as presents if his request proved successful. Amir Al-Juyush was so impressed by this gesture that he forced the Patriarch to confirm Abdun's identity and position as Archbishop (Metropolitan) of Ethiopia. The Coptic Bishop of Wisim, Abuna Mecorius, was sent to Ethiopia to confirm to the king and his court that Abdun was Archbishop of Ethiopia. But before he could be enthroned another conspiracy had been hatched by his chief supporter Ali Al-Kifti. This Muslim had falsely accused the Coptic Orthodox Bishop of Nubia of being against the Muslim rule and faith, and caused Patriarch Christodolus to be imprisoned. However, when this false accusation was discovered, Ali Al-Kifti was put to death, the Patriarch was released, and Abdun's plans came to nothing. He was willingly escorted to Cairo by an Ethiopian delegation hand-picked by the king and the senior priests. Upon arrival in Cairo he was tried and condemned to death by the ruler, Amir Al-Juyush.

When Patriarch Christodolus died he was succeeded by Patriarch Cyril II (1077–92). This new Patriarch of the Coptic Orthodox Church was an exceptionally educated Church father. All the faithful of Egypt rejoiced at his election as they knew that through his ministry the Church's life would flourish again. During the ministry of this Patriarch, Abuna Sawiros was appointed Archbishop of Ethiopia.

He arrived in Ethiopia during the time of Emperor Germa Seyoum and was enthusiastically received by the Ethiopian faithful when they learned of his previous work in his native Egypt as a teacher and confessor father. However this enthusiasm was short-lived, as Professor Tamrat shows (in his book that we have being making reference to). It was not too long before it was uncovered that Abuna Sawriwos had made many promises to Amir Al-Juyush, not only to supply him with priests from Ethiopia, but also to support the spread of Islam. As a matter of fact, before he did any work for the Ethiopian Orthodox Church, he commissioned and oversaw the building of seven mosques to encourage the spread of Islam. This act was not tolerated by Germa Seyoum and the Ethiopian Church community, and Abuna Sawriwos was imprisoned, while the mosques were destroyed. In 1088 he sent his brother Rigal to Egypt to inform Amir Al-Juyush of what had happened to him. This Sultan got angry and, after throwing Rigal into prison, he summoned the Patriarch and the Synod in Cairo. In their presence he made a savage verbal attack on Abuna Sawriwos and demanded that the Patriarch send a delegation of two bishops to the Emperor of Ethiopia with the explicit order to undo all the damage done. He also issued a threat that if new mosques were not built to replace the ones destroyed, he would destroy the churches in Egypt. But Emperor Germa Seyoum did not pay any attention to this threat and instead responded by advising Al-Juyush against such action. In regard to Abuna Sawriwos, we are not told whether he died in prison or was sent back to Egypt, because when Germa Seyoum died, he was succeeded by his son, Imra-hana Kris'tos, who lost no time in sending a delegation to Cairo to secure another archbishop. They were successful and Abuna George was appointed. However his ministry was short-lived as he was found to be greedy and power hungry. During Imra-hana Kris'tos reign the Orthodox Christian population of Egypt was under persecution from the Fatimid ruling class. He addressed letters to them warning that if the persecution did not stop they would be punished, as well as the entire land of Egypt, by the diversion of the flow of the waters of the Blue Nile. This brought great fear upon the Fatimid ruling class, for they knew that the source of the Blue Nile, upon which Egypt was dependent, was in the highlands of Ethiopia, and should Imra-hana Kris'tos carry out his threat a great famine would descend upon all Egypt. As a result, between the years 1084 and 1093 Abuna Mikael, the Patriarch of Egypt, was sent to the court of Imra-hana Kris'tos to negotiate for a settlement which would be agreeable to both sides. The Fatimid rulers also sent with the Patriarch a letter explaining to the Ethiopian monarch that no church or Orthodox Christian in Egypt would suffer if he did not tamper with the flow of the Nile which was so vital to Egypt.

Imra-hana Kris'tos agreed to this and Abuna Mikael returned to Egypt a relieved man. So, as both his predecessors had done, and his successors would do when they ascended the throne, Imra-hana Kris'tos protected the Orthodox Christian population of Egypt from the threat of Muslim persecution. When Imra-hana Kris'tos died he was succeeded by his nephew, Kiddus Harbey, who was Jan Seyoum's son, because he had no children of his own.

The new emperor was a man of vision and possessed a refined theological intellect. He wanted to generate new life in the Ethiopian Orthodox Church, knowing as he did the work of the senior priests, the monks and nuns, and also the icon painters and musicians who surrounded him. He saw that one archbishop (at this time it was Abuna Mikael) could not fill the spiritual needs of the millions of Ethiopian Orthodox believers. Therefore he asked the Coptic Patriarchate for several more bishops to assist Abuna Mikael, as well as for consecration of Ethiopian-born bishops. Emperor Kiddus Harbey (he also used his baptismal name Gabre Mariam) wrote a long letter to Patriarch Gabriel II, requesting him to grant Abuna Mikael the right to consecrate Ethiopian bishops. At first the Patriarch and the Fatimid ruling class agreed to this plan, but they later changed their minds, as some of their advisers persuaded their Fatimid Sultan that, should the Patriarch grant Abuna Mikael the right to consecrate Ethiopian bishops, they would eventually ordain more Ethiopian bishops and declare themselves free and totally independent from the Coptic Orthodox Synod. Their next step would be to stop the annual tribute of gold, salt, frankincense, and other gifts they were in the habit of sending. As a result relations now reached a very low point between Emperor Kiddus Harbey and the Patriarch, until Patriarch Gabriel II died. As soon as the new Patriarch Yohannes was enthroned, the Emperor wrote to him asking that at least two native Ethiopian priests should be consecrated as bishops to assist Abuna Mikael, who was now getting old and found it difficult to travel. This request was also refused for the same reasons given when Patriarch Gabriel II was alive.

Nevertheless Emperor Harbey's effort was not in vain, for eventually the Ethiopian Orthodox Church would have its own Ethiopian-born bishops who would lead the Church to complete freedom from its ancient sister church of Egypt.

When Kiddus Harbey died he in turn was succeeded by his nephew, Lali-bela (1185–1225), who is considered the most saintly of monarchs of the Zagwe dynasty.

Lali-bela was born in 1140 in the town of Roha in Lasta, northern Ethiopia. According to the synaxarium of 12 June, at his birth a powerful mystical sign was observed, the infant was engulfed by a thick cloud of bees, and his mother received visions from the Holy Spirit. She decided to call him Lali-bela (a name which means 'the bees know that this child is a king') because the Holy Sprit had showed her that he would be a great king one day. When the reigning king, Kiddus Harbey, heard of this mystical sign and prophesy he became jealous. He even plotted to persecute the young Lali-bela. But the Holy Spirit and the elders protected him by sending him to Jerusalem, where he sojourned for the next twenty-five years.

The famous Ethiopian historian, Sergew Habte Selassie, on pages 265–7 of his book, *Ancient and Medieval History to 1270*, describes this part of Lali-bela's life. Through a series of visions

Kiddus Harbey was forced to make peace with Lali-bela and eventually abdicated, granting permission for him to return to Ethiopia and ascend the throne in 1185.

As a young Ethiopian prince in Jerusalem, from 1160 to 1185, Lali-bela lived the life mainly of a solitary ascetic, which consisted of praying, fasting and visiting the holy shrines of the city. It is said that he used to receive visits from old monks who were revered as seers of the city. Apparently angelic beings also visited him who told him that when he reached the age of maturity, the Holy Spirit would cause to be built through him such churches as had never been seen on earth before.

When Lali-bela returned to Ethiopia and ascended the throne, the Patriarch of Egypt was Abuna Marcos IV. He now began to make plans to fulfil the visions he had received by commissioning the building of eleven churches carved totally out of rock. The architect and foreman whom he and his wife, Kibra Masqel, commissioned was Sidi Masqal. After making all his draft blueprints in the traditional Ethiopian architectural style, he informed the King and Queen that a workforce of four to five hundred including draftsmen, bricklayers, masons, carpenters, jewellers and icon painters would be needed to complete this immense project.

So Lali-bela sent him around the country recruiting. The skilled craftsmen that he could not get in Ethiopia he sent Sidi Masqal to Nubia, Egypt and Palestine to hire. While on his mission, Lali-bela's Queen, Kibra Masqal, assigned some of the ministers at their court the task of assembling a team to travel around the country to purchase the numerous tools, such as picks, chisels, axes, hammers, scrapers, etc. that would be needed. Landowners were asked to name a price for these tools and they were paid in gold.

In studying the Sidi Masqal's blueprints one sees that the eleven churches are all built in close proximity to each other. Five are located to the north of the river (named River Jordan after the one in Palestine) that flowed through the town of Roha. Four were built south of the river. And one of them, Beit Georgis (house of George) was built some distance in a south-west direction from the rest. The group north of the river are Medhane

Alem (Saviour of the world); Geneta Mariam (the paradise of St Mary); Beit Masqal (house of the cross); Beit Dengel (house of the Virgin); Beit Kiddus Mikael (house of the archangel Mikael); Beit Golgotha (house of Golgotha). The group south of the river are Beit Emmanuel (house of Emmanuel); Beit Kiddus Mecorius (house of St Mecorius); Beit Abba Libanos (house of Abba Libanos); and Beit Kiddus Gabriel (house of archangel Gabriel). The eleven churches were completed in twenty-three years. When they were completed Sidi Masqal, the architect who designed them, wrote concerning them, 'What tongue is capable of giving a description of them? Anyone who beholds them will never be able to gaze on them long enough; their sense of marvel will be so great that their hearts will never grow tired of admiring them.'

This was to prove true, for when Ahmad Gran and his army were trying to extinguish the Orthodox faith in the middle of the sixteenth century by burning the royal palaces, churches, and its literature, his biographer Arab Faqih wrote that both Gran and his soldiers were so transfixed when they beheld these rock churches built during the time of Emperor Lali-bela that they could not touch them.

The Jesuit missionaries headed by Francisco Alvarez who were in Ethiopia between 1520 and 1527 were also in amazement when they beheld these rock churches. After visiting and describing the eleven rock churches, Alvarez wrote in his book, *Narrative of the Portuguese Embassy to Abyssinia*,

> It wearied me to write more of these works, because it seemed to me that they will not believe me if I write more, and because as to what I have already written they will accuse me of untruth. Therefore I swear before God, in whose power I am, that all that is written is the truth, and there is much more than I have already written, and I have left it that they may not tax me with its being falsehood.

Like his predecessors, Lali-bela had to send a delegation to Cairo to secure an archbishop, as the attitude of the Muslim rulers had not changed, and many Ethiopian monks were leaving their monasteries, headed for Egypt, Sudan and Jerusalem. After three months the Ethiopian delegation returned with the Coptic Archbishop Abuna Mikael, who was received with great joy.

Abuna Mikael (Michael) stayed in the country only four years (1205–1209) and during this time he ordained an Ethiopian priest, Abba Gabron, as a bishop. The new bishop, who was the brother of Queen Kibra Masqel, was assigned to minister to the palace, while Abuna Mikael travelled around the country to perform the sacrament of ordination.

Because Abba Gabron was Ethiopian it caused Abuna Mikael to grow jealous, as the many students who desired ordination preferred to seek entrance to the palace to be ordained by him. They also looked to him as their confessor father. Abuna Mikael therefore went back to Cairo after four years in Ethiopia and complained to Patriarch Yohannes (the successor of Patriarch Marcos) that Abba Gabron challenged his authority after he ordained him to the office of the bishop, and even encouraged the Ethiopian faithful to ignore him, because they now had their own Ethiopian bishop. Other accounts emphasise that Abuna Mikael also lied against Abba Gabron by accusing him of stealing gold from his house. When this reached the ears of Lali-bela he had Abba Gabron executed. This was another reason for Abuna Mikael's return to Cairo, because officials at Lali-bela's court who knew the truth were looking for him. The Patriarch of Egypt sent three senior priests, headed by Abba Moses, to investigate the matter, and when it was proved that Abuna Mikael was responsible for Abba Gabron's death, he was publicly excommunicated and deposed. So the Ethiopian Orthodox Church was left again without the ministry of an archbishop, and Emperor Lali-bela had to send another delegation to Cairo to negotiate for another archbishop to be assigned. This happened during the time of Patriarch Cyril (1209–10). The delegation sent by Lali-bela brought with them as presents a gold crown for the Patriarch, a giraffe, an elephant, a lion and a zebra for the Sultan. Being successful, they returned home in March 1210 with the Coptic archbishop Abuna Yesehaq, and the bishop Abuna Yoseph, who was assigned by the synod to be his assistant.

His biographer tells us that, having supervised the completion of the rock churches and the securing of two Coptic Orthodox bishops, Emperor Lali-bela distributed all his wealth and belongings among the poor, abandoned his throne and went back to the solitary life of silent prayer and fasting in the wilderness that he lived as a young man before he became Emperor. He was succeeded by Ne-kuta La-ab, who was the last monarch of the Zagwe dynasty.

Chapter 7
The Restoration of the Solomonic Line

In 1270 Atse Yekuno Amlak became Emperor and restored the Solomonic line to power. He held these cords of power until 1285. During his time as Emperor, the province of Shoa became the centre of the nation, and the population underwent a renewal of its political, social, legal, educational and religious institutions.

To accomplish these changes – the renewal of the faith of the population – Yekuno Amlak granted one third of his kingdom to the custody of Church and its monasteries, especially the monastery of Debra Libanos. Some European writers state in their works that Ne-kuta La-ab had been persuaded by St Tekla Haimanot to abdicate the throne so that the Solomonic dynasty could be restored with Yekuno Amlak. Furthermore, the grant of land he gave to the Church was supposed to be a token of gratitude to the saint by him. But this statement is not altogether a full picture, as it had been customary for Ethiopian Orthodox emperors to donate lands to the Church and also to commission the building of new Church buildings. The book of *The Life and Miracles of St Tekla Haimanot* tells us that the part St Tekla Haimanot played was more spiritual than political or economic. He prayed and fasted on the matter, and then supported Yekuno Amlak in his plans to restore the Solomonic dynasty, which the majority of the population held in greater esteem than they did the Zagwe dynasty, despite the commitment the monarchs of this dynasty showed towards the preservation and growth of the Church.

The Life of St Tekla Haimanot (1215–1313)

St Tekla Haimanot is without doubt one of the greatest fathers of the Ethiopian Orthodox Church. He is also held to be one of its most fertile thinkers. In his long life he made twelve major missionary journeys after gaining a solid foundation in the monastic life, converting thousands to the faith of the Church, while visiting many monasteries and holy places.

His first journey was to the Karata district, where the inhabitants worshipped trees in a sacred grove in Gerarya region. Here he caused one such tree to uproot itself, an act which convinced the natives that this was a false form of worship. After teaching and getting them to accept the faith of the Church, he baptised many and supervised the building of a Church at Yateber nearby.

His second journey was from Karata and Yateber in Gerarya to Shoa going through Mt Wifat and Mt Bilat. Again he destroyed the shrines of many idols, taught the converts and baptised them. From Mt Wifat he headed to Mt Zeqwala, about thirty-five miles from present-day Addis Ababa. After resting here for a while he then set out for Wayrage on the western bank of Lake Zway.

His third missionary journey saw him travel to Zeba Fatan, a mountain range in Damot, which was another major centre of idol worship. When he came to the territory of Motalame, he was thrown over a great precipice called Tomagerer and was miraculously saved. After staying here for several years he set out for the district of the Barya and Humal tribes near the River Abbay.

His fourth journey took him from Zeba Fatan in Damot by way of Zorare to the monastery of Abba Beseslote Mikael in Ges in the land of the Amhara. It was from this monastery that he made his fifth journey to the monastery of Abba Eyesus Moa in Lake Hayq, where he stayed for ten years.

His sixth journey was through Tegray, where he went to Debra Damo in Agame, to the monastery of Abba Aragawi, one of the nine church fathers who came to Axum in the sixth century. After living here for more than twelve years, St Tekla Haimanot set off to visit Jerusalem, and on his return to Tegray travelled through the Egyptian desert, visiting several monasteries on the way. His eighth and ninth journeys saw him visit Jerusalem again before returning to Debra Damo.

His tenth journey saw him enter the land of the Zalan, a fierce tribe who provided troops to the Muslim overlords who controlled the region. His eleventh journey took him from Zalan back to Lake Hayq. His twelfth and last journey saw him head back to Gerarya going through Sayent. He spent the rest of his life in this region, and a monastic community, Debra Asbo (later called Debra Libanos after his death), grew up around him.

A SKETCH OF HIS LIFE

Descending from a family of Christian nobles who had settled on the western edge of the Shoan plateau by the tenth century, his parents, Saga Za'ab and Egzie Haraya, traced their genealogy back to Azarius, the son of Zadok the High Priest, who together with nobles from the tribes of Levi, Dan and Gad, accompanied Menelik I back to Ethiopia with the Ark of the Covenant after Menelik's visit to Jerusalem to meet his father, King Solomon.

In his boyhood, he became a student of Abba Iyesus Moa, the most famous teacher of the monastic life in Ethiopia at that time. This revered master of Ethiopian monasticism had established the monastic community of Debra Estifanos on Lake Hayq in 1248. Out of an authentic zeal, young Tekla Haimanot was attracted to this monastery and would later become himself a master of the monastic life and its spirituality. This life in Debra Estifanos was centred around the Church's cycles of daily, weekly, monthly and annual times of prayer, fasting and sacramental liturgical worship.

In this community the art of prayer was developed around the communal prayers of the Covenant which occurred three times during the day; at sunrise, 6 a.m. (the morning covenant), sunset (the evening covenant) and at midnight (the midnight covenant). However the monks were still obligated to pray what are known as 'the hours' in between their other daily activities. These hours were 9 a.m., the 'third hour', meaning the third hour after sunrise, to commemorate the descent of the Holy Spirit on the great day of Pentecost, the creation of Eve, and the hour when the Archangel Gabriel announced the Incarnation to the virgin Mary; midday or the 'sixth hour' after sunrise, to commemorate the hour when Our Lord Jesus Christ was crucified, and the hour that Adam was tempted; finally at 3 p.m. or 'ninth hour' after sunrise prayers were believed to commemorate the hour that Our Lord Jesus Christ died. The weekly cycle was centred around the remembrance of the arrest of the Lord, which according to the authors of the holy gospel, occurred on Wednesday after Palm Sunday; Friday which was the day of the crucifixion; and the main celebration of the divine liturgy on Sunday in commemoration of the first Easter Sunday when the Lord rose from the dead. Of course, this does not mean that it was only on Sundays that the divine liturgy was performed. Monday was the day that Moses and the Israelites crossed the Red Sea. Tuesday commemorated the creation of all types of plants and trees. Thursday was associated with the institution of Holy Communion and the Ascension. Saturday commemorated the day the Lord's body rested in the grave.

The monthly cycle was centred around the feast of the Saviour of World, the feast of the Holy Trinity, and the feast of St Mary. The yearly cycle was centred around the annual feasts of the Nativity, the commemoration of Baptism of Christ, Palm Sunday, Good Friday, Easter, the Ascension, New Year's Day, Pentecost, The Transfiguration and the Assumption of St Mary.

After living and studying at Debra Estifanos for a number of years, St Tekla Haimanot was ordained to the deaconhood at fifteen, in 1230. At this stage, the elder monks with the Counsel of Abba Iyesus Moa arranged for him, together with the other leading students, to go to continue their studies at Debra Damo, the Ethiopian Orthodox Church's oldest monastery in Adigrat. This was the monastery where Abba Aregawi lived and taught in the fifth and sixth centuries after coming from Constantinople. Here at Debra Damo St Tekla Haimanot became actively involved in the traditions of the ascetic and contemplative life, and prayer became for him a form of spiritual art. The monastic saints whose spirituality he mastered, besides the Ethiopian church fathers, were the great Egyptian and Syrian fathers.

These Egyptian monastic saints were St Anthony, St Amonas, St Paul the Hermit, St Pachomius and St Marcarius the Great. The Syrian monastic saints were St Apharhat, St Ephrem, St Jacob of Serough, St John of Apamea, St Philoxenus, St Babai, St Issac of Neneveh, St Dadisho and St John the Visionary. Later on he studied the great bishop-theologians, St Ignatius of Antioch, St Irenaeus of Lyons, St Basil of Caesarea, St Gregory of Nyssa (St Basil's younger brother) St Gregory of Nazianzen, St John Chrysostom, St Athanasius, St Cyril, St Dioscorus of Alexandria and St Severius of Antioch.

He stayed at Debra Damo for twelve years in deep study and in 1242 he returned to Shoa. St Tekla Haimanot now settled with a core of disciples at Debra Asbo, here he began to implement the programmes of educational reform with his spiritual father, Abba Iyesus Moa, in almost all aspects of the life of the Church, which because of its centuries-long struggle to preserve its faith in the face of the spreading influence of Islam in the northern highlands, saw many theological and canonical manuals fall into disarray. The Church needed a centralised library, and there was an urgent need for the faithful to rediscover their inner life as first and foremost a life of prayer, worship and participation in the sacraments, in their adoration of the Holy God, who lived as three co-equal divine persons in the unity of the Trinity.

Later on in this great saint's life the Holy Spirit performed many miracles (some say at least forty-four) through him, such as the healing of the sick, the casting out of devils, and the restoration of life to those who had died.

When he was sixty-nine, in the year 1284, he visited several monasteries in Egypt (St Anthony's monastery, St Marcarius' monastery, the monastery of St Paul the Hermit, to name just a few) on his way to Jerusalem, which he visited three times.

The last years of his life were totally devoted to the prayer of the silent adoration of the Holy Trinity as revealed in the holy scriptures and commented on by the holy fathers. In this silent prayer, his mind would descend into his heart and remain there in his small cell within the monastic community of Debra Libanos. In this cell he inserted nails and knives on the walls to prevent him from having any rest. And after he had been standing for quite a long time (some say at least eight years), one of his legs broke and fell off.

His disciples took it and, after wrapping it up, they buried it under the Ark of the Covenant in the sanctuary at the monastery. So he now only had one leg until he died at the age of ninety-nine just four months before his one hundredth birthday.

★

The reasons why so many became attracted to the monastic life during St Tekla Haimanot's time were various. Probably one of the main reasons was that the land on which the monasteries were located was subsidised by the monarchy, most parents wanted their children to receive a good education to preserve the Orthodox faith and later serve the Church and the throne, so they enrolled them from a young age. Others were attracted to it because they had received a genuine gift to live that life.

Many others wanted to escape the sinful life they lived in the world, and therefore sought a career in the monastic orders, hoping that the miracles that were performed by the Holy Trinity through St Tekla Haimanot could also be performed through them.

Still there were probably others who, driven by ambition and the thirst for power, knew that they could ascend this ladder of power through the life of the monastery in their community.

Within the monasteries themselves a wide variety of personalities existed ranging from healers, prophets, seers, scribes and scholars, confessors father and mothers, icon painters, musicians, vestments makers, carpenters and masons, chefs and bakers, weavers, farmers, those who lived in total solitude for five days a week and would re-emerge on Saturdays and Sundays, etc. The list was as endless as was the motivation that led them to choose the monastic life.

THE THEOLOGIAN AND WRITER

As a writer St Tekla Haimanot's style was always personal, particularly in his manner of conveying his opinions and formulating his ideas in letters with those in positions of political and ecclesiastical power at that time. This uniqueness is clearly to be seen in his manner of expressing the truths he discovered in the holy scriptures, in the tradition of the holy fathers and mothers, and in the liturgy of the Church with its fourteen anaphoras.

His manner of communication in these letters was as serious

as the profound dogmatic issues tackled in his great *Book of Dogmatic Contentions*. He seemed to have developed this trait from the thought of the greatest theologian of the fifth century, St Cyril of Alexandria, whom he quotes more frequently than the other fathers he studied. And like St Cyril, questions of how to work out one's own salvation within the life of the Church always occupied St Tekla Haimanot's thinking.

In the *Book of Dogmatic Contentions*, and also in the history of the Church which he wrote, St Tekla Haimanot achieved the perfect union of the theologian, who wants to express the Orthodox Christian faith as it has been held by the holy ancestors of the Ethiopian Orthodox Church, with the rigorous demands of the historian for establishing the facts and events of past ages without using historical sources as mere proof-texts, to support fragmented interpretations of the truth. But this did not exclude a special pastoral note, nor did it drown out his unique personal approach.

This can be seen in those chapters of the *Book of Dogmatic Contentions* that deal with the history of the doctrines about the Incarnation of Our Lord Jesus Christ, by the Coptic Orthodox bishops resident in Ethiopia from the time of Abba Selama in the fourth century until the decline of Axum in the ninth century. He gives this list as Minas I, Petros I, Mattewos I, Marqos I, Yohannes I, Gabriel I, Yohannes II, Gabriel II, Minas II, Mekael, Yesehaq, Semeon, Petros II, Mikael II, Gabriel II, Yohannes III, Mattewos II, Mikael III, Semeon II, Yohannes IV and Marqos II.

After giving this list, he then makes the observation that from the ministry of Abba Selama to the Council of Chalcedon in 451, Ethiopian Orthodox theological thought operates around three main poles.

a. Human Beings are created in the image and likeness of the Divine Co-equal Trinity.
b. Because of the fallen condition of the descendants of Adam and Eve, all men, women, and children needed one of the three divine persons to become a personal saviour, by assuming our human nature in order to restore the soiled image and likeness.

c.   The Lord Jesus Christ is that personal saviour whom God the
     Father sent, in the power of the Holy Spirit, to restore in
     purity this image and likeness.

From its close contact with the theological heritage of the famous
theological school of Alexandria, St Tekla Haimanot knew that
this theological outlook was built up side by side with Ethiopia's
affiliation with the venerable Apostolic throne of St Mark at
Alexandria.

He next shows how, from the period from the Council of
Chalcedon 451 until the decline of the Solomonic-Orthodox
Christian Axumite kingdom in the ninth century, the Church's
teaching concerning the Incarnation of the Lord Jesus Christ was
preoccupied with attacking the Dyophysite (two nature) position
of Chalcedon with regard to the mystery of the Incarnation of the
Divine Son/Word.

Like the Coptic archbishops resident in Ethiopia during these
three hundred and fifty years, Ethiopian theologians were
particularly interested in stressing the real unity of the Lord's two
natures, while at the same time avoiding any idea of confusion or
incompleteness of the union. He makes reference to the formula
which would become the most accepted one in the history of the
next centuries to describe the union of the two natures. This
formula was the one used by St Cyril, 'Jesus Christ is one
Incarnate nature of God the Word,' to describe how the divine
and human natures became one in the Lord Jesus Christ.

St Tekla Haimanot also makes reference to the *Book of Letters*
of the Coptic Orthodox archbishops resident in Ethiopia and
Faith of the Fathers, a dogmatic manual that would later be re-
formulated in the time of Emperor Zera Yacob (1434–68). In both
these books he shows how the position of the Ethiopian Orthodox Church, with regard to the mystery of the Incarnation, can
only be understood deeply when seen in the context of the
Chalcedonian dogmas.

*

Coupled with his achievement in spearheading the rebirth of

monasticism with his spiritual father, Abba Eyesus Moa, and his writing as a theologian, were his endeavours to understand the history of the Ethiopian Orthodox Commonwealth. In this regard the fundamental questions of the origins of historical writing in Ethiopia came to occupy a central place in his thinking. His book on the history of Ethiopia testifies to this. The history that really mattered to him was the history of the formation of clusters of ideas and schools of thought that emerged from the detailed study of Ethiopian historical facts and events.

This led him to an interest in the nature of the historical process itself and how this history came to be written. What was the relationship of Ethiopian men and women to their immediate family history? to that of their ancestors? and to the past in general?

How did they first begin to be aware of the past beyond their living memory, as something to take account of in their lives? By what stages in the different ages of Ethiopian civilisation did Ethiopian men and women's ideas about their past ancestors move towards history as a fully self-explanatory system of cause and effect?

All these questions can be seen in the notebooks he made about the structure of the Royal Chronicle, the *Kebra Negast*, believed to have first been compiled in the sixth century. Together with Abba Eyesus Moa, St Tekla Haimanot tried to identify and trace all the quotations and allusions of this historical work from all the Ethiopian and Asian sources present in Ethiopia: from thirty-one books of the Old Testament, and twenty books of the New Testament; from Chaldean Targums; the Talmud and Midrashim; Rabbinic commentaries; from Old and New Testament non-canonical literature, including the Syrian book of the Bee, the book of Adam and Eve, the book of the cave of Treasures, the wisdom of Solomon, the ascension of Isaiah, the book of Enoch, the book of Jubilees, the miracles of St Mary, and the Testament of Rueben; from the early fathers such as St Origen, Cyril of Alexandria, Gregory of Nyssa, Gregory of Nazianzen, Severius of Antioch and Epiphanisus of Cyprus. In his search with Abba Eyesus Moa, St Tekla Haimanot's main concern was to discover the origin of the writing of history in

Ethiopia. Of course, we know that in its present form, the *Kebra Negast* was completed later in the fourteenth century by Abba Yesehaq of Axum, together with six other scribe-priests of Tegray. But up until the time of St Tekla Haimanot, the place of the *Kebra Negast* in the history of Orthodox Christianity in Ethiopia was not pursued with such a rigorous interest in its composition, probably because, being the product of so many other written sources, its inner pattern was difficult to trace.

What St Tekla Haimanot and his spiritual father, Abba Eyesus Moa, did therefore, by revealing all the sources, was to lay bare this inner pattern.

HIS PLACE IN THE FUTURE HISTORY OF ETHIOPIAN ORTHODOX CHRISTIANITY

From the time of Emperor Zera Yacob (1434–68) St Tekla Haimanot's monastery at Debra Asbo (renamed Debra Libanos) has been Ethiopia's most prominent theological school and monastic centre. It became the site for the training of the royal family and the great Ethiopian teachers and theologians. As a matter of fact, after the Coptic Orthodox archbishop, the prior of Debra Libanos was the next highest-ranking official within the Church. After him the other high-ranking Church officials were monks as well.

For example, the Chief Priest of Debra Zion, the Church dedicated to St Mary built at Axum during the Episcopal ministry of Abba Selama, was held in high esteem. Then there was the prior of Abba Eyesus Moa's monastery, Debra Estifanos on Lake Hayq.

My teachers informed me when I was studying for the priesthood that from the time of Emperor Yekuno Amlak, the priors of Debra Estifanos formed a part of the corps of influential monk-priest advisers to the throne, until the last appointee was executed by a Muslim general in 1535 during the Islamic campaign to extinguish the Orthodox Christian faith in Ethiopia and the other nations of the horn of Africa from around 1512.

The monk-priests who were holders of these three senior positions, plus the heads of other large monasteries such as Debra Bizen (established during the life of Abba Filipos, 1323–1406),

Debra Damo, and Debra Libanos in Sheme-zana (established by Abba Yemata in the sixth century), together with the priors of the monasteries established by Abba Ewo-sta-tewos (1273–1352) formed the influential corps of around twelve to fifteen who worked with the Coptic Orthodox archbishop in organising semi-annual conferences to discuss the condition of the ordained clergy, the faithful, besides the visiting of the Church and monastic communities throughout the country to access both their physical and spiritual condition.

The Church and the Throne at the End of the Thirteenth and the Beginning of the Fourteenth Century

During St Tekla Haimanot's long life Emperor Yekuno Amlak made his capital in Tegulet, in Shoa, instead of restoring Axum. In political and military matters he suffered great losses in wars with the Arab Muslims in defence of his throne and the Church; and while spiritually it was a time of rebirth and renewal for the life of the Church, in other terms, large areas of the country, including some church buildings, were still being destroyed by Muslim armies.

After the death of this emperor, which occurred in the latter part of St Tekla Haimanot's life, the Church again began to experience various problems from the Muslim expansion, especially during the reigns of Yagbea Seyon's five sons, Senfa Ared IV, Kedma Asgad, Djin Asgad, Hezba Asgad and Saba Asgad II.

These five brothers reigned for one year each between 1294 and 1299. When Wedem Arad, a younger son of Yekuno Amlak, ascended the throne (from 1299 to 1314), he found that the whole of the Red Sea coastline was in the possession of Arab Muslims. During this time the Muslim Adal people seized the initiative and declared themselves independent. And in the first decades of the fourteenth century they urged their compatriots from Arabia to migrate to Ethiopia so as to speed up the process of extinguishing the Orthodox Christian faith to replace it with the faith of Islam.

Emperor Amde Zion was the grandson of Yekuno Amlak, and the son of Wedem Arad. He ascended the throne one year after the death of St Tekla Haimanot and held the cords of power for thirty years. During this time he engaged the Muslim Arabs in many battles in which his armies were successful, and the security of both the throne and the Church was upheld. It is said that at the beginning of his reign he could not curb his pleasure for multiple relationships with the aristocratic women around the court. This caused a series of public confrontations with some of the powerful clergy such as Abba Aaron, Abba Anorewos and Etchege Abba Phillipos (the leader of the Church's large monastic community) who rebuked him and advised him to abandon these reckless affairs and live a chaste life as befitted a Christian monarch.

In one confrontation with Abba Anorewos, Amde Zion had him whipped with a thick leather belt in the view of many until the blood of the monk-priest flowed out. In a spectacular mystical act a fire broke out that day and the entire capital of Tegulet was destroyed. The monk-priest Abba Bese-lote Mikael then told the people who saw this public beating that it was an act of the Holy Spirit, and it happened because the Emperor had beaten Abba Anorewos in their view until his blood flowed out.

Abba Bese-lote Mikael further told the people that this act had so grieved the two other divine co-equal persons of the Holy Trinity, God the Father and God the Son, that God the Holy Spirit, who was co-equal with them, manifested Himself as a wild uncontrolled fire which caused the destruction of the capital, hoping that this act would cause the Emperor to repent his reckless carnal habits. However Amde Zion was not convinced.

He believed instead that it was the monk-priests themselves who had deliberately set fire to the capital established by his grandfather, and so he persecuted them. The inhabitants of St Tekla Haimanot's monastery, Debra Libanos, were exiled to Dembeya, Begemder, and the islands of Lake Tana, while the head, Etchege Phillipos, was banished to Gesha. Nevertheless Amde Zion was forced to repent and do penance by a series of visions he received from the Holy Spirit which showed him what awaited him on the day of judgement, when the Lord would return to judge him and everyone else for all their acts, both good and bad.

So in the remainder of his time as Emperor, Amde Zion showed an abundant amount of zeal for the office of the monk-priesthood and also for the Church. He commissioned the building of many new churches and monasteries to replace the ones destroyed by the Muslim armies. Two monasteries built during this time would become famous, Kibran Gabriel and Ga-lila, both of which were located on Lake Tana.

The chroniclers of his reign speak of him as becoming a hum-bled and merciful monarch after his repentance who cared for the aged (including his parents), and the young (including his brother and sister), besides the priests, the monks and nuns. He spent much of the second part of his reign defending the Orthodox Christian faith as preserved by the Church against the Muslim armies.

He led his army against Sabr-ad-Din whose stronghold was located in the region east of Shoa called Yefat, and defeated him after he had killed many Orthodox Christians, while forcing others to embrace Islam.

He then moved on to destroy the other Muslim strongholds in Adal and Mera. By the end of his reign he had succeeded in defeating all the Muslim armies within the country who had threatened the Solomonic-Orthodox Christian throne and its union with the Church. What was also remarkable was that on every military campaign he went on, Amde Zion was accompa-nied by clergy who carried with them a replica of the Ark of the Covenant for strength and protection.

In between these military campaigns, more churches, schools and monasteries were established by devoted monk-priests like Abba Medha-nina Egzie, who established Debra Benkual in Tegray. Etchege Phillipos (who Amde Zion now restored after his banishment) now worked with Abba Ze-Yohannes on commen-taries of the New Testament and the co-edification of the canon laws. Abba Tekesta Brahan established Debra Sot, while Abba Zakarias of Ga-lila supervised the construction of several schools with funds made available from the royal treasury by Amde Zion.

One of the most remarkable of monk-priests in the entire history of the Church lived at this time. His name was Abba Ewo-sta-tewos (1273–1352), whose monastery is the most famous one in Saraye in present-day Eritrea. He came to prominence in the first decades of the fourteenth century by asserting the spiritual and financial independence of the religious life from that of the powerful but corrupt aristocrats who had carved out power bases for themselves at the royal court. Many were involved in illegal trading, especially the buying and selling of slaves from Sudan, Egypt, as well as Arabia, and would give huge financial gifts to churches and monasteries to escape paying taxes to the royal treasury. Abba Ewo-sta-tewos would attack them in his preaching and demand they abolish this practice.

Corrupt and ignorant clergy also incurred his displeasure. He called for a season of penance during which all members of the Church should renew their baptismal vows. The clergy should set the example and also go through a season of penance before renewing their ordination vows. Furthermore, all should return to the faith of the biblical saints, which included confession and regular worship, instruction in the teachings of the bible, observing Saturday as the Sabbath and day of preparation to worship on Sunday, the main worship day of the week, where the Lord's body and blood should be received by everyone. This was not a common practice. Most of the Church faithful would only receive holy communion three times a year, at Christmas, Easter and New Year's Day; others even less frequently.

As they tried to apply these reforms, Abba Ewo-sta-tewos and his followers were hounded and persecuted by the rich and powerful dynastic families who kept poor church members as slaves. They wrote to the Coptic Synod in Egypt and portrayed him as a deviant and a rebel. But in spite of the persecution he and his followers received, his ideas still continued to attract many.

*

The Ethiopian Synaxarium of 18 September states that in the mature years of his life, Abba Ewo-sta-tewos went to Jerusalem, and from there on to Armenia, where the Orthodox Church leaders received him with great joy.

When he died he was buried by the Armenian Orthodox Church with great honour and dignity, after having written commentaries on all four holy gospels as well as co-editing the canon laws. A few centuries later a bone of his hand was brought back to Ethiopia by the Armenian Bishop John during the reign of Emperor Yohannes I in 1679.

EMPEROR DAWIT (DAVID) I (1382–1411)

Etchege Phillipos was the main chronicler of the reign of Emperor Dawit I. The new monarch was held in high esteem by the Orthodox population because like his predecessors he continued the policy of support of the clergy to reorganise the canonical and liturgical life of the faithful.

He was also a great devotee of the spirituality of St Dionysius the Areopagite, the ancient mystical philosopher believed to be a disciple of the Apostle Paul (*Acts of the Apostles* 17:34) who later wrote influential books which came into circulation during the sixth century as *The Divine Names*, *The Mystical Theology*, *The Celestial Hierarchy* and *The Ecclesiastical Hierarchy*. The first book was a study of all divine names of God found in the Bible such as 'God as the source of the Good, of Being, of Life, of Wisdom', etc. The second one (*Mystical Theology*) is a summary of Dionysius' method concerning how one acquires spiritual knowledge.

In the book, *The Divine Names*, St Dionysius starts off with a consideration of Moses leaving the Israelites at the foot of Mt Sinai and climbing this mountain to enter the 'cloud' to be in the presence of God. It was in the presence of the mystical cloud that he received the ten commandments. Dionysius uses this episode in the life of Moses to highlight the two main ways of acquiring knowledge of God: the way of negation and the way of affirmation. We can come to know God by eliminating what He is not, just as we can come to know Him by describing what He is.

The third book (*Celestial Hierarchy*) is a presentation of the angelic ranks found in the Scriptures. The last one (*Ecclesiastical Hierarchy*) focuses on the Church's ministries and sacraments such as baptism, holy communion, ordination, monastic vows, funerals, etc.

★

Ascending the throne following the death of Germa Asfare (1372–82), Emperor Dawit wanted to reintroduce the teaching of these books of St Dionysius, especially in the large monastic communities and Church schools. He apparently faced an immediate crisis and had to delay these plans. It appears that the Mamluk Sultans of Egypt had decided to discontinue their payment of the tribute their predecessors had been accustomed to paying the Ethiopian royal dynasty for the water supply of the Blue Nile, upon which the whole of the Egyptian agricultural economy was based.

Emperor Yekuno Amlak had decided when he restored the Solomonic dynasty that this income should be given to the Church to help it finance its renewal projects. Because Emperor Dawit wanted those projects to continue as well as reintroducing the works of St Dionysius, he now wrote to the Mamluk Sultan in Cairo and threatened to divert the waters of the Nile at the third cataract. The Sultan gave in, and without delay the tax payments resumed. Not too long after this Emperor Dawit invaded Egypt and punished this same Sultan for his persecuting the Orthodox Coptic Christians, a situation which had come to his attention from the Ethiopian community in the Holy Land.

To show that there was a milder side to his personality, when a peace agreement was agreed between them, he sent twenty-one camels loaded with many gifts to the Sultan in his court at Cairo. In return the Sultan sent to Ethiopia through the Ethiopian community in Jerusalem many Christian relics, including icons of the Virgin Mary and the Lord Jesus Christ believed to have been painted by St Luke, and St John, the author of the Gospel.

However the most precious relic that entered the country at this time was a piece of the right arm of the Cross upon which the Lord Jesus Christ was crucified. It arrived at the Emperor's capital Tegulet on 28 September 1403. Today it is kept in Ghesan Mariam Church in Wollo.

The commemoration of this coming of the right arm of the Cross of the Lord to this Church dedicated to the Lord's mother in Wollo takes place annually on 28 September and is one of the biggest festivals of the Ethiopian New Year which begins on 11 September.

We also learn from his chronicler that between 1394 and 1400 Emperor Dawit quelled a series of Falasha raids against the Christian population in the Seimen mountains. He also began at this time a new effort at evangelising the province of Gojjam to stop the spread of the Islamic forces in the area. After quelling several campaigns in and around Adal, Emperor Dawit and his imperial guard followed the Islamic leader Sa'ad Din II to Zeila where they eventually killed him in 1403.

After these military operations against the Falasha and the Muslims in and around areas of the Red Sea coast, debates concerning the observation of Saturday and Sunday as Sabbath days (a practice the majority of Ethiopian Orthodox Christians upheld) started causing heated disputes to occur among several parts of the clergy and monastic communities.

In order to end these disputes once and for all, some of the disciples of Abba Ewo-sta-tewos from their monastic community in Seraye wanted the royal court of Emperor Dawit to make a proclamation that Saturday and Sunday were Sabbath days. Saturday was the Old Testament Sabbath and Sunday was the New Testament one. The main reason they gave for the two-day Sabbath was that these two days commemorated the Lord's body that rested in the grave, and His resurrection the following day. Other priests of the aristocratic families who had been much influenced by previous Coptic archbishops and Metropolitans held the two-day Sabbath to be a Jewish heresy.

The movement became so powerful that on the arrival of the new Coptic archbishop, Abuna Petros IV, in 1398, Emperor Dawit requested that a Council should be held to bring peace between all the parties who were involved in the dispute. The Council under the archbishop's leadership ruled against the two-day Sabbath, as the Church in Egypt did not follow this custom. Abuna Petros even had some disciples of Abba Ewo-sta-tewos confined for up to four years for refusing to accept his ruling. But despite all this the movement grew stronger and the Emperor was forced to meet Abuna Petros and arrange for their release and protection in 1404. He also advised Abuna Petros to publish an episcopal letter recognising the two-day Sabbath which he would also sign.

Another important development which occurred during Emperor Dawit's reign and which would have negative consequences for Ethiopia in the next few centuries was the fact that he invited Italian craftsmen from Florence to live at this court. In 1402 he sent a delegation to Europe to seek military support against the growing expansion of Islam on the Red Sea coast. When he finally died in 1411 he was buried in the monastery of St Stephen on the island of Dega on Lake Tana.

Chapter 8
From Emperor Zera Yacob (1434–68) to Emperor Eyoas (1755–69)

There is a third layer of Ethiopian Orthodox Christian history which begins to emerge clearly from the middle of the fifteenth century with the reign of Emperor Zera Yacob. Today, because we can look at it from a distance of over four hundred years, we can call it the emergence in Ethiopia of the notion of an independent Christian state.

I say this because Ethiopian historical documents from this Emperor's reign describe the origin of a growing relationship between Ethiopia and Europe. They also describe the revival of a profound zeal many Ethiopian monks and court officials had for making pilgrimages to the Holy Land from as early as the eighth century BC but which had subsided. Also significant during Zera Yacob's time was the mission of an Ethiopian delegation to the Council of Florence (1432–45).

*

Emperor Zera Yacob (the seed of Jacob) has been preserved in memory as the 'second Solomon' mainly because of the wisdom and reorganisation skills he displayed during his time on the throne. Receiving his education in the leading monastic communities, he was a devout Christian and regarded himself as the unchallenged head of the Church. In fact he made some very notable contributions to her life. Like many of the Emperors before him, Zera Yacob commissioned the building of several new monasteries and churches.

During the early part of his reign, he arranged a series of doctrinal debates between the leading Ethiopian Orthodox monks lead by the renowned Abba Georgis of Gascha and some European monks in the country under the leadership of the Venetian, Francisco de Branca-Leone. In their debates Abba Georgis again exposed all the followers among the Europeans as disciples of the early Church heretics such as Sabellius, Appolinarius, Paul of Samosata, Arius, Macedonius, Eunomius, Nestorius, etc.

The Emperor himself was present at these exchanges and even participated himself. Abba Georgis later wrote an account of these debates that he published under the name of *The Book of Mysteries*. Upon receiving a copy Zera Yacob ordered a team of over two hundred monk-scribes to make and distribute copies of it.

Zera Yacob was a monarch with a vision of future events. Skilled in diplomacy, he realised the importance of international co-operation to secure the latest military and commercial technology, at a time when his court wanted to pursue a more cautious approach. His main purpose in pursuing this course was to defend the throne and Church from the threat of Muslim conquest. He was determined to preserve and develop the Orthodox faith inherited from his ancestors, and sometimes did so even with the use of force.

Sorcerers, practitioners in the occult arts, and magicians who called upon and prayed to idol gods such as Dasek, Dial, Guidale, Tafant, Dino, Maku-uawze and others were to be sought out. They would be given a chance to repent by being brought to the Coptic archbishop (in his time it was Abuna Mikael and Abuna Gabriel). If they refused they would be denounced and executed. Anyone giving information about their centres and places of residence was rewarded handsomely in his presence. In displaying his intention to root them all out, Zera Yacob had three of his daughters and four sons executed who refused to give assistance to his court guard in the pursuit of their orders. A royal decree made it compulsory for all Church members to wear on their foreheads a small head badge proclaiming 'I belong to the Father, the Son, and the Holy Spirit'. They had to wear on their right arm another badge proclaiming 'I renounce the devil in the name of our Saviour, Jesus Christ'. On the left arm they had to wear another badge 'I renounce Dasek, the accursed one. I am a servant of St Mary, the Mother of our Incarnate Saviour and Creator of the World, the Lord Jesus Christ'.

Following this he also made decrees concerning the liturgical calendar of the Church. The 29th of each month, in addition to Christmas, should be observed as a festival honouring the Incarnation of the Divine Son of God. All thirty-three festivals of St Mary, the holy Virgin Mother of God, should be celebrated as Sundays, and every church throughout the country should have an altar dedicated in her honour. This decree also included monthly festivals to honour the archangels, Mikael and Gabriel, the four heavenly animals, the prophets and Apostles. On each of these occasions, alms were to be distributed to the poor.

All the priests were instructed to meet with the archbishop at least three times a year. In addition they should visit their parishioners more regularly and teach them the Creed of the Church, the Ten Commandments and the parables found in the gospels.

Supporting the decision made during the time of Emperor Dawit, which gave the followers of Abba Ewo-sta-tewos a huge victory, he further ordered that Saturday and Sunday were sacred days where no work should be done. Saturday should be kept as holy as Sunday. One commemorated the resting of Christ's body in the grave, and the other commemorated Sunday as the first day of the new creation because of the Lord's resurrection from the dead on this day. In the popular mentality of the masses it meant a two-day Sabbath.

In 1450 Zara Yacob convened the Council of Mitmaq to uphold this view of the sacred nature of both Saturday and Sunday, in opposition to Abuna Mikael and Abuna Gabriel, the two Coptic Orthodox archbishops of his reign, who taught that the Saturday Sabbath and Sunday as the first day of the week were Jewish customs no longer in effect. This ruling was proclaimed in his *Book Of Light*.

Zera Yacob explained that Ethiopians always looked at Saturday as the true Sabbath, because on this day the Lord's body was resting in the grave from all the work that He did before His Crucifixion. What in the Old Testament was only a shadow had with the death and burial of the Lord become a reality. Instead of observing it by concentrating on the laws of the Old Testament and resting from all forms of work, the faithful members of the Church should use the Saturday Sabbath (which began at sunset on Friday) to prepare themselves for the main weekly service of the Church which began early Sunday morning. In this way they could re-enter on a weekly basis the mystery of the death and resurrection of the Lord Jesus Christ, of which the service of the holy communion was a natural reflection. Weekly confession should be made before receiving the body and blood of the Lord for those who had fallen into sin.

Zera Yacob visited some of the large monastic communities and explained to the monks there that he wanted to encourage a revival in the reception of holy communion among the faithful. He wanted those poor families who lived in the arid parts of the country where access to water was limited to go to their parish church or the monastery closest to them early on Saturday to wash themselves and their clothes, as well as to attend the prayers that prepared the sanctuary for the beginning of the service of the holy communion on Sunday morning.

Being a theologian as well as an emperor, Zera Yacob's central emphasis was to teach belief in the Holy Trinity (One God in Three Uncreated Persons, and as Three Uncreated Persons). He was also very keen to stress the eternal birth of the Son from the Father without a human mother, and the historical birth of the Son from the Virgin Mary, without a human father. Therefore Trinitarian doctrine controlled every aspect of his thinking and writing. This theme is repeated many times in the books that he wrote such as *The Book of the Incarnation*, *The Book of Light*, *The Book of the Birth of Jesus Christ*, *The Book of the Abjuration*, *The Book of the Abjuration of Satan*, *The Book of Substance*, *The Keeper of the Mysteries* and *God Reigns*.

Emperor Zera Yacob also entered diplomatic discussion with the Roman papacy which at this time was pursuing a strong expansionist policy. It was better to take the initiative and contact Rome on one's own terms than to wait and be on the receiving end of any plans they were making. This was his main line of reasoning. To this end, in 1441 he commissioned a delegation to be chosen by the head of the Ethiopian community in Jerusalem,

Abba Nicodemus, to attend the Council of Florence.

This unionist Council, which was convened by Pope Eugenius IV from 1431 in Ferrara, had the purpose and hope of finding a tangible way to bring the various Orthodox Churches of Asia, Africa, the Byzantine Empire, and the Armenian Orthodox Church together into a federation under the jurisdiction of his papal administration. Eugenius IV's principal purpose of this proposed union was to rally the whole Christian world behind his ambitious plan for a Christian campaign against the Muslims, who at this time were rising to global power with the support of the Ottoman Turks.

Eugenius, like many European Christian Church and political leaders prior to himself, had been profoundly impressed by reports of the military power of Ethiopian emperors such as Kaleb, Yekuno Amlak, Amde Zion and Dawit I.

According to a letter preserved at the Vatican archives dated 9 August 1431, an Ethiopian delegation headed by a Brother Thomas arrived in Rome where it was royally received as befitting envoys of the Ethiopian Emperor (at that time it was Tekle Mariam).

Eugenius granted forty days of grace to all who contributed towards making their stay in Rome a pleasant one. After visiting and praying at the tombs of Apostles Peter and Paul, this Ethiopian delegation returned to Jerusalem then to Ethiopia. Six years later (1437) this same Pope sent a Franciscan friar called Alberto da Sarteano to visit the head of the Ethiopian community in Jerusalem, Abba Nicodemus, to explain the objectives of the Council and to seek permission from the Ethiopian throne to appoint a delegation to attend the Council which had now moved from Ferrara to Florence. Da Sarteano wrote to Zera Yacob to explain this request of the Pope. Zera Yacob's response was to write to Abba Nicodemus, giving him the authority to choose a delegation. They were to attend as representatives of the Ethiopian Orthodox Church and throne.

Furthermore, Abba Nicodemus was to encourage the members of this delegation to participate actively in the Council's deliberations, but they were not to make any final commitments on the proposed union, the phrasing of the Council's decrees, or its decisions with respect to the body of the faithful of the Ethiopian Orthodox Church.

In 1441 the Ethiopian delegation to this Council left Jerusalem for Florence. It consisted of twelve monks and an Italian merchant from Sienna. At the head of the delegation was Deacon Petros. When they reached the island of Rhodes, they were joined by the papal legate, Alberto da Sarteano, who was sent to act as their guide. Soon news reached the Council that the Ethiopians were on their way. Prior to receiving this news, two of the major objectives of Pope Eugenius IV had been achieved. The Patriarch of the Byzantine Orthodox Churches, Joseph II, and twenty Metropolitans within his jurisdiction voted to accept the proposed union with the papacy, and a document to that effect was signed on 5 July 1439. The two representatives of the Armenian Orthodox Churches had signed a similar document on 22 November of that same year, and those representing the Syrian Orthodox Churches signed as well.

Therefore, when the news arrived that the Ethiopian delegation was on its way, it was assumed that they too were coming for the purpose of signing the agreement to the same effect. For it appears that the papal legate, da Sarteano, had not informed Pope Eugenius that Deacon Petros and his Ethiopian colleagues had not been given authority by the head of their Church or their Emperor in this matter.

In addition to the Pope's strong wishes that the Ethiopian delegation should pledge themselves to the union, so that he would have their support in the big campaign he was planning against the Muslim forces, there was another reason for his enthusiasm to receive the Ethiopian delegation. His enemies had met at Basel in 1439 and voted to depose him. They even elected the Duke of Savoy, Felix V (also known as the 'Anti-Pope), to replace him. Although the rest of the Roman Catholic Church as a whole had remained loyal to Eugenius IV, he was acutely aware that the 'Anti-Pope' movement could not be ignored and might become dangerous if steps were not taken to quell its growth and influence. Having the Byzantine, Syrian and Armenian Churches on his side increased his prestige. A similar agreement with the Solomonic throne of Ethiopia would now be a powerful warning to his enemies to step carefully. We should therefore believe his chronicler, who wrote that Eugenius IV was bubbling with joy when he learned that the Ethiopian delegation was on its way to Florence.

According to another papal chronicler, when the news arrived, the Pope quickly advised that the Council should be moved at once to Rome in order that the delegation from 'the High and Mighty Emperor of Ethiopia' sent to Italy for the purpose of 'submitting his Church and Empire to the Pope' should not find the Council in such a simple town as Florence, but in the 'Eternal City itself, the great metropolis of the Christian world'. His recommendation was favourably received and the Council therefore moved to Rome.

Deacon Petros, the head of the Ethiopian delegation, made no attempt in his speeches to obscure the doctrinal differences which had long divided the theological viewpoints of the Ethiopian Orthodox Church and the Roman Catholic Church. These differences were clearly outlined by him as the following.

1. With regard to the understanding of the mystery of the Incarnation concerning the union of the divine and the human natures of the Lord Jesus Christ in the womb of St Mary, by the grace of the Holy Spirit, the teachings of three great fathers of Alexandria in the fourth and fifth centuries, St Athanasius, St Cyril and St Dioscorus, were more acceptable to the faithful of Ethiopia than those of the Latin writers St Jerome, St Ambrose and St Hilary.

2. The Council of Chalcedon (451) was Nestorian in its teaching concerning the mystery of the Incarnation by accepting the Tome of Pope Leo to Flavian of Constantinople as a document of the faith of the Church. Its excommunication and exile of St Dioscorus, the Patriarch of Egypt, Ethiopia and north-east Africa, was not canonical because he was not formally charged with any heresy.

3. The Trinitarian theology of the Cappadocian fathers is more acceptable to Ethiopian Orthodox theologians than that of St Augustine, St Hilary of Poitiers and St Thomas Aquinas, the three main Trinitarian theologians of the Roman Catholic

Church.

4. The Ethiopian Orthodox Church learned of the 'Filioque' controversy from a letter of Roman Catholic monks living in Jerusalem dated 807 to Pope Leo III. The controversy developed when some Byzantine Orthodox monks had discovered that these Roman Catholics had added to the Niceno-Constantinoplian Creed of 381, 'and the Son' to the article of this Creed which proclaimed 'we believe in the Holy Spirit, who proceeds from the Father'. With the addition this article now stated 'we believe in the Holy Spirit, who proceeds from the Father and the Son'. These Byzantine monks accused Roman Catholics of heresy for adding to this Creed, which was the prayer of faith of the Universal Church, without the authority of an Ecumenical Council.

He explained that, from what the Ethiopian community in Jerusalem had gathered, the historical background to this controversy started towards the end of 806, when an ambassador of Charlemagne at the court of the Caliph of Baghdad, Harun-al Rashid, had returned to Aachen with two Roman Catholic monks, Abbots Georg Egilbald and Felix.

While in Aachen the two monks heard the Creed sung with the addition to it that the Holy Spirit proceeds from the Father and the Son. When these two returned to Jerusalem they introduced this addition to their monasteries on Mt Olivet. Deacon Petros also told the Council delegates that from a close examination of the letter of the Roman Catholic monks to Pope Leo III, Ethiopian Orthodox theologians noted several facts. First, there was little doubt that the expanded version of the Creed had for some years not received approval from Charlemagne. Secondly, the Roman Catholic monks considered the 'Filioque clause' as only a liturgical difference, no more important than other liturgical differences between themselves and the Orthodox Churches in the Byzantine Empire. Thirdly, what had quite amazed these two Roman Catholic monks was the seriousness with which the Byzantine Orthodox monks reacted to the expanded phasing. Fourthly, it was noteworthy that the bond between the Carolingians and the papacy was so strong that the monks thought that an attack on the Frankish practices was also an attack on the Roman See of St Peter.

Pope Leo III responded by sending a letter to 'all the Churches of the East' to explain the Roman teaching concerning the procession of the Holy Spirit. In November 809 Charlemagne convoked a Council at Aachen at which his leading theologians, Theodulf of Orleans, Alcuin and Paulinus of Aquieleia, prepared arguments to defend the addition to the Creed. The Byzantine Patriarchs Thomas I and Sergius I refused to receive the explanation of these Carolingian theologians. When they met with Leo III in 810 and attempted to persuade him to ratify the alteration, Leo, though seeming to agree with the theology of the Filioque clause, refused to sanction an addition to the wording of the Creed that was made by an Ecumenical Council, although the expanded form of the same Creed continued to be widely used in Europe.

The most vehement critic of the Filioque clause was the Byzantine Patriarch Photius. When Pope Benedict VIII (reigned 1012–24) finally authorised and approved it, this drove the final wedge of separation between the Byzantine/Greek-speaking and the Roman Catholic/Latin-speaking Churches. Attempts were made at the Papal Council of Lyons (1274) to impose it on the Churches within the Byzantine Empire without success.

Throughout all the stages the Byzantine community in Jerusalem kept the other parts of the Orthodox world informed of developments. The fathers of the Ethiopian Orthodox Church rejected the addition from the start. This was because, following the trinitarian theology of the Cappadocian bishops, Ethiopian Orthodox theologians also affirmed the irreducible uniqueness of each of the divine uncreated persons within the unity of the Godhead. After their struggles with followers of Eunomius, these Cappadocian fathers began to assert the uniqueness of the divine person of the Father, as the source and origin of the divine person Son and the Holy Spirit. They were forced into this position because Eunomius (one of their chief opponents) identified the person of the Father and the shared divine essence of the Godhead as being one as the same. Therefore, from this time these three introduced a key trinitarian formula which many later Church fathers also used. This formula concerning the origin of the procession of the Holy Spirit stated 'The Holy Spirit proceeds from the Father through the Son'. Because of this formula, Ethiopian theologians could never accept the Carolingian expression that 'The Holy Spirit proceeds from the Father and the Son' as a suitable formula to describe the origin of the procession of the Holy Spirit.

Deacon Petros told the Council that the main reasons why Ethiopian Orthodox theologians proclaimed that the Holy Spirit proceeds from the Father alone were these.

a. In the text of St John 15:26, the Lord Jesus Christ promises to send us from the Father, the Spirit of Truth who proceeds from the Father.

b. Ethiopian Orthodox theologians have always been careful when discussing the origin of the existence of the Holy Spirit to make a clear distinction between the eternal procession of the Holy Spirit from the Father alone, and His temporal mission from the day of Pentecost in the life of the world, to lead all the faithful to the knowledge and path of everlasting life, through participation in the life of the Church.

c. Since the Cappadocian fathers' struggle with Eunomius and his followers, who identified the person of the Father and the shared divine essence of the Holy Trinity as being one and the same, Ethiopian Orthodox theologians like them have always made it clear that the Father is the principle and cause of the 'begetting of the Son' and the 'procession of the Holy Spirit', because it is a personal characteristic of the Father (and not of the shared divine essence) to generate the other two persons. Another way to express this same important truth was to say that the Only-Begotten Son and the Holy Spirit receive their existence from the divine person of the Father, and not from the shared divine essence.

d. However, when Ethiopian Orthodox theologians make this distinction they do not wish to give the impression that the divine person of the Father is superior to the other two, or that the Father shares out His own particular personal characteristic to either the divine person of the Son, or the divine person of the Holy Spirit, who are co-equal with Him. This is why any hint of the idea that the divine person of the Son, together with the divine person of the Father, is the source or cause of the Holy Spirit's mode of existence has always been felt by the Ethiopian Orthodox Church's learned fathers as an introduction of two causes, or sources, or principles to the uncreated ground of existence in the being of the Holy Trinity.

★

Finally Deacon Petros stated to the Council that with regard to the structure of the Church, the Orthodox Christians of Ethiopia believe that it is the entire body of the faithful (clergy, monks, nuns, lay men and women with their families) who are the guardians of the Apostolic teachings, and not just the Pope and his college of cardinals, as the Roman Catholic Church believes.

After he had finished it appears that his speech was accepted in a cordial manner, for the papal legate, Alberto da Sarteano, writes in his chronicles that Deacon Petros was asked to inform his King, Zera Yacob, that the Ethiopian Orthodox Church could establish a monastery in Rome if it was their desire. A painting commemorating this visit is still preserved in the Vatican Museum to this day.

While the Ethiopian delegation was making its way to the Council of Florence in 1441, Emperor Zera Yacob received a message from Patriarch Yohannes of Alexandria, informing him that the Muslims had destroyed the monastery of Metmaq in Egypt, because the Virgin Mary had appeared there miraculously and hundreds of Muslims who had seen this miracle had converted to Christianity. This news made Zera Yacob very sad, and as a result he commissioned funds from the royal treasury to build a church in the royal district of Teglulet in Shoa in her honour. Upon its completion he invited Patriarch Yohannes and the council of bishops of the Coptic Orthodox Church from Alexandria to attend its consecration ceremonies, during which it received the name 'Debra Metmaq' after the one that was destroyed.

The chronicles also state that Zera Yacob fought only one

major battle with the Muslims of Ethiopia under the leadership of a general called Arwe Badlay and his enormous army. In the actual conduct of the battle the Emperor insisted on leading his army despite warnings from his advisers. Eventually the Muslim general and his personal guard were surrounded and slain. This caused the remainder of the Muslims to flee when they saw that their leader was dead. There was great jubilation throughout the country as this defeat occurred on Christmas Day.

Zera Yacob's chronicler finally states that during his reign the book of *Tamere Mariam* (the miracles of the Virgin Mary) was translated from Arabic into Ge'ez. Another book dedicated to St Mary called the *Virgin's Lyre* (Ara-ga-no-ne Dengel) was composed by Abba George, an Armenian priest living at his court.

Emperor Zera Yacob died in 1468, and his remains are still preserved at the monastery of Deg Dagga on Lake Tana.

The Portuguese Mission

All of the Church fathers who helped prepare me for the Orthodox priesthood believe that it was after the successful visit of the Ethiopian delegation to the Council of Florence from Jerusalem that interest in exploring Ethiopia intensified in Europe. They believed that many European Christian leaders began to build up fantastic legends about the famous Ethiopian Solomonic/Orthodox Christian kingdom.

In 1487 two Portuguese envoys of John II were assigned to discover the exact location of this ancient African Orthodox Christian kingdom from Lisbon. And the following seven years would see one of them, called Pero de Coviha, travelling widely through the Indian Ocean, the Persian Gulf, the Gulf of Aden and the Red Sea, gathering information regarding Ethiopia. They finally arrived in 1494 during the last year of Emperor Eskender's life (reigned 1478–94). De Coviha remained in Ethiopia until his death more than thirty years later.

Having informed Lisbon of his successful landing and entry into the country, a Jesuit priest, Joao Gomez, was next assigned to travel to Ethiopia. In 1507 he arrived at the court of Empress Elleni (the wife of Be'eda Mariam), who was now regent to the throne until Lebna Dengel, who was only seven years old then, became old enough to rule.

During formal exchanges between the two, Gomez informed Empress Elleni that King Manuel of Portugal was desirous of establishing a treaty with Ethiopia in the attempt to halt the advance of Islam. Following his departure she sent a small delegation, led by an Armenian merchant and trader at her court named Matewas, with letters from her and Lebna Dengel to Lisbon in 1509. They arrived in the Portuguese capital in 1513. Seven years later (1520) the first Portuguese embassy arrived in Ethiopia headed by Roderigo da Lima, Joao Bermudez and Francisco Alvarez. By this time Empress Elleni was quite old and had retired to Gojjam where she died in 1522.

In several rounds of negotiations with Emperor Lebna Dengel, who was now the ruler, the Portuguese proposed to occupy the large sea port of Massawa so that they could secure free access to the country. However, Lebna Dengel was very reluctant to grant this.

He was more concerned with importing from Portugal the latest military weapons and armour which his army urgently needed, as some of these weapons were already in use in Yemen by Muslim armies and counted for the rapid conquest of the region. The Portuguese on their part were unwilling to concede. They remained in Ethiopia until 1526 before returning to Lisbon. In these six years no treaty was agreed upon. However, the chaplain Alvarez and Bermudez remained.

Ahmed Gran's Attempted Islamic Conquest (1527–78)

At about the same time that this Portuguese embassy was pursuing its mission for the King of Portugal in Ethiopia, the Ethiopian Muslim forces under the command of the notorious Emir Almad ibn Ibrahim (nicknamed Ahmed Gran, the left handed one) were preparing to conquer the Christian highlands. A native of Adal, the region which was located in the lowlands between the port of Zeila on the Red Sea and the highlands, Gran had been in the service of the Emir of Harar, in east-central Ethiopia, which in 1520 was already the capital of a well-structured Ethiopian Muslim state.

In 1517, the twenty-two year old Emperor Lebna Dengel and

his army had destroyed a large contingent of this Muslim force near the district of Adal, but suffered defeat at this same location ten years later. In 1529 Gran's army won a decisive victory at Shembera Kure and occupied Dewaro and Shoa in 1531. Continuing their campaign of conquest, they penetrated Lasta and Tegray in 1535. Four years later (1539) the royal mountain fortress of Quexen was captured with all the treasures that had been amassed there for centuries by generations of kings and queens. St Tekla Haimanot's monastic community at Debra Libanos, St Mary of Zion's Cathedral at Axum, the residences of the Coptic archbishops to Ethiopia, the palace where the emperors and empresses were enthroned were all destroyed. In all about fifty other principal churches with their libraries were destroyed as well. By 1539 Lebna Dengel had taken refuge at Debra Damo and sent Alvarez and Bermudez to Lisbon to get assistance before he died in September 1540.

A Portuguese force of around five hundred and thirty, under the command of Admiral Cristovao da Gama, arrived at Massawa in February 1541 and joined forces with the army of Emperor Galawdewos (reigned 1540–59). They in turn were reinforced by the armies of Queen Sebla Wengel of Tegray, and together they were able to bring about the first check to Gran's army in 1542. Gran retreated and now acquired assistance in the form of nine hundred Arab, Turkish and Albanian mercenaries from the Turkish Pasha of Zebid.

In the next encounter there were heavy casualties: half of the Portuguese contingent and Da Gama were captured and beheaded. In October 1542, Emperor Galawdewos, who had been leading his troops in Tegulet in Shoa during the first battles, linked his army with the highland warriors of the Seimen mountains. When news of Da Gama's death reached them they took the offensive against the depleted forces of Gran, and won the major battle near Woina Dega, Lake Tana on 21 February 1543. Gran himself was killed, and his army disintegrated in disarray. Other smaller battles were mounted when the Muslims, with the help of the Turks, regrouped in 1545, 50, 54 and 59. It was not until Emperor Sartsa Dengel finally defeated them in Harar in 1578 that the Muslim threat died out.

The Jesuit Mission

After the death of Ahmed Gran, Bermudez began to insist that Emperor Galawdewos should show gratitude for the assistance given by the Portuguese by submitting himself and his kingdom to the Roman papacy. Bermudez himself wrote of this in his account that is preserved on pages 180–182, and 212 of *The Portuguese Expedition to Abyssinia 1541–43*.

He arrived at the Emperor's tent, where Galawdewos' mother was also in attendance. He describes how he was received with much honour and records that, although the Emperor was a young man, he was very much devoted to the life and teachings of his Church. This now gave Bermudez the opportunity to open up a discussion about the Christian faith with the intention of getting Galawdewos to submit his authority to the Pope in Rome.

He addressed the young Emperor in these words on pages 180 and 181:

> Much beloved son in Jesus Christ, you are aware of the fact that the most Christian King, your father, now in glory, asked me to go to Rome, for himself and for myself to give submission to the High Pontiff; you may see here a letter signed by him which he gave me, that the High Pontiff might believe your father recognised him as the successor of St Peter, Chief of the Apostles of Christ – and that he considered himself subordinate to him with all his kingdoms and lordships, as were all the faithful and Orthodox Christian kings. Therefore, conforming yourself with the will of God, you should submit yourself to the Holy Father, the Roman Pontiff.

These statements amazed me when I was first exposed to them, because it appeared that Bermudez either did not possess the correct documents from Emperor Lebna Dengel, or that forged copies were made after Lebna Dengel's death which came into Bermudez' possession. In fact in the history of Orthodox Christianity no Orthodox monarch has ever submitted to the papacy.

In any case Bermudez tried to persuade Galawdewos of the

benefits he would be gaining by submitting to the Vatican. First of all he would be obeying God. Next he would gain access to an entire world-wide family, for every Christian power and community under the Pope's authority would be linked to him as well. He would not be under constant threat from Muslims.

But Emperor Galawdewos was not impressed and told Bermudez that he would not sever the centuries-long link with the throne of St Mark in Alexandria. He also warned Bermudez not to call himself his spiritual father in future. Finally he told him that he refused to submit to the Pope now or in the future. To which Bermudez records, 'I held him to be excommunicated and accursed. He [Galawdewos, that is] replied that I was excommunicated, not him.'

Not too long after this encounter, a violent conflict arose between the Ethiopians and the Portuguese. On page 212 of his book *The Portuguese Expedition to Abyssinia*, Bermudez describes it:

> There were three entrances to the camp of the Portuguese, by which the Ethiopians could attack them. The ammunitions collected at those places were concealed powder pots, which they (the Portuguese, that is) could ignite when the enemy came, and thus burn them... Before the Ethiopians attacked this camp, the Portuguese horsemen sailed out at midnight and beat up the King's camp.
>
> When the Emperor's troops attacked all three entries that led to our camp where the powder was, it was ignited, and several of the Ethiopians were burned and killed, the rest fled, scared and roasted. Bermudez added: 'The King, seeing the loss of his men, tore the rich garment which he wore, which is the sign of great grief among the Ethiopians.'

At about the same time that this violent conflict broke out, Abuna Joseph was on his way to Ethiopia from Alexandria. So in order to avoid his getting involved, the Emperor arranged that Bermudez and his Portuguese countrymen should be moved to a remote region in the district around Doara. However, when they arrived there, they started arguing with the native Ethiopian population about conversion, and fought and killed many of them when they refused to accept Roman Catholicism. The governor of the area, Calide, was one of those killed. This made many accept the faith of Rome out of fear that a similar fate might also befall them.

Emperor Galawdewos now drew the line; he imprisoned Bermudez and then later had him deported to Goa. When news of this reached Rome, the papal chronicler, Lobo Jerome, explained on pages 307–310 of *A Voyage to Abyssinia*, that

> Pope Julius III and the King of Portugal having received information of all that had passed came to the resolution of sending another Patriarch and two bishops. The person chosen for the Patriarchate was John Nuguez Barretti, the two bishops were Melchior Carneyro and Andrew Oviedo, who was dignified with the title Bishop of Hierapolis.

These three were accompanied by an ambassador and ten Jesuits.

As the Society of the Jesuits had only been recently formed in 1558, Ignatius of Loyola, its establisher, begged the reigning Pope for permission to lead this mission to Ethiopia. He was not allowed to go. Julius III did not alter his choices. However, of the three bishops, only Oviedo reached Ethiopia. The others remained at Goa. When Barretti died in 1562, Oviedo lost no time in assuming the Patriarchal rank. He was ruthless in his approach towards the heritage of Ethiopian Orthodoxy which he did not respect at all.

Sylvia Pankhurst, on pages 334–335 of her work, *A Cultural History of Ethiopia*, records that Oviedo and the other Jesuits

> prepared a treatise on the Ethiopians' errors and the infallibility of our holy faith, and issued a circular letter advising the Portuguese and other Catholics to have nothing to do with such schismatics; the circular letter also condemned the Ethiopians as stubborn and obstinate against the Church, and urged them to forsake their religion and rebel against their king. Galawdewos replied in an elegant document entitled, *Confession of Faith*, which was accompanied by a final declaration never to submit to the See of Rome.

When it was published the Jesuits were amazed by its presentation. They could not help stating how consistent it was with the faith of the Apostles, the three hundred and eighteen Bishops who met at Nicea in 325, the one hundred and fifty who assembled at Constantinople in 381, and the two hundred who assembled at Ephesus in 431. This confession is found on pages 77–78 of the book that Richard Pankhurst edited, called *The Ethiopian Royal Chronicles.*

> In the name of the Father, and the Son, and the Holy Spirit, One God. This is my faith, and the faith of my fathers the kings, and the faith of my flock which is in the fold of my kingdom. We believe in One God, and in His Only Son Jesus Christ, who is His Word and His Power. And we believe in the Holy Spirit, the vivifying Lord, who proceeds from the Father. Thus do I proclaim, and thus do I teach. I Galawdewos, King of Ethiopia, in the name of my kingdom, Atnaf Sagad, the son of Wanag-Saged, son of Noad.

The publication of this declaration sent shock waves throughout the Jesuit camp, both in Ethiopia and also in Europe. They realised now that the Ethiopian Emperor had no intention of betraying the faith of his ancestors and joining the fold of the Roman Catholic Church.

The new King of Portugal, Dom Sebastian, now faced a difficult position, and he had to do all in his power to persuade Pope Pius V to recall the agents he sent to Ethiopia, and send them further east to China and Japan where their efforts might be more successful. This proposal had to be accepted by Pius V, as he depended on the throne of Portugal for financial assistance, and in 1566 he ordered Oviedo and the other Portuguese Jesuits to leave Ethiopia and head instead for China and Japan.

Oviedo was not pleased that he had to withdraw, and the papal chronicler, Lobo Jerome records on page 310 of his book, *The Voyage to Abyssinia*, that Oviedo expressed this in writing to Pius V and Dom Sebastian:

It would be more proper to send us assistance than to recall us, and if we could obtain five hundred Portuguese soldiers, we could bring not only the Ethiopians into the Roman Church, but many other nations, and princes related to the King of Abyssinia.

Refusing to accept this order, Oviedo now joined forces with the notorious Isaac (the Bah-nagash). He was the rebel leader of the towns along the Red Sea. Isaac was in touch with other rebel Turks and Muslims who were hostile towards the government of the Ethiopian Emperor.

However, before he could participate in any campaign, Oviedo died at Fremona. The ten Portuguese Jesuits who followed him in their rebellion against the Pope and the King of Portugal also died one after the other. But the skirmishes of the combined Turkish and Muslim forces against the throne and the Church did not ease up. The Emperor was finally killed in a battle against the army of Nur, a nephew of Ahmed Gran, in which his head was severed from his body. The funeral of Galawdewos was conducted with great honour, and he was finally buried in the Church of Tad-bade Mariam, which he commissioned the building of in the early part of his reign. His head, according to page 337 of Sylvia Pankhurst's book, *A Cultural History of Ethiopia*, 'was claimed by Nur, to show to Del Wambera, Ahmed Gran's widow, and it was afterward carried to Antioch and was placed in the tomb of St Claudius, who suffered martyrdom during the persecution of the Christians under Diocletian'.

However Emperor Galawdewos' death did not mark the end of the violent conflicts between the Jesuits and the alliance of the Turks and the Muslims. It continued until the time of Emperor Fasilades, who opposed them at every step, before he eventually banished the Jesuits completely from Ethiopia and broke up the union of the Turks and the Muslims.

Civil War Breaks Out

The designs of the papacy for the submission of the Ethiopian Orthodox Church and its members under its authority took a different course from the beginning of the seventeenth century. In 1603, Pero Pias (Paes) landed in Ethiopia. Losing no time in his mission, he made it very plain that submission to the Roman curia was the purpose of his visit. He was first received with great honour by Emperor Za-Dengel. As Job Ludolphus, on pages 326–27 of his book, *A New History of Ethiopia*, writes, theological disputes broke out almost at once. 'The next day, disputes began about religion which the King was pleased both favourably and patiently to hear.' On Pais's recommendation, the Emperor wrote several letters to Pope Clement VIII and King Philip of Spain and Portugal, asking that Jesuits should be sent to his court so as to instruct the Ethiopians. Rumours started circulating among the nobility and the large monastic communities that Za-Dengel had secretly promised Pais that he would submit to the papacy once these Jesuits arrived. When these rumours were confirmed, some of the nobility, led by Za Selassie, fought with the Emperor and killed him. Ludolphus recorded, 'Pais's great hopes vanished all of a sudden.' This now caused civil war to erupt between the armies of Yacob and Susneyos, who were the main protagonists for the control of the royal throne. As the struggle increased Yacob was killed, and so Susneyos assumed control of power. Pias, who had remained aloof from the war between the two factions, now made plans to visit Susneyos' court once he realised that Yacob and his army were defeated. Again the new Emperor received him with great honour. After holding a series of discussions with Susneyos, Pais was able to get him to accept the authority of the Pope and he became a Roman Catholic. Needless to say he became very good friends with the Jesuits. He gave them land and permission to build a new church at Gorgora in the region of Lake Tana. The Jesuits even dined with him and sat at a table beside him. The only separation between them was a curtain. They started preaching all over Ethiopia.

In 1615, Susneyos 'convened a council where all the theologians of the Church had to defend their beliefs, while the Jesuits would do the same'. Again in referring to Ludolphus' book, he records that the principal theme of the debate centred around the Chalcedonian dogma of union of the two natures of Christ. No doubt having the Emperor on their side strengthened their position, and the Jesuits won the day.

Susneyos issued a decree immediately ordering all his subjects to accept the Jesuit Chalcedonian Christology. However the senior Ethiopian fathers paid no attention to his decree, they were unconvinced.

Abuna Simon, the Archbishop of the Ethiopian Orthodox Church at that time now entered the fray. Ludolphus wrote on page 329,

> He had not been present at the debate. He came rushing to the spot with loud protests and the whole discussion was renewed. It is said that the bishop was silenced and would not be allowed to speak. However, the Emperor re-issued his proclamation, this time announcing death to be the penalty for those refusing to agree with his religious views.

All the clergy and most of the monastic communities were filled with shock and horror to witness these actions of the Emperor. They openly confronted him and pleaded with him not to betray the faith of his fathers and mothers. However Susneyos refused to change his position, and as a direct result sixty monks from the monastery of Damot threw themselves from a rock rather than accept Susneyos and his Jesuit beliefs. His eldest brother, Afe Kristos, 'refused to accept the Roman religion and his tongue was cut out'.

With these acts the fabric of both the Royal Solomonic/Orthodox Christian throne and the Church was almost destroyed. The governor of Wagara and his army confronted Susneyos and advised him to change his position or face death, because there was no way that they would ever accept the authority of Rome. However, they were all defeated and slaughtered. Many other minor provincial rulers with smaller armies had similar confrontations with Emperor Susneyos, but they also suffered the same fate.

Pero Pais died from a severe fever as a result of overworking himself in 1622. However, the cause of the papacy was considerably advanced, because he was able to get the Ethiopian Emperor to accept the Roman Catholic faith before he died. Two years later on the 3 April 1624, another Papal agent, Alfonso Mendes, arrived in Ethiopia accompanied by six other Jesuits. Mendes was consecrated Patriarch of Ethiopia by Pope Urban VIII, as Susneyos' actions had given the papacy the confidence to make this spectacular move, hoping to replace the relationship that was in existence from the fourth century between the Ethiopian Orthodox Church and the Alexandrian Patriarchate.

Mendes and his Jesuits were not accepted at all by the majority of the Ethiopian faithful, only by the Emperor and the handful of believers of his palace administration, and some solders of his imperial guard.

As a result he was desperate to prove himself a strong man to the majority of Ethiopians. Pages 208–9 of Ludolphius' *A New History of Ethiopia* state that Mendes began to order Ethiopians to kneel in front of him. Secondly, he ordered that all the priests of the Church should be re-ordained by him. The faithful should then be re-baptised, as he regarded anyone not baptised by the Roman Catholic Church as heathens. The traditional architectural designs of Ethiopian Orthodox Churches should be replaced by designs more Italian and Portuguese.

In 1626 Mendes was finally able to get Emperor Susneyos to swear formal allegiance to the authority of the papacy. All the dynastic families who throughout the centuries had supported the throne were forced to do the same. The high ranking monk-priests, the heads of monasteries and churches in the royal districts were forced as well. Many of these Church and court officials signed and then ignored this ruling. As a result they were permanently excommunicated by Mendes, who was going to convince the Ethiopians that he was indeed the Pope Urban VIII's strong man. Sylvia Pankhurst on page 336 of her book, *A Cultural History of Ethiopia*, writes,

Revolt after revolt broke out, and civil wars went on without any hope of ending. The Emperor's loyal followers, including his son, began to argue with him to break with Rome; and his army began to murmur against having to fight fellow Ethiopians.

During this time Susneyos was totally preoccupied with confronting a very militant and restless Ethiopian population. Everything came to a climax when the mountain people of Lasta killed the Viceroy of Tegray, who was one of those converted by the Jesuits. The Emperor marched against them with his own imperial army, and after a series of closely contested battles Susneyos was victorious. The number of dead on both sides was terrible. On his way back to his palace he could not help hearing all along the way, the sad wailing of the people: 'How many more will you put to death? Don't you see that, as yet, they cannot understand the faith of Rome? Leave the rest of the people alone, Your Majesty, to keep to the faith of their forefathers.' This is just one variation of the complaint against Susneyos that Elaine Sanceau preserves on page 221 of her book, *The Land of Prester John*.

So Susneyos was now left with only one choice, as he finally realised that his kingdom was divided in two: either kill more of his Ethiopian subjects for refusing to accept the authority of the papacy, or expel Mendes (Rome's chief agent) and his Jesuits from Ethiopia altogether. He proposed a compromise without severing all links with Mendes. Sanceau preserves it on page 222 of her book, *The Land of Prester John*:

Hear, O Hear: we first gave you this faith which we held to be good, but numberless people have died. We therefore give you back your fathers' faith. Let the former priests re-enter their churches and replace their Tabots. Let them conduct their services, and all of you rejoice.

Upon hearing this new proclamation of Susneyos the population felt delivered. Their determination to hold on to their faith had moved the heart of the Emperor. Multitudes of men and women, including Susneyos' soldiers, danced and sang aloud. Others began to travel the length and breadth of the country chanting that Ethiopia was delivered from the clutches of the Roman devils.

Emperor Susneyos eventually died on 16 December 1632, after having been sick with a fever for a long period. His death marked the end of the papal mission to subject the Ethiopian Orthodox Church to the authority of the Pope until this century during the Ethiopian/Italian war of 1935–41.

He was succeeded by his son Fasilades, who was everything his father was not. The new Emperor was a skilled diplomat as well, and gradually began to reduce the size of the Jesuit communities. He confined them to the two locations given to them by his father, Gorgora and Dembea. Achieving success in this, Fasilades then ordered them out of Ethiopia altogether. When Mendes and his six Jesuit companions refused to comply with this order, they were summoned to Fasilades' court and told to their faces to leave. Seeing there was nothing he could now do, Mendes and his group had no other choice but to leave Ethiopia.

*

Studying the course of this conflict started by the Roman Catholic Church in Ethiopia, which proved to be both bloody and violent in terms of thousands of lives lost, and doctrinally unsavoury in terms of the different perceptions about the Christian faith that existed between the Roman Catholicism and Ethiopian Orthodoxy, is a very unpleasant and ugly matter.

Growing up Roman Catholic, I could give many other examples of similar attempts by agents of Rome to subject other Christian regions to the authority of the papacy. India and China are two other places that come readily to mind.

In the case of Ethiopia, Emperors Lebna Dengel and Galawdewos wrote to the King of Portugal and the Pope for assistance in specific areas: to secure the latest military and technological inventions which they wanted to use in their wars with the Islamic forces in Ethiopia. However, neither the Portuguese monarchy nor the papacy gave heed to these specific requests. Instead they commissioned missionary teams who entered Ethiopia and forced themselves upon Ethiopians who belonged to their own indigenous Ethiopian Church. Subjection to the authority of the papacy was the basis of their mission.

The height of insult was reached when Mendes was made Patriarch by Pope Urban VIII and ordered that all the Ethiopian

Orthodox priests had to be re-ordained, that all the Church faithful had to kneel in his presence and be re-baptised by him. The tragic case of Emperor Susneyos is even more telling. He was eventually persuaded to declare official allegiance to the papacy, but when he tried to convince millions of his subjects to join him, he saw that a huge gulf was opened up between himself and them. Civil war broke out, until Susneyos realised that even the guns and swords of his own imperial army were not enough to force the majority of the Orthodox Christian population of Ethiopia to give up the faith of their foreparents and accept the authority of the papacy.

★

Starting Over

After the Jesuits had finally left, a series of Emperors from the time of Fasilades to Eyasu II (Yohannes I 1667–82; Eyasu I 1682–1706; Bakaffa 1721–30; and Eyasu II 1730–55) began to reorganise the life of the Church again from the new capital at Gondar. New churches, schools and unique castles were built during this time, and the traditional theological books of the Church began to circulate again. Yohannes I, the son of Fasilades, gained fame and honour as a biblical scholar and as a defender of the poor and the oppressed.

In 1682, before he died, he organised a Church Council in which the following regulations were made:

a. The canon laws that up until this day regulate the sacrament of marriage. Most of the clauses prohibited marriages based on incestuous relationships.

b. Muslims should not live with Christians. They had to live in different sections of their villages. Orthodox Christians were not allowed to mix with the Muslims. The same rule was also in effect for the Falasha Jews.

c. All foreigners should leave Ethiopia and return to their homelands.

This distrust of foreigners is also evident in an interesting episode which occurred in 1679, three years before Yohannes I had summoned the Council. In that year an Armenian Orthodox bishop called John had arrived in Gondar. He had, among other things, a small bone from the hand of St Ewo-sta-tewos who had gone to Armenia in the fourteenth century and died there. The Armenian Orthodox bishop also had a letter of recommendation from the Patriarch of Alexandria, but still the people were not convinced about his identity. He was questioned by a leading Ethiopian theologian called Qostantinos and the Coptic Metropolitan Shenuda in the presence of the court.

(Q)   In what do you believe?
(A)   I believe in the Father, the Son and the Holy Spirit, in three persons and one in divinity.
(Q)   Which of these three persons assumed human flesh?
(A)   It was the Son who assumed human flesh, of our Lady Mary, the Holy Virgin, by the Holy Spirit.
(Q)   Has Christ one nature or two?
(A)   Christ has only one nature, as has been affirmed by St Athanasius, St Cyril, St Dioscorus, and their adherents in Armenia, Syria, Egypt and Ethiopia.
(Q)   Who do you worship?
(A)   I worship the Father, the Son and the Holy Spirit, and I venerate our Lady Mary, the Mother of God, and I also venerate the Holy Cross.
(Q)   If the Festival of Christmas and Epiphany fall on a Wednesday or a Friday, do you fast or do you eat?
(A)   I do not fast.

After the interview was over everyone at the court was satisfied that the Armenian Orthodox bishop was authentic and he was welcomed as one of their own. Not too long afterwards a ceremony was held to receive the relic of the bone of St Ewo-sta-tewos.

Following the death of Yohannes I, his son, Eyasu I, assumed control of the throne. It is recorded by his royal chroniclers that he ruled in a very pious manner. Eyasu was a frequent visitor to monasteries and churches in the royal districts, several of which he helped to restore. One of the more famous ones was Debra Brahan which was at Gondar, the capital. Eysau also commissioned a group of monk-scribes to re-edit the *Fetha Negast*, the manual which contained codes of practice that served both the throne and the Church. After, he died in 1706, Ethiopia began to experience much disorder; the emperors who followed him, Bakaffa and Eysau II, could hardly rule as the rich provincial families wanted to declare themselves independent. In Eyoas's reign (1755–69) Ethiopia would enter a period of internal disputes which would last until the middle of the nineteenth century. This period is known as the Ze-Mane Mesafint (the era of the Princes).

Chapter 9
The Struggle for a Sound Theology of Life and Canonical Independence from the Zemane Mesafint (Era of the Princes) into the 20th Century

The Zemane Mesafint (Era of the Princes) and the Ascension of Emperor Tewodros

In the entire history of Ethiopian civilisation this period is one of the most turbulent. Zemane Fesafint is the name given to the last three decades of the eighteenth century and first half of the nineteenth century of Ethiopian history because it resembled the period of the Old Testament history of Israel when there was no centralised administration. It actually takes its name from the last chapter and verse of the book of *Judges*: 'In those days there was no king in Israel; people did what was right in their own eyes.' (*Judges* 21:25).

Maybe only the last decade of Emperor Haile Selassie I's reign, coupled with the time of the military government who overthrew his administration (1974–1991), especially from the time that Mengistu Halie Mariam ruled (1977–91) in the more recent history of Ethiopia have there been more internal wars, struggles and conflicts.

From the last few years of Eyasu II's reign (1730–55) and for the next one hundred and five years Ethiopia's internal affairs were in disarray. It saw the decline of the magnificent city of Gondar as the capital and centre of the Empire. This capital had been established by Fasilades (1632–67). In the following one hundred and thirty-seven years, which saw the reign of six emperors, trading and commerce, the arts ranging from architecture to music, from poetry to icon painting, from metalworking, weaving, woodworking, jewellery making, house-building, shoe-making, to ivory-working and pottery, to the increase in the production of hand-copied and illustrated bibles were some of the lasting achievements of the rule of the emperors of Gondar. Even today the great castles built during the Gondar period are still standing and are a great tourist attraction.

Emperor Eyoas (1755–69), the son of Eyasu II, could hardly administer the affairs of his kingdom. During his reign the migration of the Oromo (Galla) clans and tribes from further south up to the north, coupled with a resurgence of the adherents of nature worship cults and the Muslims, were in the ascendancy. All these segments of the population were determined to have their independence. The ethnic groups of the mountain province of Lasta were resisting Eyoas's power, as well as that of the Zagwe dynasty who still controlled the province.

The powerful governors of Begemder, Tegray, Damot, Simen and Shoa had already broken off relations with the Gondar rule of the Emperors Eyasu I and Bakaffa. In Tegray, Ras Mekael Sehul ignored these two emperors and engaged in a policy of expansion. In a six-month period in 1769 he had two emperors killed.

In the central highlands, Ras Gugsa Mersu, and following him his sons, Yeman, Marye and Dori, fought local battles to eliminate their opponents.

These acts made other rulers of smaller districts look for the best opportunity to assert their independence. This had severe consequences for the life of the Church. Many of the leading Church and monastic fathers had known for a long time that the large clans and tribes such as the Darasa, the Ometo, the Anuak, the Bako, the Isa, the Gadabusi, the Darod, the Hawiya and the Dijil had only accepted the Orthodox Christian faith of the Church out of allegiance to their provincial governors and probably out of fear of the armies of the emperors. But now that these governors were trying to declare their independence they also felt free to assert themselves and their own unique religious philosophies.

The nation's Muslims saw this as an opportunity to spread their faith throughout Ethiopia. They even wanted to create a new Mecca in Ethiopia. They looked for the emergence of a new dynamic preacher/prophet/warrior in the mould of Ahmed Gran, so Ras Ali II, one of the country's powerful Muslim rulers, organised a pilgrimage to the tomb of the slain Ahmed Gran which drew thousands; he also had contacts with Mohammad Ali of Egypt, and in 1838 he was invited by this Egyptian Muslim ruler, along with Dejazmatch Ahmed and his army, to join him in the plan to conquer Ethiopia.

Theological Controversies

Because the Church itself was preoccupied with many erroneous concepts concerning the union of the divine and the human natures in the Lord Jesus Christ, it could not act as a force for the nation's unity. Priests and theologians were divided over the mystery of the Incarnation of the Lord Jesus Christ. Some of these erroneous theological formulas were brought by the Jesuits and other Europeans and had never died.

Two major factions came to the fore during this time. One was defending the traditional concept of the Lord as 'Wolde Qib-Hulet Lidet'. This formula meant that the Lord was the Son of God who had an eternal birth from God the Father without a human mother, and a second birth from St Mary, the Holy Theotokos, without a human father. 'Wolde Qib' was interpreted in a polemic sense to mean 'Karra Haimanot' which means literally in English, 'The belief of the knife as it cuts off the third birth' against those who preached a belief of 'three births' of the Lord.

The upholders of this 'Wolde Qib Hulet Lidet' theological formula concerning the Lord Jesus Christ were from the monastery of St Ewo-sta-tewos in Tegray.

The other powerful group promoted a three-birth formula known as 'Yet-Sega- Sost Lidet' which means the Lord is the Son of the grace of God who experienced three births. The eternal birth from God the Father, the birth at the moment of the conception, and the birth from the Holy Spirit during His Baptism in the river Jordan. The promoters of this formula were the clergy of Debra Libanos under the Echege and included the powerful King Sahle Selassie of Shoa. The other clergy in the large monasteries of Shoa at Menz and Merra-batie never accepted the formula of 'Yet-Sega-Lij Sost Lidet' and accused the head of the monastery of Debra Libanos of being too involved in the political plan of Sahle Selassie.

In reality these theological controversies were used by the powerful governors who vied with each other for control of the nation. The followers of the formula 'Wolde Qib Hulet Lidet, Karra Haimanot' had become popular in Gondar as the ruler, Ras Mikael Sehul, had confessed his belief in this way. It received strong support by many in Tegray as well, but was openly denounced among the Amhara and the Oromo, who had refused to recognise the power of Tegray. When Ras Mikael Sehul's army was defeated and Archbishop Yosab died, in 1803, the Amhara and the Oromo, together with Echege Wolde Yonas of Debra Libanos, vigorously promoted the 'Sost Lidet' (three births) formula. This Echege permanently excommunicated the followers of the 'Wolde Qib Hulet Lidet' belief and drove them from Gondar with the help of the Oromo and the Amhara.

Ethiopia was left without an archbishop from 1803 until 1816 when Abuna Kerilos was assigned from Egypt. Upon arrival he was escorted to the court of Ras Wolde Selassie of Tegray. During this time another formula concerning the Lord Jesus Christ had emerged in Gojjam called 'Wolde Qibat' which meant 'Son of the Anointing'. The followers of this formula also held to some of the ideas contained in the 'Hulet Lidet Wolde Qib' concept, but where they differed was in claiming that at His conception in the womb of St Mary, the Holy Theotokos, the Lord was anointed by the Holy Spirit.

Abuna Kerilos, who resided in Tegray, strongly supported the monks who promoted the 'Hulet Lidet Wolde Qib, Karra Haimanot' formula. After three years in the country of studying the ideas of the opposing faction, in 1819 he set off for Gondar to hold a council in an attempt to bring back unity in the Church.

He was not successful, however, as the Gondarines saw him not only as being in favour of the 'Hulet Lidet' (the two births) formula, but as an agent of the kingdom of Tegray as well. With the help of the Echege and Ras Gusta they forced him back to Tegray. Not too long after this, Ras Wolde Selassie died and Dejazmatch Sebaga-dis became the new ruler of Tegray. He had several disputes with Abuna Kerilos, who now returned to Gondar. But because he was a known defender of the 'Hulet Lidet Wolde Qib Karra Haimanot' formula he was hated by the followers of the 'Sost Lidet' concept. Furthermore, the population of Gondar was very suspicious of his motives for returning, thinking that he had some hidden political agenda. He was confined to one of the monasteries on Lake Tana by Ras Yeman, who was the new ruler of the province following the death of his father, Ras Gugsa. Dejazmatch Sebaga-dis of Tegray had tried to get another bishop from Egypt, however the Coptic Orthodox Synod told him that it was impossible as long as Abuna Kerilos was alive.

Abuna Kerilos finally died in 1829 at the monastery he was confined to on Lake Tana, and Sebaga-dis now sent an ambassador to the Synod in Egypt to obtain another bishop, but Sebaga-dis died in 1831 before one was appointed. It would be another ten years before another Coptic Orthodox bishop would be appointed and the condition of the Church was again in a very sad state. The disputes between the two major factors did not end.

In fact many Ethiopians who did not understand the technical language used by both sides began to be attracted to the Islamic doctrine because it was more uniform, and also because it was actively supported by many powerful Oromo leaders.

In December 1841 a new bishop, Abuna Selama, arrived in the country. He was received by Dejazmatch Wube. The 'Sost Lidet' (three births) formula was still very strong in Gondar, as its chief defenders were Echege Gabre Mariam Mahsantu, Ras Ali II, and Empress Menen (Ras Ali's mother) who was born a Muslim but had converted to Christianity.

When Abuna Selama found out this, he suspected that the Muslim tendencies may have still been alive in both Ras Ali and his mother, so he had them permanently excommunicated, together with Echege Gabre Mariam. Following this spectacular act, Abuna Selama, who was an official supporter of 'Hulet Lidet Wolde Qib' (the two births) formula, permanently excommunicated all the other known followers of the 'Sost Lidet' (three births) concept.

In other activities that were occurring at the same time, King Sahle Selassie of Shoa proclaimed that anyone who refused to accept the 'three births' concept as it was interpreted at Gondar, plus a new concept that taught that the human soul possessed knowledge of fasting and worshipping even while it was in its development stage in the womb of its mother, would be punished and stand to have all their property seized. And according to M. Abir in his book, *Era of the Princes*, King Sahle Selassie punished all the clergy by banishing them, including the head of the Church of Menz, who was a close friend of his mother.

Abuna Selama in turn wrote to Sahle Selassie and asked him to change his ideas and actions and reinstate the banished clergy, or else he would be forced to issue an excommunication order on him as well. Sahle Selassie called Abuna Selama's bluff and lost. He too did not escape Abuna Selama's episcopal authority. However, together with support from Ras Ali and his mother Menen, Abuna Selama was arrested and escorted out of Gondar back to Tegray where he was received by envoys of Dejazmatch Wube.

In the meantime King Sahle Selassie contracted an illness which took his life in 1847. He was succeeded by his son Haile Melekot. This King was the famous father of his equally famous son, Menelik II.

The Attempted Reunification Under Emperor Tewodros (1855–68)

Debtera Zeneb, one of the personal secretaries of Emperor Tewodros, writes at the beginning of his book, *The Chronicles of King Tewodros*, that Tewodros was born Kassa Hailu in Qwara in 1818 to Hailu Wolde Giyorgis and Ati-tagab who were the rulers of Qwara. When he was still a young child, his father died, and his paternal uncle, Dejazmatch Kinfu assumed responsibility for his upbringing. He was sent to the monastery of Mahebere Selassie. Here he received a traditional Church education, the Old and New Testaments, Church history and doctrine, the geography of the country, basic mathematics and law. However, while he was engaged in his education there with the monks, a rival leader, Dejazmatch Maru, attacked the monastery and massacred forty-eight students. Kassa was able to escape and returned to his home district of Qwara.

Not too long after this he joined a group of wandering bandits ('shiftas' in Amharic) in his home district and they formed a small military unit of which he was the leader. They fought local skirmishes with detachments of Ras Ali's and Dejazmatch Goshu's much larger forces. However, Kassa soon reformed and made peace with both. He distinguished himself as a warrior by fighting with a large Ethiopian force against the Egyptians at Sinnar in Sudan. His fame now grew and not too long afterwards a political marriage was arranged between himself and Tewabetch by Queen Menen (her grandmother) and Ras Ali. Their hope was that this marriage would keep him under control as they would know his every move. But things did not work out this way. Kassa had his own agenda for gaining power, and this did not involve his wife.

As he grew in adulthood he matured as a military leader as well. His fame grew and together with his own force he marched on Gondar and captured it in 1847. When the news reached Queen Menen, the mother of Ras Ali, she herself led the imperial army against him. She was defeated and taken prisoner, together with her weak husband, Emperor Yohannes III. Soon Ras Ali heard of this on his way to Lasta, to engage the forces of Birru Ali-gaz. He had to change his plan and now headed straight for Gondar so that he could confront Kassa in a big campaign for the release of his mother and the Emperor. However upon arrival his forces did not engage Kassa's own. They realised that the risk factor was too high. Instead Ras Ali agreed to give him all the land to the west and north of Lake Tana that had been in the control of Dejazmatch Kinfu as well as the title of 'Dejazmatch' for the release of his mother and the Emperor.

Having secured the release of his mother and Emperor

Yohannes III, Ras Ali could now resume his mission to Lasta to engage the army of Birru Ali-gaz. As soon as he and his army left, Ras Goshu and his son Birru Goshu, who were both followers of the theological formula of two births of the Lord (Hulet Lidet), invaded Gondar because of the way both the clergy and the people had treated Abuna Selama. They put the Echege in iron chains and took him as a prisoner to Gojjam.

Meanwhile, in Tegray, Abuna Selama became concerned by the way Dejazmatch Wube was cultivating friendly relationships with Roman Catholic missionaries. As a result, the relationship between the two became very cold and Abuna Selama left and went to the monastery of Debra Damo near Adigrat. He now published an excommunication order on Dejazmatch Wube after hearing that Wube was sending a group of soldiers to arrest him. It did not take Wube long to make peace with the bishop, especially as he still nursed a burning ambition to be crowned as 'King of Kings', but he knew that he would never get the support he needed from the bulk of the population who still held the Church in high regard, even though they probably did not understand what the dispute was all about. Wube knew that it did not look good on his part in the eyes of people to be seen to be at odds with Abuna Selama, so he made peace. However, Abuna Selama insisted that all Roman Catholics should be banished from Tegray altogether.

Back in the circle of Ras Ali and his army, an attack upon Kassa and his army was being planned. It was to be led by Dejazmatch Goshu. But he was killed not too long after engaging Kassa's army in 1852. So Ras Ali sent a stronger force under the twin command of Dejazmatch Birru Ali-gaz and Dejazmatch Belew. Again Kassa defeated this one. When news reached him that his two commanders were slain in this battle it sent waves of fear and shock through Ras Ali's forces. Ali was now forced to take the battlefield with his main army against Kassa and his army at Ayshal. This occurred in June 1853. Kassa and his well-trained soldiers again were victors. Ras Ali, knowing the tradition of the Church very well, fled from the battlefield to the Church of Mahedere Mariam near Debra Tabor to ask for asylum, which he received.

When Kassa took the title of 'Negus' (king) the following year (1854) his opponents were convinced that he also had aspirations to be 'Negusa Negast' (king of kings). Wube now gathered his army to meet Kassa's in the final confrontation. Kassa invaded Simen and engaged and destroyed Wube's army on 9 February 1855 at Deresge. Having won this battle he lost no time in consolidating his position. Two days later after he was anointed and enthroned King of Kings by Abuna Selama. He chose as his throne name 'Tewodros'. According to one of the holy books of the Church called Fikkare Eyesus, 'Tewodros' was to be God's promised king, who would come to rule the world in righteousness, peace and prosperity after a long period of war, famine, corruption, perversity and lawlessness. Kassa took this throne name because he saw himself as an incarnation of this spiritual hero.

★

After his coronation as King of Kings Tewodros still had to fight several battles. He headed south to subdue the Oromo in Wollo. He captured Magdala, which he made his base, and defeated the army of Shoa. In Gojjam, Tedla Gwalu of the ruling family of the province did not submit, and in Simen, Neguse and Tesemma Wolde Mikael, the grandsons of Wube, were also holding out.

Returning to Gondar, he burnt down a mosque built by the Muslims, after gathering various vessels and icons from the churches together with roughly nine hundred and seventy books on the history and teachings of the Church. This became the basis of his library at Magdala. He then sacked the city. Around three hundred and fifty of these books made their way back to London with the expedition of Sir Robert Napier in 1867–68.

In 1856 Emperor Tewodros issued several new regulations concerning reform of the Church. He declared that all Christians should have only one husband and one wife. Every church must cut down on the number of its clergy by having only two priests and three deacons and sufficient land to farm. All other Church land would be distributed to local farmers around the church who paid taxes to farm it. Tewodros justified this change by making reference to the way land was distributed to the various tribes of Israel in the time of Joshua. However, Abuna Selama and some powerful heads of the monastic communities held out on this by referring to the clause of the *Fetha Negast* which gave the Church the right to keep all its property.

Tewodros fell out of grace with Abuna Selama in 1860 when he seized all Church lands in the areas that he controlled. There were other reasons too. Tewodros started appointing priests, then transferring them from one church to another without the bishop's consent. He wanted the Bible read in Amharic and not Ge'ez (the language of the Church) at all Church services. To this end he assigned some of his own staff to get Amharic Bibles from some European missionaries who had established a printing press to distribute them among the people.

Tewodros further ruled that all Christians should follow the doctrine concerning the Lord Jesus Christ of His eternal birth from God the Father, and His human birth from St Mary, the Holy Theotokos (Hulet Lidet Wolde Qib Karra Haimanot) and not the three births (Sost Lidet) or the Son of the anointing (Wolde Qibat) concepts. If it came to his attention that anyone refused his ruling, they would be harshly punished.

★

It was Tewodros' foreign policy regulations that proved to be his undoing. He inherited a complicated situation in this area. During the fifty years before he was born, most of the provincial governors had started making contacts with the French and the British for specific requests to strengthen their cause internally, as well as to protect themselves from the threat they faced from Egypt. They wanted all the latest military, agricultural and industrial technology, from these two European nations. Tewodros also saw the need for latest types of technology to reunify and modernise the kingdom he inherited. He himself made several attempts to establish relations with the French and the British. The French, however, had not forgotten how he had forced the Roman Catholic Bishop de Jacobis from Gondar. Contacts with the British were not so difficult. They already had two representatives in the country in the persons of Plowden and Cameron. Tewodros wrote to Queen Victoria in 1862 and when he received no reply things became difficult. He asked Cameron to go to Queen Victoria's palace with a letter and return with a reply. Cameron, however, did not take this request seriously. Upon leaving Tewodros' court, he put the Emperor's letter in the post and visited the provinces on the border with Sudan before he returned.

When Emperor Tewodros found out, he grew very suspicious of Cameron's motives. In November 1863 an envoy from London arrived with instructions for Cameron, but still no message for the Emperor. This is when Tewodros decided to act. Cameron and his staff were arrested and chained in January 1864. Arrested also were Stern and Rosenthal, who were doing missionary work among the Felashas. They were sent to Tewodros' mountain fortress at Magdala. When news of this reached London, Queen Victoria appointed Hormuzd Rassam of her diplomatic post at Aden to mediate. When he arrived in January 1866, he was well received and the captives were released. Victoria's government now approved the opening of an Ethiopian embassy in London, but there seems to have been some fault with the translation of the letter that granted this request. It made Emperor Tewodros believe that Rassam had the authority to make arrangements with him directly. One key phrase of this letter stated, 'Consult him [Rassam, that is] concerning what you require of us, and he will do it for you.' Tewodros now decided to keep Rassam and send one of the missionaries called Flad back to London with requests for an expert infantry officer and the latest military equipment. Victoria's government did not feel comfortable with the situation, nevertheless they sent some people and equipment with Flad to the port of Massawa with the condition that Tewodros would not get the equipment until all the captives were set free. Furthermore, Flad had been instructed to let the Emperor know that the Queen had every intention of deploying a strong military force to release the captives if he did not comply.

After two more years of failed diplomatic negotiations, Victoria's government kept its promise; she sent a military force composed of British and Indian soldiers that numbered 32,000 under the command of Sir Robert Napier. They landed at Zulla near Massawa and headed inland in January 1868. The thing that surprises many Ethiopian historians today is the fact that Emperor Tewodros made no attempt to block this large army's march to Magdala. In October he deserted his other base at Debra Tabot and headed for Magdala, taking his military hardware with him. He arrived about three weeks before Napier's army did. And on Crucifixion Friday, 10 April 1868, the only battle of the entire episode took place on some fields just below the fortress.

In terms of military campaigns, this battle did not last long at all, although it was very violent. The Emperor's army of only around 4,000 faced Napier's of 32,000. Having lost, the next day Tewodros released all the captives. Napier now demanded that he submit, and when he refused Magdala was attacked on Easter Monday. However, before they could capture Tewodros, he shot himself.

*

Over the years that I have been associated with the Ethiopian Orthodox Church and its history, I have heard many assessments of this Magdala expedition and Emperor Tewodros' role (or his lack of one) in it. I must admit that I personally think that Napier's expedition to Madgala is only an isolated incident in the long flow of Ethiopian history. It suggests as well that Tewodros' plans for reunification once he became Emperor did not meet with the approval of all the power brokers around him. This is the case when one considers these facts about this expedition. Dejazmatch Kassa Mercha of Tegray (later Emperor Yohannes IV) and Wagshum Gobeze of Wag-Lasta not only granted Napier's army the right to march through their territories, once he assured them that he was only in Ethiopia to secure the release of the British captives, they even assisted by providing guides, food supplies and pack-animals. After Napier fulfilled his mission and left the country, the British government decided they did not want to have anything more to do with Ethiopia, and although several British organisations pursued their own plans, Napier's expedition was not a colonial venture in the same way that the

British government actively sought out colonies in other parts of the African continent during the nineteenth century.

We now come to considering Emperor Tewodros' act of self-destruction. If one understands the Ethiopian mind, and the way of thinking of this proud Ethiopian Christian warrior king, then it is not at all strange that Tewodros decided to destroy himself rather than face the humiliation of being taken prisoner by a group of invaders.

★

In his relations with the Church Tewodros showed himself a strong man with a determined plan. Sometimes maybe his strength and determination were a little too much for the Orthodox faithful to bear. However, when one realises that the Church was deeply torn apart with theological controversies and divisions his reform becomes understandable. These divisions would have remained if he had not been prepared to back up his reforms with the threat of harsh action.

It must be said also that from the existing records of the Zemane Fesafint, major segments of the population and its leaders had become ungodly. There is evidence that witchcraft and idol worship were on the increase before Tewodros was enthroned King of Kings. Many invoked tribal gods with names such as Waka, Tosa, Tuma, Tishena, etc. Also leading Church officials like Abuna Selama and Echege Wolde Yonas blurred the line of demarcation between the government of the Church and the politics of the rival provincial rulers. The people said that Ras Ali was never fully committed to the Christian faith, and believed that he still held the ideals of Islam, and only used the Christian faith to further his political ambitions. Furthermore, his administration did nothing to uplift the poor and the downtrodden.

The Church During the Reign of Emperor Yohannes IV (1872–89)

After the death of Tewodros in 1868 the civil wars did not end. The armies of the three strongest leaders, Menelik of Shoa, Kassa

Mercha of Tegray and Gobeze of Wag-Lasta, fought each other for supremacy. Kassa Mercha and his army finally won out, and in January 1872 he was crowned in the ancient capital at Axum as Emperor Yohannes IV. It was during his administration that one can say that the Zemane Mesafint really ended.

During Yohannes IV's time in power, a period of revitalisation in the life of the Church was witnessed which had a vital impact for the eventual securing of complete canonical freedom from the Coptic Orthodox Synod in this century.

First of all, he pursued the rebuilding of the Ethiopian Orthodox community in the Holy Land with a great amount of vigour, and it was carried on by each succeeding generation of rulers right up to our century with Emperor Haile Selassie I and Empress Menen. Secondly, the Council of Boru-Meda in May–June 1878, which he convened with Abuna Athanasius, finally put an end to the three erroneous views concerning the mystery of the Incarnation of the Lord Jesus Christ. This Council also analysed the theological outlook of the Protestant missionary movement which was growing in Ethiopia.

The Rebuilding of the Ethiopian Community in the Holy Land

Ethiopia has had a connection with the Holy Land from the time of the Queen of Sheba, Makeda, and her son, Menelik I, in the tenth century BC. It was on his way back from a pilgrimage in Jerusalem that the Treasurer of Queen Candace, Djan Darada, was baptised by St Philip. By the time that St Jerome lived in Bethlehem (386–412) there seems to have been a community there. His disciples, St Paula and her daughter St Eustochim wrote to two of their friends, Loeta and Marcella, of monks from India, Ethiopia and Persia arriving daily in Bethlehem. And by the time of the Islamic conquest of Jerusalem in 638, the Ethiopian community in the Holy Land seems to have been large enough (some figures say roughly eighty monks and nuns) for Kalif Omar to provide them protection, together with the Byzantines, the Georgians, the Egyptians, the Assyrians, the Franks, and the Armenians.

The next recorded reference to this community was during the time of the Islamic ruler Salah-al-Din, the establisher of the Ayyubid dynasty in Egypt in 1171. The military campaigns of this Muslim general gave him enormous territorial gains and saw the expulsion of the crusaders from the region. His first major attack on the crusaders began in 1187 with an important victory at Hattin, followed by victories at Arcre, Tiberias and several other cities in Palestine and Syria. By this time the Ethiopian Orthodox Church already had permanent sites where pilgrims could worship. It is said that in 1189 Salah-al-Din gave these places over to the custody of Emperor Lali-bela:

1. The chapel of the disgrace, with a fragment of the column on which our Lord Jesus Christ sat as He received the crown of thorns.
2. The two chapels of St Mary of Golgotha and St John the Baptist.
3. The chapel of the sacrifice of Issac, and the one built on the site where it is traditionally believed that Melchizedek offered Abraham bread and wine after his rescue mission of Lot (*Genesis* 14).
4. The cave of King David on Mount Zion.
5. An altar in the Church of the Nativity in Bethlehem.
6. An altar in the sanctuary of St Mary's Tomb in Gethsemani.

The decline of this community in the Holy Land started when the Ottoman Turks captured the Holy Land in 1517. When an English missionary, William Jowett, went to Jerusalem in 1823, he visited the chapel of St Helena in the Church of the Holy Sepulchre, better known as Dier-es-Sultan, and the community numbered around thirty. Their living conditions were appalling even by the humblest standards.

By 1838, when a terrible plague devastated the whole of Jerusalem, the community seems to have lost all its property. The Coptic priest who was the head of the Coptic community in Jerusalem then seized the keys to the Ethiopian chapel at Dier-es-Sultan, with the support of the Armenians, as both used to provide this community with food and financial support. The struggle to reclaim this property would reach legal proportions and last well into this century until the Israeli High Court made its verdict.

Not too long after Emperor Yohannes IV ascended the throne in 1872, the head of the community in Jerusalem, Memhir Wolde Semayat, wrote to him asking for help. Yohannes IV obliged and until his death he sent large sums of money to this Jerusalem community. This money was to accomplish two main things. On the one hand, some was to improve the living conditions of the community. And on the other hand, some was to purchase land for the building of a new church and monastery outside the walls of Jerusalem.

Being a deeply religious ruler and full of the sense of independence, Yohannes IV wanted to free the community from the protection of Anglican bishops and the British Council in Jerusalem, as in 1852 Ras Ali and Dejazmatch Wube had turned to Queen Victoria to seek aid and protection for this Jerusalem community.

In 1884 a plot of land was bought near the Russian compound to the north of the city, and soon afterwards permission was obtained from the Turkish Sultan of Jerusalem to start building the new church and monastery. The community now numbered around sixty. The construction work started at once, and although Emperor Yohannes died before he saw its completion, his successor, Menelik II, and Empress Taitu provided the necessary support and finance to see the work through. The finished building was a large round church dedicated to Our Lady Mary with the title 'Kidana Meheret' (Covenant of Mercy).

It was consecrated in April 1893. To the north-west of this new church a two-storey house was built which was to serve as the residence of the monks and nuns. This became the third house this community had in Jerusalem at the time, for in 1876 Emperor Yohannes IV had employed the Swiss Protestant banker, Johan Fruttiger, to buy a house in the Old City of Jerusalem, near the eighth station of the Via Dolorosa and the Greek Orthodox monastery of Hagios Xaralampos. In 1887 it was rented out to the Roman Catholic convent, the Sisters of Charity. However, this arrangement ended in 1891 and the house became the residence of the head of the Ethiopian community in Jerusalem. When I met His Eminence Abuna Matthias, who was the Archbishop of Jerusalem from 1979 to 1982, he told me that this house purchased in 1876 still served the same purpose.

Having successfully completed this project, Menelik II and Taitu were determined to purchase more land to build more houses in the neighbourhood. Empress Taitu bought some land halfway between the new monastery, called Debra Gannet, and the Damascus Gate, built a house on it and acquired the adjacent land in 1903. These were presented to the community as a gift. Some misunderstanding surrounded this project. Memhir Wolde Semayat was falsely accused of slander and dismissed. When he arrived back in Addis Ababa, he was confined to the monastery of Debra Libanos. He later went to Egypt to live and eventually died there.

The house that Empress Taitu built in 1903 was rented out in 1936 to the Palestine Broadcasting Service, and today it houses its successor, the Israeli Broadcasting (Shiddurei Israel).

In 1905, Emperor Menelik II donated the sum of 200,000 Thaler which was deposited in the Crédit Lyonnais Bank. This was to provide a regular income for the community through an annual investment payment. The regulations which were drafted by the bank and the community in connection with this donation would become the basis for a constitution of this community in 1925.

One year later (1906), two more houses were built in the names of Emperor Menelik and Empress Taitu, very close to the Church of Our Lady Mary, Kidana Meheret, which was built in 1893. These houses were rented out to provide additional income for the monks and nuns, as well as to provide for the welfare of pilgrims from Ethiopia.

From 1910 to 1920, various noble Ethiopian men and women followed the example of Emperor Yohannes IV, Emperor Menelik II and Empress Taitu and donated to the monastery of Debra Gennet more houses and land both within and outside the city walls. These houses were all built at close proximity of the monastery. This caused the area to acquire the name the 'Ethiopian Quarter'. Empress Zewditu and Empress Menen (the wife of

Emperor Haile Selassie I) added to this 'Ethiopian Quarter'. Between 1925 and 1928 Empress Zewditu built a huge house on Prophets' Street. It was her intention eventually to retire there but she died without realising this ambition.

One of her cousins, Woizero Amaretech, also bought land and built two houses near Jericho. She entered in the nunhood and when she died in 1969 these two houses were left to the care of the community.

In 1933 Empress Menen purchased land and built a new monastery near the River Jordan close to the site where it is believed the Lord was baptised.

Finally, in the 1950s more land was acquired in Bethany for a new monastery and a cemetery. The foundation was laid during the administration of Abuna Phillipos, the Ethiopian Orthodox Bishop of Jerusalem from 1951 to 1966. However, this building project was not completed until the time of Abuna Mattewos (1972–77).

The Council of Boru-Meda, May–June 1878

This Council was convened by Abuna Athanasius with the support of Emperor Yohannes IV a few months after he was able to finally get Menelik of Shoa to submit. This Council was able to achieve more than the two Councils held during the time of Emperor Tewodros, as Yohannes IV was able to bring about the political unity of the nation in a way that Tewodros was not able to. The leaders of Gojjam and Wag-Lasta had been defeated before Yohannes IV ascended the throne. It was only Menelik of Shoa who was holding out, but now that the new emperor finally got his submission in the early part of 1878, the Council could do its work knowing that its decisions would be implemented nationwide.

Its main aims were three:

a. to affirm the final elimination of the three heresies concerning the mystery of the Incarnation of the Lord that was done in 1856 during the reign of Tewodros.
b. to assess the views of the various Protestant missionary groups that were then current in the country.

c. to make plans to install a new education and evangelisation programme.

★

The followers of the three erroneous teachings concerning the union of the human and the divine natures in Christ came under heavy attack.

As we have shown earlier these were:

1. Those who emphasised the adoption of Son of grace view concerning the Lord Jesus Christ (Eyesus Kristos Wolde Tsegga).
2. Those who emphasised the Son of the Anointing theory (Eyesus Kristos Wolde Qibat).
3. Those who emphasised the three-birth theory (Sost Lidet).

These three views were again formally denounced, and an episcopal letter, given formal canonical strength by the Patriarch of Egypt, Abuna Cyril V, and the Emperor Yohannes IV, was made restating the Church's position regarding the mystery of the Incarnation of the Lord Jesus Christ. This episcopal letter used all the gospel and Apostolic passages which spoke about the mystery of the Incarnation, as well as considering all the main concepts of the Creed the Apostles composed at the first Apostolic Council held at Jerusalem, a summary of which was found in *Acts of the Apostles* 15. The clauses of the Nicean-Constantinoplian Creed formulated at the second Ecumenical Council held at Constantinople in 381 that referred to the Lord Jesus Christ were also discussed in Abuna Athanasius' letter.

Separate paragraphs dealt with such topics concerning 'Jesus Christ – The Only-Begotten Son' as 'He is co-equal with the Father'; 'Light of Light'; 'Very God of Very God'; 'Who for our Salvation became Man'; 'Incarnate by the Holy spirit from the womb of our Lady Mary'; 'Was crucified in the days of Pontius Pilate'; 'He suffered, died and was buried'; 'He rose up from the dead on the third day'; 'Forty days after He rose up from the dead He ascended into Heaven to sit at the right hand of His Heavenly

Father'; 'He will come again on the last day, which is the Day of Judgement, to judge the living and the dead'.

Other paragraphs dealt in summary form with the work of the Holy Spirit, the Church (its sacraments and its use of the Bible); community and personal dimensions of prayer and fasting were also considered, as well as other related items.

The nation's monastic communities were to be used as centres to explain Abuna Athanasius' letter to the population in the villages and rural districts up and down the country, as Emperor Yohannes IV wanted the Orthodox faith of the Church to be the only faith of the nation.

Anyone who was found promoting the three outlawed teachings concerning the Lord Jesus Christ stood to be harshly punished by having their tongues cut off.

*

In his remarks concerning the Protestant missionary groups then active in the country, Abuna Athanasius makes several interesting observations.

First of all he notes how they make a false division between two types of language about God, the mystical and the theological. This false division is then stiffened between the actions of the thinking mind, the healing heart, and willpower in the human apprehension of religious truth. By appealing to a private mystical knowledge, Abuna Athanasius stated that the Protestant missionaries who had been active in Ethiopia earlier in the century such as Samuel Gobat, Christian Kugler and Henry Stern aimed at trying to get Ethiopians away from the framework of theology as a series of revelations of the Living God made known through the Incarnate Son and the Holy Spirit, based on the witness of the biblical authors that the worshipping and sacramental life of the Church had preserved from the age of the Apostles. To him these three Protestant leaders were trying to establish a personal and individualistic approach to God as a distinct orientation away from the polemic theology of the Roman Catholic Church. This is why their views were not really relevant in a nation like Ethiopia whose Christian heritage was totally independent of

Christianity as it had developed on the European continent.

The Christian Missionary Society in particular had earned his disdain because it tended to undermine the fundamental truth of Church unity and participation in the sacraments. It tended to approach the mystery of salvation in Christ as an individual event, and not primarily as the fact of life in the Church.

Abuna Athanasius held that the mode of the Church's unique existence was established on the teaching of the Holy Trinity as essentially a teaching of the unity and inter-communion of three uncreated divine co-equal persons. In the case of the Church community, this unity was revealed in the relations that existed between men, women and children. This was the truth that the Protestants tended to ignore or failed to realise.

*

A new evangelisation programme was also agreed upon which became the basis of modern Church education. A group of senior Church teachers were assigned to design a new catechism. It had to consist of knowledge of the seven sacraments, the worship of the Church, its liturgy, and its calendar and history, the two creeds, and the basic message of the Bible, prayer and fasting, as well as Abuna Athanasius' episcopal letter that was mentioned earlier. After receiving instruction in the catechism, non-Orthodox Christians who did not accept membership in the Church could not hold any government office, and those already in such posts were given three months to gain Church membership or resign. All other non-Orthodox Christians were given three years to embrace the faith of the Church after their period of study was completed.

Just as important at this Council was the request made by Abuna Athanasius and Emperor Yohannes IV to the Patriarch of Egypt, Abuna Cyril V, for more bishops to be assigned to Ethiopia to train and then ordain more clergy to make these programmes effective. In 1881 four arrived: Abuna Petros, Abuna Lukas, Abuna Matewos and Abuna Markos. With their arrival dioceses were created in Shoa, Gojjam, Begemder and Tegray. And one can say that from this time onwards the Ethiopian Orthodox

Church's drive to gain complete freedom from the Coptic Synod to elect its own bishops, archbishops and Patriarchs began. However, another seventy-eight years of negotiation and struggle would elapse before this goal would be achieved in 1959, when Abuna Basilos became the first Ethiopian-born Patriarch of the Ethiopian Orthodox Church.

Into the Twentieth Century with Emperor Menelik II

Even by the most conservative estimates, the life of Menelik II (1844–1913, Emperor from 1889), the son of King Haile Melekot and Ejje-gayehu of the illustrious dynastic line of Showa, saw some of the most profound changes in the entire course of both Ethiopia's and Africa's recorded history. Externally probably the most important change was the full-scale venture of the European governments of Britain, France, Holland, Belgium and Portugal to carve out colonies in Africa. By the time of Menelik's death on 12 December 1913 this process was complete and most of the continent was under colonial rule, except Ethiopia.

Internally the entire length of Menelik's life saw the reunification and consolidation of the government of the nation. Through the efforts of his father and grandfather, Shoa emerged as the centre of the nation after the collapse of the Gondar dynasty during the Zemane Mesafint. Neither Tewodros nor Yohannes IV could get either of them to submit. To break his father's independence Tewodros even captured the young Menelik and his mother and took them north as political prisoners. Menelik escaped in 1865 as a young man of twenty-one and returned to his native Shoa where he began to build up his political career as ruler of the province. Within the next two decades he had become so powerful that the only way that Emperor Yohannes IV was able to get him to submit was by crowning him King of Shoa and the Galla (Oromo) lands in March 1878.

Menelik's fame became eternal after he defeated the Italians at Adowa in March 1896 and secured Ethiopia's independence in the European scramble for Africa. But Menelik was much more than a soldier. Like Yohannes IV and Tewodros before him, Menelik II was just as sensitive to the fact the he could not linger in the past glories of Ethiopian history. He knew that he had to co-ordinate both the preservation of Ethiopia's illustrious past and the modernisation of all aspects of its society. Modernisation meant for him the same thing as it did for all the nineteenth-century rulers: securing all the latest technology in the fields of military hardware, farming and industrial equipment, medical science, communication systems, etc.

Through Menelik II's administration Ethiopia became a member of the International Postal Union. The first railway line of the nation, the one from Massawa to Asmara in Eritrea via Keren and Agordat in Tegray, started construction in 1888, and work on the second one from Djibouti to Addis Ababa, started in 1897.

However, both would not be completed until after his death. The one hundred and ninety mile-long Massawa-Asmara line via Keren and Agordat saw completion in 1920, and the five hundred mile Djibouti-Addis Ababa line in 1917. The introduction of the telegraph and telephone systems were also notable achievements under his administration. It was through his skills as a diplomat that Menelik was able to negotiate treaties with the British, the French and the Italians to secure these latest forms of technology for his nation. Furthermore, Menelik encouraged all Europeans who had expert knowledge in any area of modern technology to settle in Ethiopia on fixed work contracts.

*

Building upon the educational programmes of his predecessors, Menelik was innovative and established in 1908 the multilingual Lyceum school in Addis Ababa. It was an elementary and secondary school and instruction was given in Amharic, French, English and Italian.

Its principal was the renowned and distinguished Ethiopian surgeon and educator, Azaj Charles Worqneh Martin, who had studied in India and Scotland, and received degrees from both the Universities of Punjab in India and Edinburgh in Scotland. In the same year Menelik also commissioned the opening of a secondary school in Harar, which had acquired the status of Ethiopia's second city mainly because it was the centre of commerce and banking.

★

Menelik also purchased a printing press in 1893, which had a font that could print the Amharic alphabet, and in around 1900 the first Amharic newspaper was printed on it by Blatta Gebre Egzaibeher. Five years later, in 1905, the French Roman Catholic priest, Father Marie-Bernard, whom he had given permission to open a hostel to care for lepers at Harar, purchased another press with Menelik's approval and printed a news sheet about his mission's work on it. After four years of publication, Father Bernard visited his native France to acquire the latest equipment for his press, and on his return to Ethiopia his printing establishment was moved from the small address in the capital to Dire Dawa, where he was given a larger establishment.

Being inspired by Father Bernard's project, a Greek printer in the country, called Andrea Kavadia, established an Amharic periodical called *Aimero* (Intelligence) and printed about thirty copies on a duplicating machine. When Menelik saw this production he immediately made an order to purchase one from Europe. When it arrived, he presented it to Kavadia, who now published the *Aimero* on it until the beginning of World War One, when he had to stop because of difficulties. However, this press was not allowed to remain idle. It was now used to publish Ethiopian government decrees and memos.

Inspired by this innovation, in 1923 Emperor Haile Selassie (then Ras Tafari Makonnen) established a second printing press in the capital which printed the weekly newspaper *Brahanenna Selam* (Light and Peace). It had an original circulation of five hundred copies.

★

Menelik also created a cabinet that consisted of Ministers of Justice, War, the Interior, Finance, Commerce and Foreign

Relations, and Agriculture. There was also a Minister responsible for the affairs of the Palace and one for Public Works. This Council of Ministers first met at the Imperial Palace in July 1908. The following year two more Ministries were created by Menelik. A Minister was to be responsible for the Postal, Telegraph and Telephone services, and the Ministry of Education also came into being.

With the creation of the Ministry of Education under the leadership of the Egyptian educator, Professor Hanna Salib Bey, who moved over from the leadership role he shared with Ajaz Charles Worqneh Martin at Menelik's multilingual Lyceum school, the education of the nation was no longer in the sole custody of the Church.

This innovation reflected Menelik's view that the pluralistic nature of Ethiopian society was now a fact. The new Ministry of Education, in the design of its curriculum and programme of learning, was no longer to be guided only by the syllabus of the Ethiopian Orthodox Church schools. Of course, knowledge of the Orthodox concept of Christ and His Church was still taught, but it was now only one of many subjects students would learn.

Unlike Emperors Yohannes IV and Tewodros, Menelik's educational philosophy was not dominated by a vision of creating a nation where all the segments of the population would eventually be members of the Ethiopian Orthodox Church. Although a devout Orthodox Christian monarch himself, Menelik learned as he grew into adulthood that the different non-Orthodox Christian groups which made up the Ethiopian nation could not be forced or threatened into holding the faith of Church. This was one of the issues that had caused so many problems for Tewodros and Yohannes IV as well as for the Coptic Orthodox heads of the Church, Abuna Kerilos, Abuna Selama and Abuna Athanasius. And whereas their educational philosophy, which was supported by Tewodros and Yohannes IV, proclaimed 'One State Religion', Menelik II proclaimed that, whereas all religious beliefs had public expressions in terms of worship and rituals, the relationship between each believer and God was a private matter with which his Solomonic/Orthodox Christian government would not interfere.

The Movement to Ordain Ethiopian-born Bishops as the First Stage Towards Complete Canonical Freedom from the Coptic Orthodox Synod of Egypt

As was described in greater detail in chapter 4, the relationship between the faithful believers of Ethiopia and Egypt went back to the Old Testament times. In the first three centuries after the Incarnation this relationship continued. Ethiopians always associated themselves with the church faithful in Egypt for the following reasons:

a. the venerable Apostolic Throne of St Mark, the cousin of St Barnabas, disciple of St Peter, and author of the gospel which bears his name.
b. the legacy of the sojourning in Egypt of the Infant Messiah; St Mary, His Mother, and St Joseph, His guardian.
c. the fame of the theological school in Alexandria.

In a similar fashion the faithful of Egypt associated themselves with Ethiopia for these reasons:

a. they knew that the source of the River Nile, which was their main water supply was in the highlands of Ethiopia.
b. the illustrious Solomonic/Orthodox Christian monarchy which Ethiopia possessed.
c. Ethiopia's guardianship of the Ark of the Covenant.
d. the fact Ethiopia possessed frankincense-bearing trees meant that they could always have a constant supply.

While the Church in Egypt was organised very early around the ministry of a bishop and priests, this was not the case with the Church in Ethiopia. We know that Djan Darada, the Treasurer whom St Philip baptised, practised some sacraments before he died in AD 55, but he never ordained anyone to continue this work.

With the consecration of St Frumentius as Ethiopia's first Archbishop in AD 330 by St Athanasius, the Holy Synod of the Coptic Orthodox Church assumed canonical jurisdiction over the

Ethiopian Orthodox Church. From this date until 14 January 1951, at least one Egyptian archbishop or Metropolitan was always assigned from Egypt. However, there was always a group of influential Ethiopian monk-priests to assist and advise him in his duties. These were the head of Debre Libanos, St Tekla Haimanot's monastery; the head of Debre Zion Church in Axum, which housed the Ark of the Covenant; and the head of Debre Estifanos on Lake Hayq, established by St Eyesus Moa in the twelfth century.

The only time that the Coptic Orthodox Synod failed to keep this practice was when Egypt was overrun in the seventh and eighth centuries by the Islamic armies, and again during the sixteenth century when the forces of Ahmed Gran tried to conquer Ethiopia. However, there were always problems with this arrangement. Sometimes it caused a lot of animosity on both sides. The main reason was that the Coptic archbishops who came to Ethiopia were usually young and did not always speak Amharic or Ge'ez, let alone the other regional languages of the country. Their visitation of all the churches, monasteries and convents in a vast country like Ethiopia was always limited. Since the archbishop was the only one who had the gift to perform ordinations and settle disputes among the clergy, pastoral care and counselling activities were neglected. Ordinations only took place twice or three times a year, and sometimes there were hundreds of candidates, as described in chapter 6.

There exist records of five separate occasions of influential monk-priests and scholars trying to get the imperial family to support them in a movement to gain freedom from the Synod of Alexandria to elect a Patriarch and archbishops from among themselves. This occurred in the ninth century after the campaign of the Felasha Queen Yodit destroyed Axum. The second time occurred during the lifetime of St Tekla Haimanot (AD 1215–1313). The third occasion was during the reign of Emperor Zara Yacob (1434–68). The fourth time occurred during the time of Emperor Fasilades (1632–67) following the expulsion of the Jesuits. The fifth occasion was during the reign of Emperor Yohannes IV (1872–89). On each of these occasions the Coptic Orthodox Synod would always invoke canon 42 supposedly composed at the Council of Nicea in AD 325, which they said forbade Ethiopians from electing their own leaders. This is what usually caused the movement to die out. This 42nd canon was a forgery that came into existence after the Islamic invasion of Egypt. At Nicea in AD 325 only twenty canons were actually composed, and at that time Ethiopia had no bishop.

The well-known German Roman Catholic canon law doctor and historian, K.J. Hefele (1809–93), on page 36 of *A History of Christian Councils*, supports this view. A similar explanation is given by Henry Percival on page 46 of volume 14 of *The Nicean & Post Nicean Fathers*.

The movement during the reign of Emperor Yohannes IV (1872–89) met with some success because of the influence of the Coptic Archbishop of Ethiopia, Abuna Athanasius. The Church was able to gain four other Coptic bishops in 1881, Abuna Petros, Abuna Lukas, Abuna Matewos and Abuna Markos. This was a major step in the direction of freedom, but political and economic conditions in both Egypt and Ethiopia prevented any further efforts along this line. However, for the first time the Church administration was organised into four large dioceses: Shoa, Begemder, Gojjam and Tegray. Nevertheless by the end of the century all four Coptic bishops had died and they were not replaced.

It was not until March 1922 that negotiations between the administration of Empress Zauditu and the Coptic Patriarch Abuna Cyril V began for the case of the Ethiopian Orthodox Church. Emperor Haile Selassie I (then Regent to the throne, Ras Tafari Makonnen) played a leading role in putting the Ethiopian delegation together. Five meetings were held between April 1924 and November 1928. At this last meeting a list of candidates to travel to Cairo for ordination to the rank of bishop was agreed upon. These were Abba Desta, Abba Haile Mariam, Abba Wolde Kedan, Abba Haile Mikael and Abba Gebre Menfes Kidus. Deacon Gebre Meskel was also selected to travel with these venerable Ethiopian Orthodox monk-priests. On 29 May this delegation left Addis Ababa and travelled to Cairo. Upon arrival on 30 May they were met by the Deputy Patriarch, Abba Yosab. The following day they were taken to the offices of the Holy

Synod where they met the Patriarch, Abuna Yohannes.

From this conference they learned that the Coptic Orthodox Synod was not planning to give them the full powers of the office of the bishop because they feared that this would diminish their power in Ethiopia. They were presented with a document of the Synod's decisions and were asked to sign it. Three main clauses stated that once elected the Ethiopian bishops would not have the gift to ordain without the presence of the Coptic archbishop. Nor would they have the gift to consecrate replica arks of the covenant that each new church received.

Finally, they would not be able to consecrate the various holy oils used in the sacraments of unction of the sick, marriage, chrism or ordination. These activities would be reserved for Abuna Qerolos, the Egyptian archbishop resident in Ethiopia.

The Ethiopian delegation refused to sign and a stalemate was reached. The following day (1 June) the conference continued and the Egyptian bishops told them if they wanted to be ordained as bishops they must sign. They refused again and said they would go back to Ethiopia. 'We came here to increase, not to decrease the independence of our Church in Ethiopia,' was the protest of Abba Wolde Kidan and Abba Haile Mariam.

The college of Egyptian bishops now did not know what to do, and a division arose among them. Finally the Patriarch, Abuna Yohannes, said he would make a decision later in the day, and in the afternoon it was announced that the office of the bishop would be granted to the Ethiopian fathers without any conditions. So the following morning, Sunday 2 June, all five Ethiopian fathers were duly ordained and anointed as bishops.

These newly consecrated Ethiopian bishops left Egypt on 8 June and visited the Ethiopian Church community in Jerusalem, staying there three weeks before returning to Ethiopia on 28 June 1929 to take up their new duties.

1. Abba Desta became Abuna Abreham and his diocese was Gojjam and Begemder.
2. Abba Haile Mariam became Abuna Petros and his diocese was Wollo and Yajju.
3. Abba Wolde Kedan became Abuna Yesehaq and his diocese

was Tegray, Lasta, Wag and its surrounding districts.
4. Abba Haile Mikael became Abuna Mikael and his diocese was Keffa, Illubabor and Wollega.
5. Abba Gebre Menfes Kidus became Abuna Sawiros and his diocese was Gomu Gofa, Bale and Sidamo.

Abuna Qerolos, the Coptic archbishop, was the primate, and his diocese consisted of Shoa, Hararhe and Arussi. In February 1931, Abuna Sawiros died and responsibility for his diocese was shared between Abuna Mikael and Abuna Qerolos.

These five Ethiopian bishops and the Coptic archbishop now worked hard in organising their diocesan administrations until the outbreak of war with Italy in October 1935.

Besides practical arrangements for their new administrations, theologically speaking one of the key problems of Orthodox thinking and living that now confronted them and the primate, Abuna Qerolos, was that of the present function of the Apostolic tradition within the context of Ethiopian Orthodoxy. This problem was all the more acute precisely because these newly appointed bishops took up their episcopal responsibilities at a time when everywhere else in the Christian world the need for adaptation, for change and for a radical self-questioning was to be seen.

In Protestant and Roman Catholic theological faculties (despite the fact that Pope Pius X had issued in 1907 an Encyclical condemning modernisation) there was a revolt against a kind of theology of repetition and concern for the past, till even articulating the Apostolic faith to one's contemporaries seemed mere reaction.

To our four bishops and Abuna Qerolos these theological faculties seemed unable to establish a living relationship between the faithful of the first century and the subsequent centuries of the Christian era. With their diocesan administrations in place the two crucial questions they had to address were these:

1. How long would it take the Ethiopian faithful, with their beliefs rooted in the nation's past, but who depended on the Coptic Orthodox Synod to appoint its leaders, to adjust to the

new situation?

2. How were they as bishops to distinguish between the 'local Ethiopian traditions' and the 'Apostolic tradition'? That is, between the relics of earlier ages which no longer had any significance for their generation, and the living tradition of the gospel which is always made new, with the newness of eternity, by the power of the Holy Spirit.

The first important item to was to translate into Amharic and print as much as possible of the Ge'ez biblical, liturgical and theological materials so that the teachings of the Church would be more accessible to the members.

From 1929 to 1931 the government press published Church calendars which listed the Bible passages, the hymns of St Yared and the Anaphora, for the cycle of fasting and feasting days over the Church year. Books were also published in Amharic on the five pillars of the mystery, the principles of prayer and the New Testament.

From the Old Testament, the Psalms, the books of Moses, Solomon, and the prophets Isaiah, Ezekiel, Jeremiah were published with commentaries written by monks and scholars of the nation's two main monastic fathers, St Tekla Haimanot and St Ewo-sta-tewos. The same was the case for the teachings of the Lord to the twelve Apostles, and sacred songs dedicated to St Mary (Waddase Mariam). These songs are a collection for each day of the week which is chanted during worship services.

With this body of literature in place each diocese embarked on its own education programme and more and more of the Church faithful who never had any formal education were taught to read and write Amharic.

The next issue that would slowly arise from this time until the present day as more and more Ethiopian bishops were consecrated was for this body of printed biblical and liturgical work to be translated into the main language of each diocese, as for many Ethiopians Amharic is not their mother language.

Epilogue

We have now come to an end of part one of my planned trilogy *Towards a Fuller Vision: My Life and the Ethiopian Orthodox Church: A Short History*. As I said at the outset, inspiration for this project began one day early in March 1972 when I was seventeen years old, living in Brooklyn New York City and attending South Shore High School. This is when I had my first exposure to the world of Ethiopian Orthodoxy. In terms of population density, Brooklyn was the most populated of the five boroughs which comprise New York City. The other boroughs are Queens, Manhattan, Staten Island and the Bronx.

When I think of New York City now, the memory of the destruction of the twin towers of the World Trade Centre in lower Manhattan, where over three thousand people lost their lives on 11 September 2001 in the attacks on that ominous morning, still lives with me. I was actually working on the second manuscript in the trilogy when the attacks happened. The twin towers had particular personal meaning for me. First of all my mother who used to work for First National City Bank (now called Citibank) on Wall Street from 1970-76 would have literally seen the twin towers erected stage by stage after its foundations were laid in 1969, and construction was completed in march 1973, before it was officially opened the following month.

Secondly, my sister (Sharon Briggs-McDougall) who is now the Assistant Commissioner of the Department of Children's Services within the New York City's Division of Child Protection responsible for the boroughs of Brooklyn, Manhattan and Staten Island, has her office a few minutes away at 150 William Street.

The geographical layout of this city is unique in the sense that three of its five boroughs are islands connected to each other by bridges and tunnels. The only borough that is actually connected to the North American main land is the Bronx.

While Washington D.C. is the capital city of the federal state of the USA, Manhattan borough within New York City is one of the main international diplomatic, financial, educational and religious centres of the world, housing as it does the United Nations headquarters, the Stock Exchange and the banking district on Wall Street, and prestigious universities like New York, Fordham and Columbia universities.

It is also home to the headquarters of the National Council of the USA, in the Inter-Church building on Riverside Drive on the upper West Side, where the World Council of Churches also has an office.

Brooklyn borough in New York City is made up of smaller communities with names like East Flatbush, Bushwick, Greenpoint, Red Hook, Bay Ridge, Brooklyn Heights, Bensonhurst, Midwood, East New York, Carnarsie, Sheepshead Bay, Crown Heights, Brownsville, just to name a few that come to mind.

In March 1972, I was a seventeen year old junior attending South Shore High School in the Carnarsie community of Brooklyn. We were the first group of students to enrol in South Shore when it opened in September 1970.

I lived about eight miles away with my family in the East Flatbush community where it came near the boundary that leads into the Brownsville community.

*

In order to give the reader a feel of the Carnarsie community of Brooklyn where South Shore was located, if you have ever seen the late 1970s' musical film, *Grease*, which stared John Travolta and Olivia Newton-John, the environment that forms the background to the high school in the film is the best series of images I can think of. It was a white European-American middle-class community in every respect. Carnarsie in Brooklyn is very similar. It also is a white European-American middle-class community, and the Europeans were mainly from Eastern Europe.

Where we lived in East Flatbush was less than five minutes

away from the border with Brownsville, and while East Flatbush had a substantial size African-American community, you would see some Puerto Rican, South American and Caribbean families.

Once you entered Brownsville however, you were in a black African-American community. By 1972 many families in this part of Brooklyn had made a few visits to Africa (mainly the West African nations like Nigeria, the Gambia, Ghana, Senegal, Côte d'Ivoire and Guinea Bissau) and on their return took up the task of assisting the newly independent African nations.

Now the majority of the black students who attended South Shore were African-Americans who lived in a four square mile pocket of southern East Flatbush northern Brownsville.

★

If you were a visitor to New York City and travelled through Brooklyn, as my friends and I did on our bicycles, you would see for yourself that there were only two main ethnic groups in this borough: white European-Americans and black African-Americans. In the other boroughs you would meet other nationalities from the Caribbean, Central and South America, China, India and Africa. However, in Brooklyn these other nationalities were definitely in the minority.

As part of the Federal Government's efforts to combat the racial tensions among the 16–23 age group across the USA during the 1960s, President Nixon authorised a year-long nationwide analysis in the spring of 1969. Each state government was required to produce a report of the causes of riots within its borders, especially in the big cities.

When New York State published its own report in February 1970, it quoted heavily the analysis produced by officers on the State Board of Education Department. They had concluded that after thorough examination, one of the main reasons for the race riots among the youth in four large cities of the state, Albany (the state capital), New York City, Rochester and Buffalo, stemmed from the fact that the ratio between blacks and whites in each high school was not balanced. Some high schools had too many whites, others had too many blacks.

*

South Shore was opened six months after the publication of this report. It was the first effort in the state to put into practice the new federal policy where each new high school would have an equal balance, in terms of the composition of student population, the teaching staff, and the curriculum.

The multicultural design of the syllabus is where the change was felt immediately. In the literature, social studies, geography, music and art classes, we studied contemporary African, African-American, European and European-American authors, musicians and artists. In this milieu it was hoped that the African-American and European-American student population of the school would come to appreciate and respect each other by the time they graduated.

This type of education philosophy did a world of good for everyone. For me and my circle of friends, it brought Africa closer and closer into our mental and emotional horizon.

*

One day at the beginning of March 1972 (I can't remember the exact date, but I know it was near the beginning of the month) I made a discovery that changed my life for ever. At my friend Frank Johnson's house, I saw a World Council of Churches magazine called *The Ecumenical Review*. It was dedicated to the meeting of the Central Committee of the WCC. This meeting was held in January 1971 and the Ethiopian Orthodox Church was the host. The head of the EOC was Abuna Theophilos. I flicked through this magazine, and when I came to the pages where Abuna Theophilos' opening speech was recorded, I read it.

From then a magnetic force drew me closer and closer to the Church of Abuna Theophilos until I found a worshipping community of this same ancient African Orthodox Christian church in London in May 1975, becoming a member the following year. The rest of the story is what I have tried to share with you in Part One and which I plan to continue in the next two instalments.

Another seven years would elapse before I was in a position to make the first outline for this book. The time now was the beginning of August 1979. I had completed my studies and exams for the ordained ministry, and was awaiting the results. On 3 August 1979, as a member of the staff of the Church's magazine, *Brahane Misraq*, we received the first unconfirmed report, through the office of Amnesty International and also the WCC's news service at the Inter-Church building in Upper Manhattan, that His Holiness, Abuna Theophilos, the Patriarch of the Ethiopian Orthodox Church, who was deposed in February 1976 and imprisoned, had now been strangled to death by some soldiers of the government of Mengistu Haile Mariam. The date for my ordination as a deacon on 16 September would be fixed four days later on 7 August.

It was now very significant that the parish where this ordination service would take place was the Holy Trinity parish, first established on Lennox Ave in Harlem, by Abuna Theophilos on 25 October 1959. The address of this parish had changed twice since then.

Its current site was 140–142 West 176th Street in the Morris Heights community of the Bronx, a huge building with three floors which had four self-contained apartments (each of which had three bedrooms, a living room, kitchen and bathroom) with a fitted basement. A piece of land about half an acre in size was located next to the building. This property had been purchased by the faithful with assistance from the administration of the Patriarch Abuna Basilos on 5 December 1969, and moved into on European Christmas Day, 25 December. It was consecrated when Abuna Theophilos visited the USA in May 1973.

The archbishop, whom God would use to confer the spiritual rank of deacon upon me on 16 September 1979, would be Abuna Yesehaq. As a priest he was Abba L.M. Mandefro and served as one of my mentors. Now he was in charge of the archdiocese of the Western Hemisphere.

The book really began to take shape since my ordination to the deaconhood when I started the research project to produce a full-length biography of the life of Abuna Theophilos.

I soon realised that I had to set his life, which extended into so many segments of the history of twentieth-century Ethiopian Orthodoxy, as well as the twentieth-century ecumenical movement on the largest historical canvas that I could possibly construct. This is when I knew I would have to publish the book in three parts.

Only one priest, who was visiting New York at that time, gave me some information concerning Abuna Theophilos's work with the Inter-Orthodox Theological Commission for the Reunion between the Oriental and Eastern Orthodox Churches.

★

I knew there would be an external market for such a book. None of the bookshops in New York, Washington DC, or London, where Orthodox Christian literature was sold had anything about the Ethiopian Orthodox Church. One could find a wealth of material by Russian and Greek Orthodox scholars. Even books by Coptic and Armenian Orthodox authors were available, but nothing by any Ethiopian Orthodox scholar.

Internally I knew there was a demand for such a book as well. When I became a deacon in September 1979, the archdiocese had many African-Caribbean and African-American born clergymen within its parishes. In England (two parishes), in the USA (ten parishes), in Canada (one parish) and in the Caribbean (twenty-one parishes). The age group of the majority was between twenty-five and thirty-five.

The official membership if one went by the records kept at the diocesan HQ was 75,000. The majority was in the same age group as the clergymen. However, in reality the active worshipping membership of the diocese was probably around 30,000. Furthermore, this entire Diaspora membership like me, were all products of the African decolonisation decades of the 1950s and 1960s. A good number had belonged to various Rastafarian organisations before accepting membership.

★

Being a product of the African Diaspora, I knew I would have to start part one of my narrative by discussing my birth in Grenada, in the south-east Caribbean; my family background; and my early life in London and New York City, until I first discovered the Ethiopian Orthodox Church in 1972 and joined it as a member four years later in 1976. This would then enable me to carry the reader in the main body of the book.

Chapter 1 is an introductory chapter that describes the training and areas I studied at the Holy Trinity Ethiopian Orthodox Church located at 140–142 West 176th Street in the Bronx, the borough situated at the northernmost point of New York City, as well as at other Orthodox Christian centres in the New York metropolitan area.

Chapter 2 is now called 'A Brief Description of my Studies for the Priesthood'. It summarises the studies of the fossil discoveries of European and European/American scientists and their teams along the Great Rift Valley of Africa. The discoveries made in Ethiopia in 1974–75 by Donald Johnson and his team from the University of Cleveland in the USA is looked at with particular care, as well as how this new body of knowledge has been received by Ethiopian Orthodox scholars who know about it.

This chapter also gives an account of the work done by African and African-American historians on the relationship between the growth of the early African civilisations of the Nile Valley and its connection with the growth of other African civilisations, as well as the Greek-speaking civilisations of the Mediterranean. In this chapter I also try to show how this body of African studies on the origins of life is related to biblical studies. The distinguished and renowned African scholar, Cheikh Anta Diop of Senegal, and the impact of his work features strongly in this chapter.

Chapter 3 deals with the biblical references of 'Ethiopia/Cush' Old and New Testaments.

Chapter 4 covers the time span 290–356. It deals with St Frumentius, Ethiopia's first archbishop (330–356). The relationship established with the Coptic Orthodox Patriarchate of Egypt, when St Athanasius, consecrated St Frumentius, would affect the life of the Ethiopian Orthodox Church for sixteen centuries. Although done with mutual consent by the faithful on both sides, from this time in the fourth century, the Ethiopian Orthodox Church was under the canonical authority of the Holy Synod of the Coptic Orthodox Church, who appointed its archbishops. This arrangement generated a lot of tension in the history of both Churches, until June 1959, when the Ethiopian Orthodox Church finally became an independent body.

The emergence of Arius, an African churchman of Libya in North Africa, and his 'strange' theology that led to the convocation of the First Ecumenical Council at Nicea (present-day Ismir in Turkey) in the summer of 325, out of which the Nicean Creed was produced, is also discussed.

In this chapter I have taken particular car to show the reader how the victory won at this First Ecumenical Council over Arius and his followers gave the Patriarchate of the Coptic Orthodox Church of Egypt in the person of Patriarch Alexander, and then Patriarch Athanasius, the lead in any future discourse about the mystery of the Holy Living God in Trinity, and as Trinity, as well as the mystery of the Incarnation. I have tried to show how the entire 'Arian crisis' grew out of an African base.

This chapter also deals with the reigns of the twin monarchs, Ezana and Shaiazana (Abraha Asbera).

Chapter 5 deals with the theocratic structure of Orthodox Christian Axum from the fourth century to its decline in the ninth century. Constructed in three segments, the first one describes Axum's srtucture. In the second segment I have taken time and care to deal with the Council of Chalcedon (present-day Kadikoy in Turkey) in October 451, and its reception by the Ethiopian Orthodox Church. There is no doubt that this Council is the most controversial Church Council ever held.

From this time until the modern twentieth-century ecumenical movement, the Council of Chalcedon 451 had the distinction of being one of the major causes for the division of the Christian world into four main camps: Roman Catholic camp (and by extension the Protestant Reformation in Europe during the fifteenth and sixteenth century which was a reaction to the abuses of the papacy); the large Byzantine Orthodox camp; and the

Oriental Orthodox camp.

Segment three deals with some of the major events and personalities from the sisth century to Axum's decline in the ninth century.

The life of St Yared (506–563), the composer of all the Church's music is outlined, as is also the relationship of Axum with its colonies in South Arabia, and the advent of Islam.

This period ends with Axum's destruction by Queen Yodit (Judith) of the Falasha and her savage army. The centre of power now moves to the Showa province further south.

Chapter 6 deals with the Church and the Zagwe dynasty from the tenth to thirteenth centuries.

Chapter 7. The restoration of the Solomonic line with Yekuno Amlak, the impact of the long life of St Tekla Haimanot and the reigns of Emperors Amde Tsion and Dawit I are dealt with in this chapter.

Chapter 8 deals with the time from Emperor Zera Yacob (1434–68) to the beginning of the Zemane Mesa Fint (Era of the Princes) during the reign of Emperor Eyoas (1755–69).

In this chapter I have given full coverage to the attendance of the Roman Catholic Council of Ferrara/Florence by an Ethiopian Orthodox delegation from Jerusalem. The attempted Islamic and Jesuit conquests have also been given ample space in this chapter, as well as the emergence of Gondar as the new capital of the nation during the reign of Emperor Fasilades (1632–67).

Chapter 9. This is the last chapter of Part One. In it I have outlined the struggle for a sound theology of life during the Zemane Mesafint (1769–1855) and the first attempt of unification by Emperor Tewodros and Abuna Selama, during the years of Tewodros' reign (1855–68). It also goes into the changes to the life of the Church during the administrations of Emperors Yohannes IV (1871–89), Menelik II (1889–1913) and Empress Zauditu (1916–29). Part One comes to an end with the process that led to five Ethiopian Orthodox monk-priests being ordained and consecrated as bishops for the first time in the history of the Ethiopian Orthodox Church in 1929.

In the second instalment called 'Links to Part Two', I start off by describing how it felt to make it into the ranks of published authors for the first time to fulfil the dream I nourished since I was a teenager. I also give some more biographical details of my intellectual formation as a writer, historian and priest. I try to chart the journey that I made from being a US marine to an ordained priesthood in the Ethiopian Orthodox Church.

This is without doubt the biggest change to have occurred in my entire life. While I was working on this second instalment, the attacks on 11 September in America occurred, as well as the initial days of the campaign in Afghanistan and I could not ignore making some comments on these matters.

I also describe in the second part, the challenges I have faced from the hierarchy of the Ethiopian Orthodox Church, to do the vital research I need in order to complete my trilogy.

The longest part of 'Links to Part Two' discusses the major changes that have occurred in my life since I became a priest. I lay out the contours of the canonical case that surrounded the deposing and eventual execution of Abuna Theophilos. I also discuss for the first time the difficulties in the relationship with the Archbishop, who the Holy God in Trinity chose to bestow the priesthood upon me and his book.

Part Two

Part two was originally written as a twenty-five page essay 'The EOC in the Twentieth Century' between September and November 1986. I wrote it under the guidance of Abuna Matthias, the Ethiopian Orthodox Archbishop of Jerusalem from January 1979 until he resigned this office in 1982.

Abuna Matthias had made this brave decision to spearhead an attempt to have the heads of the Oriental Orthodox Churches approach the Executive Committee of the WCC for a hearing about the violations of the canons that regulated the sacrament of ordination, with the unlawful removal of Abuna Theophilos on 18 February 1976.

The entire Synod around him is then removed from this time until the end of December 1978 by the Revolutionary Military Government of Ethiopia, officially led first by Gen Aman Amdon (June–November 1974), then Teferi Bante (November 1974–February 1977), and finally Mengistu Haile Mariam (February

1977–May 1991). In July 1979 this military government murdered Abuna Theophilos.

That original essay formed part of the portfolio two other priests and myself hand-delivered to the WCC's Deputy General Secretary for Orthodox relations, in December 1986.

Chapter 1: I will go into the Italian invasion, war and occupation of Ethiopia of 1935–41, and the role of the League of Nations during this time.

Chapter 2: I will focus on the decades from the 1940's to the end of the 1970's, following the expulsion of the Italians, describing the two major initiatives that were undertaken.

a. The movement to have more Ethiopian priests consecrated to replace those murdered by the Italians to restart the process for complete canonical freedom from the Coptic Orthodox Synod which occurred in June 1959.

b. The emergence of the ecumenical world of Ethiopian Orthodoxy: the joining of the World Council of Churches (WCC) at its inaugural assembly in 1948. Its work in this organisation up to the unlawful removal of Abuna Theophilos in February 1976 and his murder in 1979. Secondly, the joining of the All Africa Conference of Churches (AACC) in 1963, and its work with this organisation until the same time frame.

Chapter 3: here I will focus upon the life and administration of Abuna Basilos as archbishop of the EOC from January 1951 to June 1959 and Patriarch from July 1959 to October 1970 when he died.

Chapter 4: I will discus the establishment of new parishes outside of Ethiopia in other parts of Africa, the Caribbean region, North America and Europe.

Chapter 5: the life of Abuna Theophilos 1910–1979.

Chapter 6 will be the last chapter. It will cover the effects of the September 1974 military revolution on the life of the Church until the destruction of the Dergue government in May 1991. It ends with the election of Abuna Theophilos' disciple, Abuna Paulos (formerly Abba Gebre Medhin Gebre Yohannes) as the new Patriarch of the EOC in July 1992.

A series of appendices will include material on the current state of biblical studies, a list of theological schools, monasteries, the sacred music of the Church, and icon painting.

★

In order to compose Part Two I will have to spend some time in Ethiopia to do extensive research. I intend to compose the second part as an exercise in twentieth-century ecumenical history. All six chapters will be an attempt to show the reader the connections of the world of Ethiopian Orthodoxy, with the wider twentieth-century ecumenical world, and the WCC membership.

The ecumenical baton which Abuna Theophilos received in 1948 had previous carriers going back as far as 1902. These were a group of theologians and churchmen like Metropolitan Meletios of Athens, Metropolitan Nicholas of Caesarea, and Professor Alivisatos who all belonged to the Ecumenical Patriarchate of Constantinople (Istanbul) Turkey.

A second group was led by Metropolitan Germanos of Thyateria from 1925. They attended various meetings and conferences in the three decades before the establishment of the WCC in 1948.

This group all belonged to a generation which shared the faith of the Orthodox Church, not as a confessional or a historical body, but as the continuation of the Church built upon the foundation of the Holy Apostles, and the bishops/theologians of the age of the seven Ecumenical Councils.

Several Russian Orthodox churchmen, theologians, and religious thinkers, who fled Russia following the 1918 Bolshevik revolution, settled in Paris and established St Sergius Theological Seminary in 1925, also joined this group under the leadership of Metropolitan Germanos. They extended the ecumenical cause by establishing a number of principles and convictions, particularly when discussing the inner nature and structure of the Church. The names of Metropolitan Evlogi, Sergius Bulgakov, George Florovsky and Nicholas Berdaief of this Paris community were the most outstanding voices.

Their style of sharing the Orthodox way of life with the Protestant Churches in the ecumenical movement was centred around discussing such topics as iconography, sacraments, prayer and worship, the transfiguration of the creation, the in-dwelling of the Incarnate Saviour in each believer through the power of the Holy Spirit, etc.

This was the stage reached when Abuna Theophilos received the ecumenical baton from them at the establishment of the WCC in Amsterdam 1948.

But in spite of almost one hundred years' participation in the twentieth-century ecumenical movement from 1902 and fifty years in WCC, Orthodox Christianity in general, and Ethiopian Orthodoxy in particular, is still relatively unknown in the Diaspora. Links to Part Two and Part Two, are a humble attempt to address this problem.

Brahana Selassie
Feast of the Holy Cross
28 September 2002
19 Maskariam 1995 (Ethiopian Calendar)